THE BIRD and THE BEEB

LIZ KERSHAW

THE BIRD and THE BEEB

LIZ KERSHAW

The facts of a life at the BBC

Trinity Mirror Media

Dedication

For...
the record

Trinity Mirror Media

THE BIRD AND THE BEEB

Copyright: Liz Kershaw

Edited by Chris Brereton

Published by Trinity Mirror Media
Managing Director: Ken Rogers
Publishing Director: Steve Hanrahan
Executive Editor: Paul Dove
Executive Art Editor: Rick Cooke
Design & Production: Graeme Helliwell, Vicky Andrews, Simon Monk.
Senior Marketing Executive: Claire Brown
Senior Book Sales Executive: Karen Cadman

First Edition
Published in Great Britain in 2014.
Published and produced by: Trinity Mirror Media,
PO Box 48, Old Hall Street, Liverpool L69 3EB

ISBN: 9781908695819

Photographs:
Liz Kershaw, Mirrorpix, PA Photos, BBC.
Every effort has been made to trace the copyright.
Any oversight will be rectified in future editions at the
earliest opportunity by the publishers.

Printed and bound by CPI Group (UK) Ltd, Croydon, CR0 4YY

Running Order

Intro

HIYA

Liz here...

Coming up in the next few hundred pages is my story of 30 years at the BBC. From being signed up on the spot at Radio Leeds in 1984. To notching up five years on Radio 1 and then four years on Radio 5 Live and now, in 2014, 12 years on Radio 6 Music, plus plenty in between. All the thrills and... er... spills along the way.

I was, and still am, essentially a music fan wanting to be close to the action. I never set out to be a famous face myself. Which is a good job. Because I'm not really.

Fame is a funny thing. If you're an A-Lister like, say Lady Gaga, you hire a retinue of hangers-on to get you around, to wait on your every need. But being a bit famous for being a faceless voice on the radio, like me, means I just go about my business. Until I open my mouth! Then people are naturally curious about my world. The world of wireless that touches their lives every day.

It's very flattering when people still remember what I did decades ago. And want to know what's happened since.

So I decided that one day I should just put it all in print for the people who've paid for it. Hopefully coming up are the answers to all the questions I've ever been asked. Like whenever I get into a black cab. And the conversation goes like this...

Me: Broadcasting House please.
Cabbie: 'Ere, don't I know you?
Me: Erm, do you? I'm not sure.
Cabbie: You're that bird from the Beeb aren't you?
Me: Yeah, yeah, that's right I'm on the radio.
Cabbie: Yeah, you're that Janice Long.
Me: No, no I'm not Janice.
Cabbie: Oh, don't tell me, it'll come to me. 'Ere, go on, what's your name then?
Me: It's Liz Kershaw.
Cabbie: That's right. You used to be on Radio 1 didn't you?
Me: Yes, 20 years ago.
Cabbie: How's that Bruno?
Me: Erm, well, he's OK.
Cabbie: D'ya ever see him?
Me: Usually go out for his birthday.
Cabbie: What's he up to?
Me: He runs his own company these days – making radio for Topshop and others.

HIYA

Cabbie: Oh, right – so are you still on the radio?

Me: Yes, yes, I'm heading there now.

Cabbie: Really? What you on these days then?

Me: Well, I'm on BBC Radio 6 Music.

Cabbie: What's that then?

Me: Oh, it's a digital station. You can get it on DAB radio or the internet and stuff.

Cabbie: What do you play then?

Me: Oh, all sorts really. Anything that's good.

Cabbie: Nah, I can't get that on 'ere. You must've met some famous folk then. Who's the most famous person you've ever met?

Me: Well, probably...

Cabbie: And who's the nicest you've ever met?

Me: Oh, I'd say that's got to be...

Cabbie: And what about the biggest idiot?

Me: Oh, I don't really want to say. But now you mention it...

Cabbie: 'Ere, ow's that brother of yours doing?

Me: Oh, Andy – he's fine. He's really well thanks.

Cabbie: No, not 'im. Nik.

Me: I've not got a brother called Nik.

Cabbie: Yeah, yeah you have. Nik Kershaw.

Me: Nope, he's not my brother.

Cabbie: Yeah he is. I had him in the back once. 'Ere, 'ow did you get into radio?

Me: Well I...

Cabbie: 'Ere what's that Steve Wright like?

Me: Oops, sorry – we're here, keep the change...

I've enjoyed the ride. I hope you'll enjoy the read.

Chapter One

WE ARE FAMILY

"Why are all songs about 'lovey-dovey' stuff Mummy?"

My mum smiled back at me in the rear view mirror of our little Austin A40. "Because love makes the world go round Libbeth!" She seemed surprised I'd even needed to ask.

It was a hot summer's day in 1962 and she was driving us to 'The Riviera'.

Not the swanky Mediterranean coast of France, but Rochdale's very own lido, then nestled at the foot of the Pennines next to the town's smelly tannery. Both now long gone.

We were off for a picnic in the sunshine and a swim in the unheated pool. I was plonked on the back seat with my chubby little legs sticking straight out of a 'sticky-out' frock with my gaze fixed on the reflection of her glowing young face framed by neat curls. The sloppy song she was singing along to was Bobby Vinton's 'Roses Are Red My Love'.

Her dinky red leather covered Perdio with its gold mesh front was, as ever, perched precariously on the dashboard. It was her most prized possession.

And no wonder. She'd bought it from Lovicks, the poshest shop in Rochdale, for a small fortune and most of her weekly wage. But this little radio introduced me and my brother to a lifetime passion for pop and the BBC.

So it was probably the best £12 19s 6d she ever spent.

As we set up on the grass by the outdoor pool for our typical '60s spread of sweaty Spam sandwiches and stinky boiled eggs from a warm Tupperware box, that 'tranny' was plonked beside us on our itchy tartan travel rug.

Wherever we went, that wireless went with us. And when we weren't out and about it was constantly on in our kitchen.

Because if my mum had her way, whenever we could, whatever we did, we did it to music.

The soundtrack for Saturday mornings was provided by Children's Favourites. Play me some Pinky and Perky or 'There's A Railway Runs Through The Middle of Our House' and I'm right back in my highchair watching our sausages sizzling away on top of the Baby Belling cooker.

Just say the words Cyprus, British Forces Broadcasting Service or Doris Day and I'm instantly looking down that yellow gloss-painted kitchen again, with its black and white checked lino tiled floor, open coal fire, huge old butler's sink, and, until it was replaced by a gleaming white Fridgedair, a green wooden meat safe.

On Sundays, the twin tub would be pulled out and cranked

up. Steaming, shaking and quaking, it would do its best to drown out the sounds of the BBC Light Programme and Two Way Family Favourites.

From the vantage point of my high chair I'd watch at eye level as my mum rolled out pastry on the new Formica worktop, wiping her eyes on her frilly pinny as she cried with laughter at the hilarious innuendos of Beyond Our Ken – which were, as yet, way beyond me.

Two hundred miles, and a world away from the BBC, was our Edwardian end-of-terrace red brick house, 28 Greenhill Avenue, next to a park in what was still a thriving and rapidly expanding Lancashire mill town.

We didn't have gardens. Just small backyards. But it was a leafy area within walking distance of the bustling town centre and even handier for the daily errands we were sent on with a list and a string bag to the butcher's, baker's and greengrocer's, in a nearby parade of busy local shops on the main road.

We were only tots but it was quiet and safe. Hardly anybody had cars and Greenhill Avenue became our playground. Me, my little brother, and Andrew and John Binks at number 10, who are best friends to this day, would spread our bikes and toys across it, untroubled by traffic.

There was the occasional mishap when purple iodine would be liberally applied to grazed knees but, on the street and in the park, we'd play out in all weathers without a care in the world.

My mum and dad, both teachers, (in fact my dad was already a deputy headmaster), had bought this four bedroomed house for £1400. In 1961, that got you a rather grand entrance hall with oak panelling. This was home to the new telephone (Rochdale 40617) on its very own wrought iron glass-topped stand with integral seat and matching wall mirror, and a huge navy blue Silver Cross carriage pram.

My brother, henceforth always known and referred to as 'Our Andrew', had come kicking and screaming into my life not long after my first birthday. Legend has it that while he was very fast at learning how to talk, he was just too lazy to bother to walk. And why should he when he could sit in that pram, issuing orders to his 'big sister'? I'm told I was only too happy to play the little mother, so willingly did his bidding. I'd like to be able to say, 'until I got wise to him' but actually, I don't think I ever really have.

Greenhill Avenue was grand enough to have a dining room where, once the fire was lit and the room and the valves of the cube shaped TV had warmed up, we watched grainy black and white programmes. On Mondays I could choose between the usual bedtime story or a new show set down the road in Salford.

I always plumped for Coronation Street and the gossip of Minnie, Martha and Ena in the snug over their bottles of Milk Stout. Or the antics of Elsie Tanner as my mum lamented her succession of unsuitable men and her wayward son Dennis. And Annie Walker of the Rovers Return because she reminded me so much of my grandma, the landlady of her own pub, who we only saw on Sundays then because she lived so far away (11 miles) in Manchester.

But not Top of the Pops. Oh no. If my dad came in and caught us trying to watch that he'd switch it off. According to this schoolmaster – who'd gone round ripping pictures of Elvis Presley out of his pupils' desks, rounding up truants from cinema queues for films like 'Rock Around The Clock' and who'd ended up in The Sun for banning trouser suits for girls at his school's Christmas party – this new-fangled pop was subversive and so was this show. Ahead of his time maybe?

On Saturday teatimes, the telly was all his. After coming back from watching his beloved Rochdale Hornets play rugby league, he'd tune into Grandstand to watch the results of other matches miraculously coming through live on the teleprinter before the final football results from far away places were solemnly read out.

While that was happening we'd be sent to play in the front room, with its velvet three-piece suite and fringed lamps, and a shiny polished piano. Any respectable parlour had to have a piano. Even if nobody could play it yet. But we'd seen what Russ Conway and Mrs. Mills could get out of one on BBC TV's The Billy Cotton Band Show.

And Miss Whitely too. She was our headmistress at Howard Street Nursery School. Miss Whitely was already too far the wrong side of 30 to appreciate the Hit Parade and, anyway, along with crisp frocks, thick red lipstick and tightly permed hair, she favoured the classical composers. Every day after 'school dinners' she'd start plonking away at the piano, barking at her young charges in our hand-knitted cardies and knee socks while we flailed around trying to interpret Grieg and Prokofiev in our daily music and movement sessions.

Once we were suitably worn out we'd be tucked under grey ex-army blankets on canvas camp beds for our regulation afternoon snooze. Thanks to her, 'In The Hall of the Mountain King' and 'Peter And The Wolf' still fill me with awe and have a place in my heart and on my shelves.

And I tried to bash them out like Miss Whitely on our piano. So my dad thought he had a child prodigy on his hands, and as soon as I was able to reach the pedals, he enrolled me in lessons. I did reluctantly learn to play Beethoven and eventually even passed some exams at the Royal College of Music. But in 1963 I wasn't really interested in mastering classical chords.

My dad only wanted the best for us and was a clever man too. He had enrolled me at Rochdale Convent for a top-flight Catholic education – on the very same day he'd registered my birth – and the choice of my middle names, Mary and Marguerita, was no coincidence either.

Dad had picked them in order to win over the Sisters of Saint Vincent Palotti.

Sister Marguerita was the headmistress and so dad's choice of name was entirely strategic. The convent was the best private school in town, popular with 'left footers' and heathens (as my grandma called anybody who didn't have a picture of the Pope on the wall) alike, so was always oversubscribed. My namesake must have fallen for the flattery because I was guaranteed a place straight away.

Even here, music was part of everyday life. Well, hymns anyway. Every morning would start with: 'By the blood that flowed from thee, in thy grievous agony' and 'Faith of our fathers living still in spite of dungeon fire and sword'.

This would set the mood for an hour of colouring in pictures of Jesus on the Cross or drawing hearts dripping with blood, complete with severed tubes and always with 'INRI' splashed across the top.

But otherwise it was just lovely. The nuns had made their base in what had been three adjacent and very grand mill owners' mansions set in woods just off the Manchester Road. One for infants, one for juniors and one for the senior school.

Our playground was a sprawling estate of inter-connected formal gardens, lawns and bluebell woods.

Every playtime, me and my friends, all Beatles fans, became the Fab Four. I can't remember which of the girls played John, George or Ringo, but I was totally in love with Paul McCartney so I bagsied being him. And Gillian Taylor was my best friend so she had to be Jane Asher, Macca's then girlfriend.

When those harsh German nuns discovered us acting out these childish fantasies in the grounds, they instantly banned our silly games. Oh, well. I could dream. That Paul McCartney wouldn't get married until one day, when I grew up, he'd meet me. I was gutted when Linda Eastman beat me to it in 1969.

Never mind. Within a few years I'd switched my affections to Rod Stewart anyway.

We didn't have any Beatles records at our house. In fact me and Our Andrew didn't have any records of our own yet. But the front room now had a Dansette which took pride of place on a new teak coffee table in the corner by the piano. If we were well behaved we were allowed to listen to my dad's LPs by local girl-made-good Gracie Fields, Bing Crosby and American big bands. Or my mum's ever growing collection of 'lovey-dovey' albums by crooners like Nat King Cole and Perry Como. And, showing her Irish roots, Val Doonican with his trademark natty knitwear, rocking chair and sickly sentimentality. And also rebel rousers by some rather angrier Irishmen.

So, by the age of five, my party pieces included the Republican anthem 'The Wearing of the Green', ('Oh the wearing of the green. For they're hanging men and women for the wearing of the green'), Our Gracie's 'The Biggest Aspidistra In The World' ('For years and years I've been a lonely spinster on the shelf') and 'She Loves You (Yeah Yeah Yeah)'. For a while, my singing was put on hold when a tiny virus made me really poorly – but dead happy. I'd got chickenpox so wasn't allowed to go out or to have anybody round. Taking pity on her quarantined seven-year-old staring longingly out of the window at her friends playing in the street, my mum slipped out and came back with my very own record player (well, like everything else, as usual I had to share it with Our Andrew).

It was small and portable with a white plastic handle attached to its red leather case. I could now play music in any room in the house or even take it round to my friends.

And this was much more fun than LPs. Just by switching the knob from 33 and a 1/3 to 45 rpm and stacking up a pile of 7" singles we could marvel as they dropped down in turn to reveal the midnight blue or dark green Pye and Decca labels of my mum's new favourites, up and coming heart-throbs like Tom Jones and Engelbert Humperdinck.

Soon I had my own red plastic record box which was filling up fast with the psychedelic coloured 7" plastic discs that arrived in the post each week. I'd started filling my face with Weetabix so that I could collect and send off the necessary tokens from the packets. I'd order fairytales set to music. They were very American and pretty ghastly. Meanwhile Our Andrew had his own blue box which he was filling with more masculine Weetabix releases featuring cowboy songs.

And we'd also been bought Max Bygrave's 'You're A Pink Toothbrush' and Tommy Steele's 'Little White Bull' from Bradley's Records in the town centre.

My heroine at the time, though, was the one and only Dusty Springfield. How I longed to be like Dusty one day.

"How would you like your hair doing today Elizabeth?" The hairdresser was only humouring her young customer. But this was my big chance at glamour.

"I'd like it blonde and flicked up at the ends please. Like Dusty."

"You'll have the usual and like it!" piped up my mum. I didn't think she could hear from under the hood dryer.

I felt equally thwarted when it came to getting a new winter coat. I wanted the red one with the white fur collar. Dusty would have gone for that one. But I came away from the children's department of Senior's, the bespoke gentlemen's tailors where my dad got his made-to-measure suits, in a traditional rust number with brown velvet trim.

I would get a blonde bob and a fur coat, and sing on a record myself eventually. Because as my dad always told me "you can get whatever you want in life if you want it enough."

But for now it was another of his mantras. 'Education. Education. Education.'

For the first few years of my life, Rochdale was my entire world. In fact the edge of the world might as well have followed the skyline of the surrounding moors. I knew it didn't because sometimes we went 'over the tops' to Blackpool for the nose-to-tail 50-mile drive 't'ert Luminations'. Or our summer holidays.

Everybody went to Blackpool for their holidays then and until 1963, we always went to the same hotel. Long days were spent in our matching hand-knitted jumpers, huddled in deck chairs behind windbreaks on the beach, warmed up by the tea sold in white pot jugs from a kiosk. Or digging with our rubber buckets and wooden spades before the obligatory donkey ride.

But then my grandma suggested Butlins. So for the next few

holidays we headed off to Filey, Ayr or Pwllheli. (Which was eventually bulldozed because of me!) Once installed in our adjoining chalets me, Our Andrew, Cousin Linda and my grandma launched ourselves into everything from riding the chairlifts to entering talent contests while my mum tripped the light fantastic in the massive ballroom. My dad, on the other hand, soon decided he wasn't cut out for this forced camaraderie and regimentation so he bought a tent.

After being washed out for the umpteenth time in the Lake District and being given shelter by some kindly caravanners, he then decided that towing his own mobile home was the future.

And, like everything else he did, he took his caravanning very seriously, planning the itinerary for educational expeditions with military precision. So for the next few years, we trawled up and down, taking in every coastline and county, every city, through the highlands and islands, exploring every castle and nook and cranny in England, Scotland and Wales.

His mission? To make sure that we saw and knew our own country inside out before we inevitably started venturing abroad. (Which we did in 1972 on our first package holiday to Majorca for £17 each).

Just before I turned 10, we headed off to Cambridge. I'd just got the highest marks of any primary school pupil in Rochdale in some tests or other and I'd been moved up a year at school.

I think his plan was to inspire me to aspire to Oxbridge. So we trudged round all the colleges. As usual I had to collect postcards because every evening on these trips, we'd have to stick them in scrapbooks and write about what we'd learned that day. I still have those projects. Even though the Sellotape holding the postcards to the pages has now withered and they're falling to bits they're still a reminder of how we weren't always happy being made to do 'homework' on our holidays. But I came to appreciate his motives. Later on at the BBC, even some of my brightest colleagues evidently had absolutely no idea about the lie of this land. I'd get asked things like "can you go to York for 9 in the morning and then be in Bristol for 12 o'clock?"

No. That's just not geographically possible.

On one occasion I drew a blank outline of the country and gave them a list of place names. But they just couldn't place them. Basic stuff? You'd think so. I'm not being smug. My dad was a one-off who had the time to spend with us and I know I was very, very lucky.

Every day of Jack's Tours would end with one of my mum's latest new-fangled finds; Vesta Ready Meals. Particularly the never-entirely-rehydrated Chicken Supreme. Combined with the Calor Gas, it created a particularly memorable smell. Then we'd be tucked in, tired but cosy in our bunk beds, swaddled in heavy cotton sleeping bags, and reading Famous Fives in the flickering lamp light with the deafening sound of rain beating down on the roof, whilst Friday Night Is Music Night resonated throughout our metal boom box on wheels from the Perdio perched on the shelf.

Me and Our Andrew got the best of both worlds. A curious and conscientious educator for a father. And a fun-loving party girl for a mother.

Sadly they weren't all that compatible in the long term.

Ultimately those differences started to grate. Soon they were to go their separate ways.

And it all started when my mum had her head turned by another man.

Chapter Two

YOU'RE THE ONE FOR ME, FATTY

In 1964, Cyril Smith came into our lives. 'Big Cyril' was so called not just because of his burgeoning 24 stone bulk and 60" waist. But also because he effectively ran Rochdale. He was the leading light in the local Labour Party and asked my dad, his old classmate from the boys' grammar school, if he fancied standing as a councillor.

He didn't. He was very active in his trade union, as president of the local NUT, and with a school to run he said he had enough on his plate. But my grandma, the daughter of Irish immigrants who'd worked her way out of abject poverty, was very ambitious for her college-educated only child and so thought my mum should go for it. In May that year, having won her seat for the Balderstone ward, where my grandma and grandad were well known and respected having run a pub there, Councillor Eileen Kershaw took her seat on Rochdale Council.

By day she was working full time as a teacher. In evenings she would be down at the town hall attending committee meetings until long after our bedtimes. In the mornings, when I opened my eyes, I'd instantly look for the evidence that my mum was home: the reassuring little Milky Bar that she'd placed on my bedside table at some ungodly hour.

Some nights weren't so peaceful. We'd be woken by the front door bursting open and the booming voice of 'Big Cyril' as he and his entourage piled back to our house after some meeting having stopped off for double helpings of pudding and chips from the chippy on the main road. Now wide awake again, me and Our Andrew would hang over the bannisters earwigging in on the conversation bellowing up the stairs from the front room.

Late one night we watched as my dad grabbed his coat and hurriedly left with Cyril for some destination unknown to us. I only learned recently, when my mum took part in a documentary about Cyril Smith, that he and my dad had set out that night to enlist the help of the local MP, Jack McCann, because Cyril was facing accusations about the sexual abuse of young lads in a local council-run home.

My mum related on camera how he'd sobbed and swore blind to her and my dad that the claims about him were unfounded and malicious and that, actually, he was the victim here. So, as lifelong friends, they rallied round him.

But me and Our Andrew didn't have a clue back then about

what was going on. And, apart from having our sleep interrupted, we weren't yet disturbed in any way by Cyril and these late night comings and goings.

In 1966, he became Mayor of Rochdale. And the icing on the cake on my eighth birthday was the arrival of his official car at our house during my party. Most of my friends' families didn't have cars. So they immediately abandoned Musical Chairs to run to the window when the chauffeur-driven limousine bearing the town's crest and the famous number plate DK 1 pulled up outside. There were squeals of delight when Cyril, in full red ermine-trimmed regalia and heavy gold chain, had all us kids hop in, taking turns for a ride round the block, sitting on his lap or squeezed in beside him.

Later that summer there was more drama during our long school holidays. I don't know how he got in touch with us in those days before mobile phones, but our idyllic stay in Dornoch in the north-west of Scotland was thrown into turmoil by a frantic exchange of phone calls via the caravan site's office.

Listening in, I gleaned that Labour's local top dog was defecting to the Liberals and he was trying to persuade my mum to cross benches with him. But she refused to be bullied by her political mentor and remained a Labour stalwart in local politics for nearly 50 years.

My dad was now the headmaster of a middle school in Cyril Smith's Comprehensive Utopia. Cyril was in charge of education in Rochdale and had been quick off the mark to scrap the very system that had given working class lads like him and my dad a leg up from an otherwise inevitable life in the mills.

The grammar schools had made them what they were. Obviously now, the best endorsement for Cyril's modern vision of equality and opportunity was that it was seen to be good enough for their own children. Cyril didn't have any for reasons we now know. Instead, Jack Kershaw's oldest child, me, had to be the flag-bearer for the experiment.

So in 1968, aged just 10, I started at my dad's school. It was hell for someone who'd been taken out of a sheltered convent school, full of children from fee-paying families. Now I found out what it was like to be a poor kid from Rochdale's toughest estates as I witnessed real deprivation first hand. And it wasn't just about money.

Some of the 12-year-old girls talked about how they were already having sex with older boys. And one of them boasted quite openly that her mum was in a lesbian relationship with Dusty Springfield whenever she was in Manchester. It was all so shocking and unlikely at the time. But now I know that was entirely possible.

To them I was a posh swot. On a school trip to Coventry Cathedral, nobody would sit next to me because I was 'Jack's daughter'. So I spent the coach journey of 120 miles each way on my own fighting back tears and just looking out of the window. It was the most lonely and humiliating day of my life. But I didn't want to burden my dad.

Some of his staff went out of their way to show there was no favouritism towards the boss's kid. So they were especially strict and harsh with me. A games teacher in particular seemed to revel in humiliating me in front of everyone. Until I spied her holding hands with the deputy head one night on a school trip. She was lovely to me after that. But I soon had a real supporter.

Mr. Tinkler was our English teacher. He was so full of energy and enthusiasm and so was I when he cast me in starring roles in his musical productions. As the tallest girl in the year, and with a surprisingly deep singing voice for a child, I always ended up playing the leading man. But I loved it and I loved him for it. He gave me back my confidence and inspired and encouraged my lifelong love of language and books. You never forget a good teacher and we're still in touch.

One day, towards the end of that summer of 1970, and at the end of the school day, I went to sit outside the headmaster's office to wait for a lift home from the man I had to call Mr. Kershaw. That sunny afternoon we were driving home when my dad suddenly swung into the curb outside a row of terraced houses on the main road. "Wait here Elizabeth. I won't be long," he instructed me, jumping out and slamming the car door. I watched him run up the steps of one of the houses just as its door was closing behind some boys in our grey and maroon school uniform.

He banged on the door and was let in. Before long he was back in our car and speeding home. He was muttering that now he knew where some persistent truants had been spending their afternoons and something about Jim, Cyril Smith's constant companion.

I don't know who he found there that afternoon or what he did about his grim discovery. It's since come to light that around that time Cyril was questioned again by police about his sexual activity with boys.

I do know that very soon after that, Cyril turned on my dad and tried to get him sacked.

This was ostensibly over the issue of Our Andrew following me to his school. Because it was so highly regarded it was oversubscribed and the education committee introduced 'zoning'.

This meant you couldn't get a place there unless you lived in the immediate catchment area. We didn't. We'd moved out to the suburbs.

So my dad had put the address of my grandma's pub on his son's application form. And both me and Our Andrew had gone to live with her for a while. She loved it. And so did we. My mum was always so very busy with the council that we'd learned to fend for ourselves but my grandma spoiled us rotten with big, hearty home-cooked meals, feather beds, unlimited crisps and pop on tap from behind the bar (the fizzy drink variety) and no rules at all. And we made what seemed like loads of money collecting and washing glasses and scavenging under the seats for loose change dropped by 'the regulars'. I suspect it was placed there by my grandma to teach us about work ethic.

But we were soon back home. And so was my dad. All day and every day for weeks on end. He'd been suspended from his job for misleading the education committee over our domestic arrangements.

After what seemed like an eternity the committee decided to take the view that he was an excellent headmaster who'd made a bad judgement whilst trying to demonstrate his faith in his own school. That it was good enough for his own kids. And he was reinstated. But throughout that ordeal, it was understood by us that Cyril Smith was orchestrating a vengeful campaign against him.

In 1972, Cyril Smith, MBE, turned on our local Labour MP, the very man who'd given the Rochdale police an ultimatum to produce the evidence and prosecute or leave Cyril alone. He ran what my mum describes as a very personal and dirty campaign. Cyril won the seat and headed off to Westminster.

THE BIRD AND THE BEEB

By the early '70s it seems Cyril's penchant for young boys was the worst kept secret in town. It was 'common knowledge' that one of the shops in the town centre had been set up with hush money given by Cyril to a young man who'd once lived in one of the homes Cyril ran.

One day my mum decided to tackle the issue head on. So she picked up the young shopkeeper in her car and challenged him about those rumours.

But he refused to be drawn and just stared straight ahead and wouldn't utter a word on the matter.

In 1979, I was gobsmacked when Cyril turned up unannounced at my 21st birthday bash at my grandma's pub. In front of all my relatives and friends, he made a generic glowing speech about me and presented me with a silver necklace. I never wore it. It stayed in its box until more stories came out about him after he died. Then I gave it to a charity shop.

All I'd ever wanted was to go to Rochdale Grammar School for Girls. Ever since I'd encountered its sixth form girls in the nearby sweet shop, on my way home from Howard Street Nursery School.

They'd be sitting at the counter on high stools chatting away over a Dandelion and Burdock as we ordered our Fairy Drops (like pastel coloured rice crispies) served up in a little white triangular paper bag, or four-for-a-penny Fruit Salads or Black Jacks. Being only knee high to them I was most impressed that they didn't have socks. Instead they all wore tan coloured stockings. How sophisticated. One day I'd be one of their crowd.

But by 1970, that crowd was mixed. Boys went there too. It was now Greenhill, thanks to Cyril Smith.

YOU'RE THE ONE FOR ME, FATTY

It was a comprehensive school with about 1200 pupils. If my dad's school had been a culture shock, I was in for a real eye opener now. It was a jungle. Sometimes I wonder how I kept from going under.

The old grammar school building had been massively extended for its new role. A maze of corridors linked new 1970s airy glass blocks to the dark recesses of the original 1930s building. And some of those had quickly become no-go areas for a goody two shoes like me.

Like the toilets. With the light bulbs removed and swirling with stale cigarette smoke and daubed with eye poppingly 'informative' graffiti, these were the dingy dens of Greenhill's baddest Bad Girls. In 1972, the school leaving age was raised to 16, trapping even more 15-year-olds who really didn't want to be in school.

And neither did I at lunchtimes. Apart from anything else I really needed a wee. So my grandma decided I'd better go to her pub for my dinners. This meant speed walking through the park and across Cronkeyshaw Common. My poor bare knees (uniform rules meant I still had to wear knee socks) would be red raw in the wind. But singing songs by the likes of Slade, T Rex and The Sweet kept me trudging along on that 20 minute hike. Then I'd have another 20 minutes to wolf down her homemade broth and pies before setting off back again.

I especially loved this arrangement on Tuesdays. Because in those days the new chart would be announced at lunchtime on Radio 1. I could go back and tell everyone in registration whether our favourite records, like Alice Cooper's 'Schools Out', had made it to that 'all important number one position'.

But I never went back on Wednesdays. The whole of that

afternoon was for sport. My grandma knew I dreaded compulsory sports because I was so hopeless. "You can't have brains and brawn Our Elizabeth." And anyway, with all the walking and growing (I was 5' 8" by now) the weight was dropping off me so she reckoned I was getting enough exercise and could always do with new clothes.

So instead she'd grab her big handbag stuffed with cash (her pin money made from selling her pies in the pub) and take me on the train to Manchester. She'd patiently spend the afternoon on a chair outside the changing rooms of Chelsea Girl or Miss Selfridge while I tried stuff on, popping out for her approval. "Is that the fashion nowadays? OK. If you say so." She'd splash the cash on the understanding that I'd pay her back by working in the pub that weekend. Which I did from the age of 14. I could have whatever I wanted, as long as, like her and my grandad, I worked for it.

And blimey did they work hard. Starting at 6am, seven days a week and then, apart from a bit of shut-eye in the afternoons, up until around 1am locking up, clearing up, and cashing up the tills. And I never forgot that. If ever I've started to feel sorry for myself over the years, dragging myself out of bed before dawn or working through the night, I've remembered that I never had to clean toilets or lug heavy casks of beer around in a damp cellar after only a few hours' sleep.

And they'd been grafting like this since they were children. By the time they were 14 they were old hands in the mills. So what had I to moan about? Not much. Best not let them down then.

The teachers we'd inherited from the grammar school were mainly spinsters of this parish who simply couldn't cope with what the newly comprehensive intake was throwing at them.

But for those of us who showed an interest in learning they could still manage a very decent education. Even the classics, a hangover from the grammar school, were still on offer. So, with his heart still set on Oxbridge, my dad made me 'choose' Latin and Greek. I particularly hated those subjects. But, I hate to admit, the rigour of grappling with all those declensions, grammar and etymology, might have helped when I sat my first two O-Levels – in French and English Language – at just 13.

So, as a kind of reward and acknowledgement that I was doing OK and that his master plan was on track, my dad lightened up and gave us permission to buy pop records with our own money. As long as we only played them when he was out. Deal.

Chapter Three

ROCK 'N' ROLL
HIGH SCHOOL

Dad's timing couldn't have been better. 1972 was a belting year for music. Soon we had singles by Roxy Music ('Virginia Plain'), David Bowie ('Starman'), Mott The Hoople ('All The Young Dudes'), Status Quo ('Paper Plane'), Slade ('Mama We're All Crazy Now'), Lindisfarne ('Lady Eleanor'). And... ahem... Gary Glitter's 'Do You Wanna Touch Me?' (All the clues were there).

And before long we'd got our first albums. Elton John's 'Honky Chateau' and 'Don't Shoot Me I'm Only The Piano Player' and Rod Stewart's 'Every Picture Tells a Story' and 'Never A Dull Moment'. I just loved Rod Stewart, even after I nearly died listening to him. On the morning of April 13th, 1973, when I was home alone and supposedly revising for my latest O-Levels, but actually listening to the DLT show on Radio 1, I suddenly felt really sick. Then, just as Johnnie Walker cranked up Python Lee Jackson's 'In A Broken Dream' (everybody knew it was Rod Stewart), the squits kicked in. I always associate JW with that. As I was able to tell him when, amazingly, I became his great mate less than 15 years later. By early afternoon I was rolling around in agony. When my mum got home at tea time she sent for the doctor. He put on some rubber gloves, shoved two fingers up my bum and diagnosed appendicitis.

I was swiftly stretchered into an ambulance and taken, sirens blazing, to Rochdale Infirmary. Emergency surgery was followed by violent vomiting which nearly burst my stitches so I'm still absolutely petrified of ever having another general anesthetic. In fact, I've since had four operations with an epidural instead. (It's always worth asking when it involves procedures below the waist).

My grandma, who harked back to pre-NHS days when it was (officially) down to your own family to feed you in hospital, did her best to build me up. Every afternoon when the pub was closed she'd arrive with whatever pies hadn't sold that lunchtime. And tins of fruit salad, which I had no way of opening or eating. But I suppose it was all she could do for me and it made her feel better. So I just stashed them in my locker. Years later the roles were reversed and I found myself fighting to keep her from dying of starvation in the 'care' of Rochdale's NHS 'Trust'.

After finally being discharged and to celebrate finishing my exams in seven more subjects, I was allowed to go to my first gig. The Faces in Manchester. With Rod Stewart!

I'd been invited by a 22-year-old Rochdale Corporation bus driver who was also moonlighting in my grandma's pub as a barman. He was seen as a 'nice lad' so we headed off with my grandma's full blessing. But blimey. Looking back, it was all a bit rum. What was a 22-year-old doing hanging out with a 14-year-old? I suppose he seemed a safe enough bet. He was bound to bring me back in one piece. He was owed a week's wages. And his 'wheels' were an old Morris Minor rather than a flashy Capri or souped up Escort, so he certainly didn't seem racy.

I did look older than my years, with Rod-style feather cut hair, and a skinny stripey t-shirt under red dungarees with 32" flares. And, nudging six foot in my platform shoes, I was bigger than my escort for the evening. So, unlike him, I was lofty enough to see the band. Just about. Everybody between me and the stage, just like the stars on stage, had spiked up hair and huge heels. And that was just the guys!

It was so exciting to see a hero just feet away and in the flesh, strutting around. And three dimensional, not just flat on an LP cover. Packed in shoulder to shoulder, I could feel the excitement, and the heat, and smell the sweat of the crowd. I could feel the drums and bass in my stomach. And I'd never re- alised anything could be so loud. It wouldn't faze me now after hundreds of live concerts and thousands of hours of wearing headphones. But that was the most deafening thing my young ears had ever taken in. They were ringing for days. But it was worth it. Unlike listening to a record this was the real deal. This was a feast for all the senses. I absolutely loved it and it fed a hunger for music that has never gone away.

It's worth pointing out here that my love for Rod was not blind or unconditional. I fell out of love with him when he fell in love with leopard skin lycra leggings.

'Do ya think I'm sexy?'

No Rod. You look a right tit and you've completely lost the plot.

But in November, 1973, I'd saved up just enough to get his recent compilation 'Sing It Again Rod' which included songs from his first two albums which I didn't yet own. And Our Andrew, now a big Bob Dylan fan, had money burning a hole in his pocket. So one wet Saturday afternoon, we persuaded my mum to take us into town in her new car. A purple metallic Austin Allegro. With its uniquely square steering wheel this was the epitome of '70s style.

Bradley's Records was our destination that day and every Saturday. Woolworths sold MOR albums and ghastly LPs on the Hallmark label featuring bad cover versions of chart hits and bikini clad dolly birds on their sleeves. But Bradley's sold the proper stuff. It was rammed with vinyl, listening booths, a busy counter and was always so packed that its young customers would spill out and hang out on the corner of this tiny shop at the bottom of Rochdale's busiest shopping street, discussing which single to buy that week or showing off their latest LP. This was the hub of teenage life in the town.

This particular trip to Bradley's stands out – but for all the wrong reasons. We couldn't wait to get home and put on our new LPs. We were excited but our mum drove us back in virtual silence. It was a grey, miserable, drizzly day. Even so, we couldn't understand why she was so grumpy and short tempered. Glen Campbell was crooning out from the cassette player set in the mahogany dashboard. We'd yet to fully appreciate country music. So I thought our chatting and giggling over Wichita Lineman must have got on her nerves when she suddenly stopped the car and turned on us.

"Your father's got another woman!"

That's all I remember her saying.

Something had been puzzling me for a few months now. I didn't know much about sex but I did know that you couldn't get pregnant if you'd had your ovaries and womb removed. And my mum had. Recently I'd gone rummaging in dad's jacket pockets for a pen, but had found a Durex instead. My mum's outburst finally confirmed my suspicions. I knew it! I'd been right to wonder if he was having it off with someone else. It was unthinkable. My uptight dad having a passionate fling. Yuck! It turned out my mum had been trying to spare us for a few weeks. But today she'd reached the end of her tether. Was it the pissing weather? Our incessant banter about Bob vs Rod? Or trying to steer a car with a stupid square steering wheel? Whatever. She just couldn't keep it in any longer. To be honest, I wasn't surprised and we weren't particularly upset. The atmosphere at home had been so bad that just knowing the reason why was a relief. In fact – good! If they split up perhaps we'd have a bit more peace about the place.

So how had my dad been caught, quite literally, trousers down?

Well imagine yourself in this nightmare. You tell your wife that you are off to a rugby match. But actually you're going round to your new girlfriend's for some afternoon delight.

Meanwhile, on the other side of town, your children, after helping in their grandparent's pub, are getting into a tinny two door Austin 1100 to drive to a restaurant for a late Sunday lunch. Their grandad's just turned onto the main road and a car's coming towards them at speed. It tries to overtake them. But there's a bus coming in the opposite direction and the idiot overtaking tries to pull back in, ramming the car with your children in it and forcing it off the road and into the shopfront of the local chemists.

I was sitting with Our Andrew in the back behind my grandma who was in the front passenger seat. Because I was turned towards Our Andrew I could see the other car level with us at our side before it started shunting us onto the pavement. Then I looked straight in front and realised we were heading for the shops. It is a cliche but what happened next did seem to be in slow motion and I actually thought 'Is this it? Am I about to die? It's not going to end well anyway.'

The next thing we'd ploughed into the plate glass floor-to-ceiling window and I was covered in suntan lotion and Dr Scholl sandals. My leg was trapped under the front seat and I was dripping in blood. None of us were wearing seat belts so as my grandma's seat had tipped up and she went through the windscreen, I'd slid forward. And the seat had then fallen back, with her still in it, after the impact. Now her considerable bulk was pinning me down.

My grandad was first into an ambulance and, still conscious even though he had obvious head injuries, he was crying out to know if we were OK. He'd lost his glasses and teeth and suddenly looked much older than 65.

At the infirmary I had my face stitched up. Chins bleed a lot. Hence all the blood collecting in my lap while I'd waited to be released. My leg wasn't broken but it got such a bashing that I still have a big chunky dent with no feeling in it to this day. But where was all the other blood on the trolley coming from? "Oh don't worry. That'll be from earlier on."

Actually it was from my buttock. A spring from the seat had pierced it and when they got round to spotting that, it had to be stitched up too. My grandma and grandad were taken away. (They were kept in for weeks and never fully recovered). But where was Our Andrew?

Well he'd bashed in his teeth but managed to get out of the car OK and stood watching on the pavement while the ambulances took us away. Nobody took any notice of the little lad who walked to the Infirmary in a daze.

And where was my dad?

A call had been put out for him over the tannoy at the Rochdale Hornets' ground. But he wasn't there to hear it. So when he eventually rolled home he had some explaining to do and he had to collect us from the Infirmary. I didn't understand why he was so unsympathetic and was shouting at me to get in the car. Understandably, after what I'd just been through, I wasn't too keen on another ride so soon. But he wasn't having any of it. And he wasn't any more helpful through the next few days when I could hardly walk the few steps to the toilet at home.

My legs were swollen and black. And red and yellow and pink and green. Orange and purple and blue. This wasn't like my dad. What the hell was going on?

Suddenly, on that journey home from our record buying trip, with me clutching 'Sing It Again Rod', it all made sense.

He didn't move out straight away. Or for long. I understood why. He'd fallen out of love with his wife but not with us. And it was his home too. He just carried on courting.

One night, me and Our Andrew were home alone – again – when we were woken up by banging on the door. It was the police. And my mum and dad. "Keep these two out of trouble will you kids?" The boys in blue were pushing our parents through the front door. The cops had been called to my dad's girlfriend's house following reports of a disturbance. He'd been there enjoying himself when my mum had spotted his car.

One day, arriving home from school, as I put my key in the lock, I spotted my dad's legs sprawled across the dining room floor. He was covered in tea leaves. "Get her away from me!" he yelled as I bent over him and he came to. My mum had ambushed him by hiding behind the front door and whacking him over the head with a big wooden clog as he came home. In a panic, trying to revive him, she'd then emptied the tea pot over him.

This couldn't go on. My dad moved out and my mum then took the view that we should cut him out of our lives. But I couldn't do that. So the peace I'd hope the split would bring just never came. She had good reason to be distraught but I didn't see why, just because I wanted to keep in touch with my other parent, I deserved to have abuse – and more – thrown at me. Things calmed down when my mum found a new love interest.

She'd brought him straight from a Labour Party meeting one night to my grandma's pub when I'd been working behind the bar.

"This is Jim. Don't you think he'd make a lovely boyfriend?" What? Not only did he look like a poor girl's Jason King. He was 25! Surely she wasn't trying to fix me up with a man 10 years older than me?

Obviously not.

If I didn't see his appeal my 40-year-old mother sure did. Soon he was practically living with us. When I shared my Christmas Day photos with my friends they were bound to ask:

"Who's that sitting next to your grandma at the table?"

"Oh it's my mum's boyfriend."

"And why's your dad there?"

"Oh he's moved back in. He still has a girlfriend. So he sleeps in the spare room."

The upshot was that I now felt I could do whatever I liked, all previous notions of normality having gone out of the window. So, aged 15, I went clubbing. Not that anyone really seemed to notice. Or mind. Well I was with trusty Cousin Linda I suppose.

Now 20, she'd got her first car. Her mum and dad were busy running a pub (most of my mum's family did that) and making a mint. So as soon as she passed her test they bought her a brand new sporty Triumph Toledo. She'd pull up at our house or my grandma's pub, I'd hop in wearing the latest clothes I'd got that Wednesday and with a few quid I'd earned from my grandma on the Friday, and off we went – both still in our heated rollers – to the bright lights of Manchester and beyond. The new M62 motorway had opened up the entire north west to anyone setting out and belting along at 11pm on a Saturday night.

So we found ourselves in Oldham, Ashton, Heywood, Bury, Knutsford and other hotspots in deepest Cheshire.

To clubs like Carriages, Tramtracks, The Richmond, the Brown Cow, The Farmer's Arms and The Valley Lodge. And in Manchester at Placemate, Reubens and Pips. Pips was a bit different. There were several rooms, each one dedicated to a distinct artist and their music and fashion. So a T. Rex room was full of Mark Bolan lookalikes, another full of Rod Stewarts, there were wall-to-wall Bryan Ferrys in the Roxy Music area. And of course there was a David Bowie shrine.

Plastered in make up, I always breezed past the bouncers. Then, inevitably I'd have to go back to the door and vouch for little Cousin Linda being over 18. Once inside we'd make straight for the dance floor (we weren't interested in drinking except for the occasional Britvic Orange) hoping the DJ would play our current favourites. George McCrae's 'Rock your Baby'. The Detroit Emerald's 'Feel The Need In Me'. Lou Rawls' 'You'll Never Find'. Johnny Bristol's 'Hang On In There Baby'. And everything by The Three Degrees, Harry Melville and The Bluenotes and, most of all, Barry White. In fact anything on the Philadelphia label.

We were genuinely happy just to be dancing. But we'd usually get hit on by one of the suited older guys eyeing up the dance floor. And sometimes I'd accept a lift if they dropped a hint of a posh sports car. One night a guy called Barry, who must have been over 30, drove me back home in his Jensen Interceptor. That really was the business. Princess Anne had one of those. How glam was that? How alarming is it looking back? But I never came a cropper because, thank God, nobody ever turned nasty when all they got was a quick snog in the front seat before I'd totter safely back down our drive.

'Romance' aside, most weekends me and Cousin Linda would head home in the early hours together. And then sleep until lunchtime when I had to pay my dues glass collecting and washing up in my grandma's pub and Linda had to do the same in her mum and dad's.

If you've ever seen the TV sitcom 'Early Doors' set in a Manchester pub, you'll have an idea what life was like then for me and Linda. We provided a bit of a floor show for the regulars who never went anywhere else, always sat in the same spot, but like an extended family, fondly followed our comings and goings. "Are you off out again love? Is that a new frock? Eeh. Dunt she look smashin'. Where yer off to then? Manchester! Ooh be careful there. Did you have a good time then? Eeh. These young uns eh. Have you got a boyfriend yet? Never mind. Yer've got plenty of time."

On Sunday tea times I'd rush through my homework listening to the Top 20 on Radio 1. By Monday morning we'd both have recovered just in time for Linda to breeze back into work at Barclays Bank and me to slope into school.

Sixth form was a haven anyway. Very civilised. We never had to leave our own purpose built block. Between lessons we'd hang out in the common room where distinct tribes would decamp to their own areas. The Greebos, lads with long greasy hair, centre partings and ex-army coats but no girlfriends, would pore over Yes album sleeves between physics lessons. They despised all that 'commercial' stuff so loved by us Bowie, T. Rex and Roxy Music fans. Why did those guys have to be so anal? Why couldn't they just appreciate everything? I did. Well except for Yes and similar pretentious shite.

In the end, and against all odds, I passed 4 A-Levels. I'd been expected to stay on to take the Oxbridge entrance exam in February but unsurprisingly I hadn't quite made the grades. And I just wanted to get away. So, two months after my 17th birthday, I started a new life in Leeds.

But first there was a life lesson to learn. One more rite of passage. A night of passion. I had to get that out of the way before I became a student. And I knew just the man for the job.

In 1969, my dad had said goodbye to his trusty tow bar and hello to the keys of a luxurious 32-foot static caravan on the Yorkshire coast. We'd spend every weekend and holiday there as a family. My mum and dad would sit out their days in deck chairs reading books while we'd go off, Famous Five style, on our bikes down hedgerowed winding lanes exploring the countryside and coast with our new friends, bags of ham sandwiches and lashings of ginger beer. One of the gang was a year older than me but because he was a lad he was first and foremost my little brother's mate not mine. For now anyway.

After my dad's hanky panky had been discovered and my mum had taken up with Jim, she'd take us there with him. That was fine. We liked Jim. He was really kind to us and a good laugh. Sometimes, though, because my mum and dad were so busy actively pursuing their new love lives, me and Our Andrew would be left to our own devices there for weeks on end with just enough money for food and no limits to what we could get up to.

In June, 1975, aged 16, I had finished my A Levels and headed off to the caravan on my own. But not for long. One lunchtime I was stretched out on a sun lounger, in a white cotton bikini, all oiled up and getting thoroughly burnt because, although Ambre Solaire was dead sophisticated, I might as well have covered myself in chip fat.

The peace was suddenly shattered by the distinctive din of a clapped out Ford Anglia approaching. My heart, and everything else, leapt.

Back home, for a couple of years now, I might have been attracting a lot of unsuitable older admirers around the clubs of Manchester, but ever since I was 13 I'd only ever loved one boy.

And now Our Andrew's cheeky older friend had just turned 18, was 6' 2" and drop dead gorgeous. And here he was.

Squinting into the sunshine I could see his white shirt was unbuttoned. His stripey tie was askew. The little school cap he'd long outgrown was perched defiantly on the back of his head. His arm, bronzed and muscular from water skiing, was resting on the open window of his souped up old banger. Huge brown bedroom eyes burnt right through me and a big beaming smile was coming straight at me.

He'd just finished his last exam and sixth form and had roared straight over from his nearby boarding school to see if 'anyone' was around and up for celebrating. He admitted later he meant me. I was. And I was!

"Fancy going down the pub Kershaw?"

By the time I'd pulled on my cut-off denim shorts and tie-dye t-shirt he'd turned the car round and we were hurtling down the empty coast road with his eight-track stereo blasting out Free's 'Wishing Well'.

We spent the rest of that summer exploring his record collection together. And each other.

He opened my mind and a lot more to Muddy Waters, Rory Gallagher and Pink Floyd, struggling in and out of wetsuits and his speed boat and fumbling around with each other's buttons and zips.

But I held out on the full thing until our very last weekend before Uni. Even though my intention was to get properly laid before I became a student, us nice convent girls just didn't do that kind of thing without a pretence at resistance. And, anyway, I really couldn't see how I'd fit all that lot inside me.

In the end, that fateful Saturday night, we made a dash to his parents' empty executive detached house complete with sauna while they were, as ever, knocking back the gin, Jag parked up outside, in their caravan.

I've not read Fifty Shades of Grey. But I bet its erotica doesn't involve catching your toenail in purple nylon sheets, and demolishing a pyramid of empty beer cans stacked in the corner of the bedroom to a Pink Floyd album. Well, five minutes of it anyway. Was that it? He kissed me on the forehead, pulled on his pants, and drove me back to the caravan.

I've still got the funny affectionate letters he sent me in my first year. But then it just fizzled out and I never heard from him again. I did hear that after graduating he went off to join the RAF as a fighter pilot. I didn't get over him until six years later in 1982, when I was taken to the pictures in Leeds to see An Officer and a Gentleman by my then boyfriend.

Seeing Richard Gere in his uniform having second thoughts about abandoning his girlfriend and coming back to carry her away opened the floodgates. I bawled my eyes out that night. And then, and only then, was I finally over my first love.

If I ever compile an album called 'Your 100 Shagging Greats' – the soundtrack to my first night of 'passion' – 'One Of These Days' by Pink Floyd would be the opening track. It's perfect. Starting with a bit of tinkering around and building to a mighty climax. It rocks.

Chapter Four

SHE'S LEAVING HOME

That October, after deciding on Leeds University, I found myself rattling around an empty flat near Headingley cricket ground. This leafy bohemian suburb of north Leeds was to be my home for the best part of the next 12 years. My dad had dropped me off with all my worldly goods. Two new pairs of jeans, an assortment of colourful t-shirts, our old family Dansette along with my entire record collection of no more than a dozen LPs, and enough cash to see me through the term. Oh and a new winter coat with a big fur collar. At last. Thanks Dad! Bye! See you at Christmas.

I was too naive to be scared. But my dad wasn't. I didn't know then that as I unpacked he was parked up round the corner sobbing over the steering wheel. Just as he'd done when he first dropped me off at nursery school 14 years earlier. And at the convent when I was five. But now I was just excited and waiting to see who else would turn up to share this student home for the next year.

The first of my new flatmates to burst through the door was Helen, a second year medical student. With long flowing Titian locks, a ruddy well-scrubbed smiley face, cheesecloth maxi skirt, long Dr Who style knitted scarf and flip flops, she was our resident Dylan fan. Then came Maggie. A second year design student in a vintage frock, huge platform shoes, sculptured short hair and a painted face she'd copied from a Roxy Music album sleeve. Finally Alison. She was in her final year of English, very straight, and seemingly untouched and unliberated by two years of student life.

The fifth bedroom of this unit, in one of the seven purpose-built blocks that made up the Lupton Flats complex, saw different people come and go over the next three terms. Including an ex-nun studying theology. I suspect we might have unwittingly driven out this timid reclusive woman with all the different styles of loud music from each of our rooms constantly clashing in the corridor.

But me, Helen and Maggie hit it off straight away. And, when Alison – who was already engaged and liked to cook cosy suppers for her fiancé – wasn't hogging our communal kitchen, it would be full of the friends we each brought to the party. Medics, artists, engineers, toffs, scruffs, country bumpkins and townies from Woking to Wigan. And exotic, unbelievably rich foreign students from Portugal, Lebanon and Istanbul who, in flashy suits and dripping in Paco Rabanne, whisked me and Maggie off to nightclubs in their Mercedes and BMWs.

What a melting pot. I was in my element. And also in heaven from the moment I'd found out that, on my first Monday there, October 5th, 1975, Roxy Music were headlining in the Union. The Leeds University Student Union Refectory was legendary. This had been the venue for already historic concerts by The Who and The Rolling Stones. All we'd ever got in Rochdale was Mud passing through on tour with chart toppers like 'Tiger Feet'. Now my favourite bands were all here right on my doorstep week-in week-out and me and Maggie made sure we always had tickets.

And our cushions. I was quickly learning the ropes. In those first terms, whether it was John Martyn or Hot Chocolate, the concert crowd would sit respectfully cross-legged on the floor watching the gig.

But that all changed with punk. And so did the hairstyles. And so did my collection of albums. Suddenly during the long hot summer drought of '76, as the Sex Pistols, The Clash and Buzzcocks came onto our radar, all the guys we knew wanted their long lank hippy locks chopped off. I was only too happy to crop them and spike them up in exchange for a now unfashionable rock LP. So that's how I became the tardy but proud owner of 'Led Zep IV' and a lifelong fan of 'The Led'. How was I to know then that, in time, I'd get to meet and get matey with their front man?

By 1977, us girls had left the comparative luxury of Lupton behind, having opted for the obligatory decadence of a student slum down the road. Helen, Maggie and me now shared with a couple of guys doing town planning and one landscape architecture student from Leeds Polytechnic.

Our circle was widening and so was our musical education.

SHE'S LEAVING HOME

These lads introduced us to prog rock from the likes of Wishbone Ash and Caravan as well as funky new stuff by The Crusaders and the latest from Stevie Wonder. And one of their mates, Steve the Colour Chemist, was keen on a new band from New York. He told me I had to hear their songs 'I Don't Wanna Go Down To The Basement' and 'Now I Wanna Sniff Some Glue'. Yeah, right Steve. Are you sure you're not on something yourself?

But I was soon hooked on The Ramones and wearing out their debut album on my new stereo. A Sanyo music centre with a smoked glass lid and integral deck, cassette player and radio. And the biggest speakers in the house. I'd just got my compensation from our car crash (three years earlier) and had finally ditched the Dansette.

On May 17th the whole household went on a pilgrimage to see The Clash at the Poly. For a week after that my badge of honour was a big black eye. I'd got headbutted by a Siouxie Sioux look-alike with jet black hair, heavy eye make-up and a basque when I'd got in her way down the front. Maybe it was her! Whatever. I was, briefly, the coolest kid on the block.

As the nation celebrated the Queen's Silver Jubilee, we did our bit for anarchy in the UK with a copy of the Sex Pistols' 'God Save The Queen' and a poster of Her Maj stuck on the wall over the gas fire in the front room. It was soon adorned with tattoos (I 'heart' Phil on her bare upper arm), a real safety pin through her nose, and various bits of anti-establishment graffiti. Otherwise we were all still being dutiful middle class kids, revising and taking exams to make sure we kept on the right side and the payroll of our parents and could carry on into third year.

THE BIRD AND THE BEEB

Before we'd even got our results we'd all started working shifts in a frozen food factory for 63p an hour. We were on nights and sleeping all day, so not spending anything. Just stashing it away. Every night for 12 hours I'd sit beside the women who worked there all the time. Not just for eight weeks to save enough for a four-week backpacking trip around Turkey later in the summer. Most of my new mates had loads of kids and no men to help. This wasn't a hoot for them. It was their life. And it was grim and cold and crushingly boring and low paid.

Note to self. Never get stuck like this.

I was now going out with one of the lads in the house. We stuck together for over three years but in the end we split up because his dream was to get married as soon as he got a proper job after Uni. He'd pissed me off when he'd put me down, telling me any dreams I had were silly and could never come true. Who did I think I was anyway? He wasn't into Bruce Springsteen!

Nevertheless I was really upset when he quickly married someone else and I was left wondering if I'd made the biggest mistake of my life. But I know it could only have ended in tears if I'd settled down and had children so soon and before I'd had chance to explore more of the world and to experience all I've been able to since. He was a lovely lad. And I hope it's all gone to plan and he's been happy and contented. I really do.

That September, having got back from roughing it round Turkey, a bit older, a lot wiser and having caught the travel as well as a tummy bug (I'd lost a stone!) I spent my last few bob on a copy of Ian Dury and The Blockheads' new album 'New Boots and Panties'. I'd got the single 'Sex and Drugs and Rock and Roll' just before we went away. That song was banned by Radio

1 but John Peel and Annie Nightingale rebelled by playing the B side, 'Razzle In My Pocket'.

We still listened to Radio 1 all day and every day even though its DJs refused to play any of the music we owned.

Apart from Peel and Annie.

Her show, which she always started with a deep throaty 'Hi' (inspiring me to open with a somewhat less sultry but cheery 'Hiya' years later and to this day) was a fixture on Sunday afternoons. Not least because our Uni got more mentions than any other. So she got bombarded with more and more requests from Leeds students and it became a standing joke on her show. As it has on mine. I'm told there's a drinking game where some 6 Music listeners in that city sit round the radio with a bottle of vodka and every time Leeds gets a namecheck they knock back a shot. They must get quite sozzled some Saturdays.

Anyway, even before I ever heard her on Radio 1, Annie Nightingale was already my heroine. I'd first spotted her in Petticoat magazine. She was pictured at the top of her weekly column wearing a big, fun fur coat and huge flares and to a 13-year-old pop fan in Rochdale this blonde music journalist, living the life in London, was just the bees knees.

And everything I wanted to be.

On one quiet grey Sunday afternoon in my first term at Leeds, Annie played a song that would change my entire attitude to life. Bruce Springsteen and 'Born to Run'. Coincidentally, from Greenhill Avenue, Andrew Binks (Binksy) was watching Tony Wilson on Granada TV as he introduced the same song. That was it. We've been devotees of Bruce ever since. 'Tramps like us' had discovered the greatest poet of the 20th Century who pleaded with us to 'share our dreams and visions'. Who inspired us to believe that with a 'can do' ethos, no matter how lowly or mundane your beginnings, you should go out and grab life by its blue collar, live it to the full and make the world yours.

It was six years before I saw Bruce 'live' with Our Andrew in 1981 in Birmingham but since then, me and Binksy have travelled the world to see him play. Thanks, Annie. Three minutes of BBC radio. A lifetime of passion.

I still liked pop and prattle though. And that's why I was tuned to Radio 1 on the day that Tony Blackburn famously went into meltdown on air, playing the same record over and over again and pleading with his wife "Tessa, me old darlin'" (as Smashie and Nicey parodied it in their 1992 spoof documentary The End Of An Era) to come back.

And I still loved disco so went to any and every boogying event put on by the students' union, various societies and the halls of residence. And by me. I'd been elected Events 'Sec' of my department and thrived on organising every kind of social function from sweaty discos to formal black tie balls with sit-down dinners and live bands. But my little brother was soon to take this to another level. I kept Our Andrew fully informed of how much fun it was in Leeds. And, because of my feedback and its already established reputation, he was also interested in... er... studying at the iconic home of The Who Live At Leeds.

When Bob Dylan played in early 1978 he bagged a ticket and came to stay with me. That was it. He was hooked and, though still small for his age, looking about 12 and painfully shy, he started his short-lived Politics course that autumn. Before the end of his first year he'd grown (in height and confidence), blossomed big time, turned into something of a babe magnet, and was running the Refectory gigs full time.

SHE'S LEAVING HOME

Meanwhile, it had suddenly dawned on me that maybe I'd been partying a bit too hard and it was time now to get down to some work if I was actually going to leave Leeds that summer with a degree. So after Easter I took to my bed. With books and lecture notes for revision, bunches of bananas for handy nourishment and Kate Bush's and Elvis Costello's debut albums for company.

I scraped a Third. My dad cried with pride and joy. Actually, mainly with relief. While I, still only 19, packed my bags and headed for Liverpool.

I know this sounds a bit old farty but 'ooh, I do feel sorry for the kids of today'. Really I do. The hoops they're put through to get a job is just obscene. I say that because the whole recruitment process just seems so dishonest.

It appears to be designed to put as many hurdles as possible in the way so that, despite all their best efforts and because there are simply too many of them, it will knock back the majority of earnest young hopefuls.

So if you just want to stack shelves for the minimum wage you're asked to submit a CV listing all your previous employment experience, voluntary work and extra curricular activities. If you want a proper graduate job it can take six months of psychometric testing and interviews. And that's only if your CV suits in the first place. I know this first hand from my own sons who are going through all this now. Even with a 2:1 Masters degree in engineering after four years at a top 10 Uni.

In my final year all I had to do was to turn up at the careers centre on campus for what they called 'The Milk Round'. All the big companies came to hoover up new recruits. I was snapped up on the spot by Littlewoods.

They did mail order catalogues, high street retailing and the football pools and they didn't mind what grade I got or even if I passed at all. Brilliant. Result. No worries. I had a job to go to after I left Uni. I could have gone with the more prestigious and better paid Marks & Spencer (I was intent on fashion retailing) but that offer was dependent on me getting a 2:1 and I knew damn well that was never going to happen.

Actually, to be honest, there was one further hurdle. I had to go to Littlewoods' HQ in Liverpool for a final interview. But I still maintain that was just a formality. Especially after what happened on the day.

Before boarding the train bound for Lime Street Station I hurriedly stuffed down a pepperoni pizza. Maybe it was that followed by the running to catch the train on time, or the motion of the filthy old rolling stock, or the hangover from the skinful I'd had, in nerves, the night before, or all of the above. But not long into the journey I started to feel a bit queasy.

My dad had bought me a sharp suit and my grandma had paid for the matching accessories, a shirt, handbag and shoes. Now I was sitting there all dressed to kill on the Trans Pennine Express wondering where I could be sick.

Before I had time to decide, my lunch was already swilling around in my lap. My new skirt was all that was keeping the rounds of spicy sausage coated in tomato sauce and mozzarella off the floor. Fantastic. I was a stinking mess and due at my new employer's posh office block in just a couple of hours.

That was that then. I cleaned up as best as I could in the train's revolting toilet and headed for the showdown. They wouldn't want me now would they.

Oh well. Fuck it.

Maybe my blasé 'couldn't care less' attitude suggested a certain confidence. A self belief. I dunno. But they instantly confirmed, as I answered a few questions while covered in reeking Italian vomit, that I had a job to go to that September.

Hey, kids. I wouldn't recommend this method of psyching-up for a major career challenge. But it certainly worked for me.

Chapter Five

CAREER OPPORTUNITIES

Not long into my new career, two things dawned on me. The first was that I'd made a 'forever friend' while I was sitting in the canteen with a fellow graduate recruit. I had an advert from the Liverpool Echo for an affordable, smart, rented house, a three bedroomed semi for £120 a month in a nice suburb. She had wheels. So we teamed up to go and have look. We took it and lived there for a year, sharing our Donna Summer, Police and ·Blondie albums and going to gigs. And 35 years later Sheena Bullen is still my best friend.

The second realisation was that this job was not for me.

Littlewoods was an archaic, privately owned family firm. John Moores was the elderly head of that family and a patriarch in every sense. He'd arrive at his flagship HQ like Young Mr.

CAREER OPPORTUNITIES

Grace from the TV sitcom 'Are You Being Served' with an entourage of sycophants, expecting to be greeted by obsequious staff doffing their caps. Meanwhile we employees, even those at the highest level of management, were apparently so untrustworthy that we had to succumb to the ritual humiliation of clocking in and out at a machine by the entrance every morning and night.

Plus your status in the firm (or lack of it) was constantly on display due to the state of your workspace. Only when you got to a certain level were you allowed to sit with your back to a window. Further promotion meant men in brown coats came and ceremoniously plonked a glass top on your desk. Really?

I might have hated working for Mr. Moores but, amazingly, it was in his flagship store that I got my first big break in broadcasting! As part of our induction into his mighty empire, us management trainees had to experience life on the shop floor in Littlewoods in Liverpool city centre.

So I spent a couple of months trudging miles along the aisles for 10 hours a day, checking stock levels and monitoring sales.

"What's the sales per foot on men's underwear today Miss Kershaw?"

"Six pounds so far Sir."

"Jolly good Miss Kershaw. Carry on."

After a few weeks of checking tills, re-folding jumpers, putting bras back in their packets and wrestling with shoplifters, it was a relief to be consigned to a glass booth overlooking Ground Floor Ladies Fashions.

Ding dong. "Good morning customers. In our Lower Ground Floor Food Hall today you will find Silk Cut King Size (I had a lot of trouble with that one) for only £1 a packet."

Ding dong. "Ladies, we now have Tricel twin sets in a range of pastel colours and sizes for only £1.99 in our Ground Floor Separates Department."

Ding dong. "Our men's action slacks now come in waist sizes 28 to 48 on the upper sales floor. Why not relax in our cafeteria with a pot of tea and a toasted teacake while you're there. Thank you for shopping at Littlewoods. Enjoy your day."

Ding dong.

Well at least I got the chance to sit down.

And for all this, I was being paid the princely sum of £3,100 a year. One day, I calculated that, after paying my rent, utility bills and travel costs, I had 10p a day for lunch. That would just about buy me a 6p soup from the machine by the lifts. A few years earlier I'd met a fellow Rochdale girl who'd won Miss England and married into the Moores family. She'd been draped in chiffon and mink. I was now on a treadmill paying for all that while being half-starved.

Bollocks to all this.

I soon decided this was against all the principles that had been drummed into me from birth by my socialist relatives and because of my heritage – hailing from the home of the co-operative movement. So I announced to Sheena that I wasn't going to spend my life kowtowing to old Mr. Moores, and lining this multi-millionaire's already bulging pockets. I wasn't prepared to simply be 'a pawn in the capitalist machine'.

Oh, get me. I now realise, of course, that Littlewoods was good for Liverpool, creating loads of jobs and bringing millions into the otherwise depressed local economy. And that capitalism is OK if it cares.

But hey. I was young and idealistic then and soon started

scanning The Guardian for opportunities elsewhere. Ideally in the non-profit public service sector. Oh here was a job with the Post Office. And back in Leeds! For £4,800 a year. Bingo.

Another interview triumph followed.

"You'll have to supervise male staff. Some of them much older than you. How do you feel about that?"

"Well I can tell you now. I've been on the job with all kinds of men before."

Shit! Did I really just say that? Oh well. Never mind. Back to Liverpool then. Or so I thought...

"I see. Can you start in early September?"

Sadly, before I could begin my life of selfless public service, Margaret Thatcher decided it would be best if the Post Office was flogged off to the electorate so I now worked for British Telecommunications PLC, or BT, instead.

Anyway, back to Leeds where Our Andrew was now following in my footsteps. He'd spent his first year at Leeds University in Lupton Flats and was moving into the same decrepit house where I'd spent my second year. 16 Norwood Terrace. Luckily there was a spare room going in the attic and, thanks to my brother, my name was on it. I had a few bob coming in now so I splashed out on matching wallpaper and fabric from Habitat and a fitted carpet to make it more habitable than it had ever been in our day there.

It was still bloody freezing though. You still had to keep your t-shirt on just to survive a bath. There was no promise of central heating and dodgy wires hung out of the walls. The bannisters were all wonky. The floor in the front room was covered in slugs and threatening to collapse into the cellar. The gas fire was hanging off the chimney breast. The back of the sofa was long gone. But hey!

This was the best of both worlds. I was holed up with my beloved brother while earning good money and living the life of a student again. What was there not to like? He was still supposedly on his politics course but actually running all the gigs in the students' union Refectory. So I got 'Access All Areas' passes for everything. Iggy Pop, Bob Marley, Ian Dury and The Blockheads, Kid Creole and The Coconuts, Stray Cats, Black Uhuru, UB40.

By day I was suited and booted and oozing corporate respectability (or so I thought). By night it was back to jeans and t-shirts and sex and drugs and rock 'n' roll.

After yet another bloody freezing winter, the novelty of roughing it in Norwood Terrace had worn a bit too thin. One day I was driving along by the university when I spotted two elderly men in suits going up the front steps of a large terraced Victorian villa on the corner of the park. I pulled over and pounced. They were a bit startled but confirmed that they were property developers and about to do the place up. What a dump. But, as they say... 'location, location, location'. And I was in there. They agreed that as soon as they'd given it the once over, the keys would be mine.

By now I had my first convertible. Well... a bright yellow Citroen 2CV which was easily converted into a removal van by rolling back its plastic roof and sticking Our Andrew's seven foot rubber plant on the back seat beside boxes of LPs and the kitchen table over my head. And so, with a few trips, I moved us, frocks, rock, and (biscuit) barrel, into 159 Hyde Park Road. Our Andrew enjoyed telling everybody that he'd come home to

Norwood Terrace that evening to find everything gone except for a note informing him of his new address.

But he soon calmed down, impressed by the miracle of central heating and hot water, a gas cooker that wasn't actually lethal, a toilet that flushed, brand new fitted carpets (bright orange and quite obviously the cheapest in town) and picture windows giving us panoramic views across Hyde Park to the university. Luxury. And at the centre of the universe... as we knew it then.

Now we could unpack our records including the latest from Bruce Springsteen – 'The River' and soon after 'Nebraska' – and the debut album from ABC, 'Lexicon of Love'.

We made a pilgrimage to Birmingham to see Bruce. But ABC were actually coming to town, to the Queens Hall. That was a cavernous old tram shed with a much bigger capacity than the Uni Refectory and I'd seen the biggest crowd pullers, like The Police, there.

Before the show I witnessed Sting being driven up to the stage for the soundcheck in a Jag. That was a bit of a contrast to my first Police gig in Blackburn in 1978 with Sheena when we'd paid £1.50 for our tickets and the stage lighting consisted of just three small static spotlights.

But now Martin Fry, resplendent in his trademark gold lamé suit, was centre stage in front of a string orchestra and I was singing along word-perfect to the amazing album that's still in my Top 10. There and then I decided I didn't want to be just a face in the crowd. I wanted to be part of all that. And not as some groupie. But as an equal at the heart of the music industry.

I was getting there. I was now writing a weekly music column for the Yorkshire Post after meeting their reviewer at a gig one night. I wrote about as many bands as I could – under the name 'Dawn Chorus' – and I picked up about £25 a month. This was the life. I could blag more tickets than ever and the kudos was great. It was quite amazing to see my name at the top of a newspaper page – even if it was a false one!

When I wasn't out seeing live bands, The Warehouse club in Leeds city centre was a favourite haunt. Marc Almond was the cloakroom attendant for a while and it was from his little booth, that he'd famously first heard 'Tainted Love' by Gloria Jones. I picked up on 12" singles by The Sugarhill Gang, Grandmaster Flash and The SOS Band there. And Soft Cell.

Their 12" version of 'Tainted Love' mashed up with 'Where Did Our Love Go?' was an immediate staple at Hyde Park Road. Because we were all in the students' union watching and working on gigs every Friday and Saturday, our parties then had to be fitted in on Sunday afternoons. And they were always heaving with Rude Boys (fans of The Specials), Goths (who idolised The Cure and Sisters of Mercy) and New Romantics (Duranies and Spands fans). But the floor would clear when one guy, who thought he was Adam Ant – so whatever the weather would turn up in his tight leather trousers, Hussar's jacket and full make-up – would 'Stand And Deliver' on the opening blast of the song's hunting horn.

It was alarm bells that Our Andrew was hearing now. So far those nice bearded academics in the university Politics department hadn't yet kicked him off his course. Perhaps they hadn't noticed that he'd not set foot in the place for nearly 12 months. Or maybe they enjoyed free passes into all the gigs he put on. But at the end of his second year came a reality check. It was time for exams.

CAREER OPPORTUNITIES

One sunny Saturday morning, I bawled at him to get out of bed and set the table for breakfast. He said he'd have something when he got back. We both knew it was a waste of time but I sat alone at the table in the front window watching him stride across the park. Before the tea pot had time to get cold he was strolling back. And that was that. He wasn't a student anymore and his triumphant two year as Entertainments Secretary were nearly up too. He needed a job.

A new local radio station – Radio Aire – was just starting up with a lot of publicity and noise. I decided to give it a whirl and tuned in to find out if it lived up to all the fuss. I hated all the ads but pricked up my ears when I heard one for the station's Promotions Manager. I persuaded Our Andrew that he had nothing to lose by going for it so he did and was snapped up on the spot. What he lacked in experience he must have made up for in charm.

Before long they'd spotted that he knew more about music than marketing and they gave him his own show. His own promotion left an on-air vacancy as the compiler and presenter of the weekly five minute Gig Guide during the Martin Kelner show. Martin was only too happy to replace Our Andrew with Our Elizabeth and gave me a go.

This was pre-internet so I'd spend hours ringing round all the venues in West Yorkshire from pubs to clubs to big halls and colleges finding out what was coming up.

After a few months, the boss, an ex-BBC man who liked a long lunch and sometimes came back to the office with half of it stuck in his beard, had really taken to me, and offered me a little slot of my own. 'The Saturday Sizzling Sounds of the Sixties Show'.

Having got my top set around that I set about showcasing my growing collection of old singles.

Martin Kelner is a brilliant broadcaster and has long since moved to the BBC in Leeds. He likes to joke that he is responsible for discovering both the Kershaws and has had to hang his head in shame ever since! Radio Aire has certainly punched above its weight finding talent.

In our time there, the roll call included the future BBC correspondents Mark Easton and Mark Mardell, Helen Boaden who is now BBC Director of Radio, Peter Levy and Christa Ackroyd, who became the BBC's biggest stars in Yorkshire, and many many more down the years including Chris Moyles and Radio 2's Alex Lester.

Martin had another on-air sidekick, a local carpet fitter called Tony. AKA Chip The Ginger. AKA Edouard Le Paglier. We only lived just up the hill from Radio Aire so when we found we'd somehow got locked in and couldn't get out of the flat, naturally Our Andrew called his colleagues for help.

The next thing we knew, all hell let loose outside with the fire brigade having been called, the Radio Aire Range Rover in the middle of the road with its mighty broadcast aerial fully extended, and Edouard Le Paglier in a red white and blue ra ra skirt and wig giving a full live commentary on the rescue in his comical, slightly French, but mainly thick Yorkshire accent to an excited bank holiday crowd.

It just shows how free wheeling and creative it all was back then. Or maybe the boss was in the pub. Or maybe he'd had just about enough of all this tomfoolery when he had a hissy fit and a massive clear out about a year later and sacked Our Andrew, Martin and a couple more top turns on the same day.

CAREER OPPORTUNITIES

I think we'd have quite happily stayed in Hyde Park Road forever. But then, by pure chance, I heard that the most amazing flat in the most elegant house in the poshest road in Headingley was up for sale. It belonged to a friend of a friend who'd taken me round there once. Wow! Nestled in the eaves under exposed oak beams, it filled an entire floor of an imposing Arts and Crafts-style Edwardian mansion. Its leaded windows overlooked extensive grounds and a long driveway behind a high stone wall and sturdy gates.

Buying this three bedroomed £24,000 penthouse seemed just pie in the sky. I hadn't got two halfpennies to rub together never mind any kind of deposit but I soon discovered that on paper, now on a mighty eight grand a year in a secure job at the rock solid BT, I was a good bet. And these were the days of 100% mortgages. The maths stacked up so I decided to go for it before it got snapped up on the open market. Miraculously, we moved in a couple of months later.

The silver-haired residents of the other three flats probably feared the worst as soon as they saw their new neighbours lugging tons of vinyl, guitars and amps, shabby chic furniture and a massive fish tank up the communal stairs. When they saw the jukebox arrive they must have thought the peace of their previously exclusive enclave had been shattered forever.

I'd always wanted a jukebox and I'd come across a 1963 Rockola Capri in the back of a junk shop in Leeds. It was covered in cobwebs and full of mouse droppings but the guy assured me it worked and just needed a good clean and a good home. For 50 quid, he was glad to get shut of it and I was happy to take a risk.

With its chrome and glass now polished up and gleaming in its own pink neon lights, and filled with all our favourite 7" vinyl singles, it was now cleaned up and cranked up and standing proud, and very loud, in the echoey central hall of our spacious new pad. For the next four years this was party central.

The neighbours did complain. I suppose we were annoying. But so were they. They blamed us for everything. I suppose the weaselly, smug retired bloke on the ground floor who'd wearily climb the stairs to come banging on our door had a point. We nicknamed him 'Hi-Fi' because of his stock phrase which he'd whine in a thin, pained, posh Scottish voice. "Won't you turn down your Hi-Fi equipment?" Fair enough. Especially as the jukebox would burst into life at all times of the day and night because Our Andrew always insisted on letting us all know he'd just got his leg over with The Thunderbirds theme tune. OK. Then I'd do the same with selection A6. A US No. 1 from 1963 by Paul and Paula, 'Hey Paul'. That worked well for me as I had three successive boyfriends with that name.

So, yes, we were noisy. But dogshit on the grass? That was an accusation too far. We didn't even have a dog. Neither did anybody we knew. So Our Andrew went and indignantly sprinkled multi-coloured hundreds and thousands all over the offending pile and left it like a big steaming cake on the lawn. Our real crime? Being upstarts. They'd worked all their lives to afford to live here so in their book we were just too young to deserve to be able to do that.

And yes it must have been galling to open the curtains on a Sunday morning only to see everything from doormats to traffic cones hanging high in the trees after yet another party.

But whether they liked us or not, we owned it. So as long as we kept up with the mortgage payments nobody could ever throw us out. We had a secure home at last. A happy place that worked because of our distinct and important roles. I was the practical 'grown up' one, juggling to pay the mortgage, papering over the cracks, doing up junk shop finds and filling the fridge. Not always very successfully. On one occasion we opened it to be faced with just half a dried out onion for dinner. A tuna sandwich was all I could rustle up one lunchtime. And we had to share that.

We might have been living it large in luxury. But we were always skint even though we were both earning, me at BT and Andrew at Radio Aire. Why? Because we partied hard. While I was head of housekeeping Andrew was social secretary, throwing himself into organising parties with his trademark gusto and bringing home all sorts of characters he met through his job. "Oh come round to ours. Our Elizabeth will feed you."

And that's how I met Dixon, who became like an older brother to us. I'm sure he told me in 1981 that he was 33. And yet, 30-odd years later he's still only 55. Apparently. Perhaps I made a mistake. Or maybe that just sums up what a loveable rogue he is. Chris (we've never called him that) Dixon was a right ducking and diving Manchester geezer and had worked for years for record companies in his home city, plugging new releases to radio stations there. He'd crossed the Pennines to take up a lucrative job at Yorkshire Television, making trailers for its top productions like Emmerdale Farm and Countdown. YTV was next door to Radio Aire and when Our Andrew met Dixon in the staff bar there they instantly bonded over several pints and talking bollocks about bands.

Ever since then he's worked his way unashamedly through my friends, breaking hearts and promises along the way. But to his credit, none of them seems able to bear a grudge. The original party guy, he's up for anything with anybody and likes a laugh. Especially at himself. I'd say that he is the most amoral man I've ever known. Except he has a heart of gold, is utterly generous in every way, would do anything for anyone, and still spends Christmas with us.

On another day Our Andrew arrived home with a real glamour puss in tight coffee-coloured leather trousers, with Tina Turner style spikey blonde-streaked hair and a sweeping black poncho. "This is Carol."

Bloody hell. Carol Vorderman?

I hardly recognised her. Wasn't this Richard Whiteley's sidekick who I'd seen on the telly a couple of years earlier when Countdown launched Channel 4? The brainy bird with the sickly smile who did the sums while gazing disturbingly into our living rooms. I'd thought she looked like Morticia from the Addams Family with long, lank, dark locks and a dowdy line in catalogue clothes. What a transformation.

Now she'd just won Our Andrew's song-writing competition on Radio Aire, and was guffawing in my kitchen. Years later her mum Jean took me aside. "You remember those leather trousers Liz? They cost £50 at Lewis's Department Store on The Headrow. That was a lot of money then Liz. A good investment though, eh?" Yes, a major dent in anyone's budget at the time, especially for poor Jean Vorderman. But, like Jean's lifelong dedication to her youngest daughter, one that paid off big time. It was Jean who actually wrote the winning song but, typically, she'd put her Carol's name on the entry. It had been Jean who, whilst reading the Yorkshire Evening Post on the bus ride home from her lowly admin job, had spotted Yorkshire TV's ad for a girl who could add up.

CAREER OPPORTUNITIES

Carol and her mum were completely devoted to each other and fiercely loyal. I've always envied, but never resented, the constant love and practical support that Carol's had throughout the years I've known them. Carol is the first to say she couldn't have done it without 'Mum'.

By the early 1980s, now in her fifties, Jean was divorced for the second time, penniless and living in a women's hostel. Carol was just out of Cambridge with a third class degree (now commonly known among students as a "Vorderman"), a job in engineering that was taking her all over the country and getting her down, and with most of her possessions stuffed in her old banger. A brown Datsun. The kind favoured by dodgy mini cab drivers.

Carol took an unusual step for someone just out of university but typical for Team Vorderman. She jacked in her job and sprang her mum from the hostel, and together they set up home in a humble house, just round the corner from us in Headingley.

Jean Vorderman was one of the loveliest, most ladylike, sweet, and generous women I'd ever met. A cross between the film star Jean Simmonds and Miss Marple with her pretty, delicate features, constant curiosity about people, soft, rather refined Welsh voice and genteel ways. She genuinely wanted the best, not just for Carol, but all of us.

She never poo-pooed our wild schemes. Instead her eyes would twinkle even more with every plan we came up with to escape the nine to five routine of 'proper jobs'. If her dreams hadn't come true, she was damn well determined ours would.

And so when we decided, like Bananarama or Madonna, that we'd storm the charts by forming our own girl group, Jean, then 55, was like the fourth member of the band. While the three of us, me, Carol and Lindsey, (then Miss Radio Aire and another of Our Andrew's finds), as Dawn Chorus and the Bluetits, practised, Jean, after a long hard day at work, would open up her living room, serve up tea and biscuits, type out lyrics and video everything. Jean's tapes still haunt us years later.

I thought our flat was a bit basic. We didn't have curtains until we got to Radio 1. 'Why spend money on 'luxuries' when you can go on a road trip across the States or have another party?' being our policy on interior design.

But everything about the Vordermans' unmodernised 1930s semi was second hand and shabby. From their cold kitchen with its original butler's sink, to the dowdy sitting room with snagged moquette '60s settee and frayed flowery '50s curtains. Nevertheless, like Jean it had a cheerful, welcoming, soothing gentility about it.

I felt right at home round there. While we fretted over the latest fella to dump us, Jean would serve constant coffee and cakes. We spent whole afternoons blubbering about lost loves while Jean kept the kettle on and me and Carol comforted each other while Phil Collins' 'Against All Odds' played on repeat on the old radiogram.

In 1997, after the best part of two decades climbing the TV tree, Carol was invited onto This Is Your Life. The Bluetits had gone belly up a long time ago but Jean, the fiercely proud mother, still had her video tape. No wonder Carol sat with her head in her hands when I popped out from the sliding screen. Only recently Carol suggested that "you and me and mum must watch it sometime for a laugh together. But that video must never be shown to anyone else!" Agreed. I'm not sure it would do me any favours either.

CAREER OPPORTUNITIES

As I arrived that night at This Is Your Life, Jean grabbed me and gave me a big squeeze. She was proud as punch and obviously bursting to tell me something.

"Look Liz," she whispered, beaming and twirling around in her new chiffon gown. "It's Frank Usher!" It was so touching to see her genuine pleasure in owning something beautiful. And, for Jean, who'd had nothing much for years, brand new and pretty expensive.

Her Carol had made it and, at the age of 70, that finally meant spangly frocks from a proper posh shop for 'Mum'.

Nobody deserved it more.

Back in our Headingley days, it got a lot wilder whenever Jean went to visit her family in Wales. One weekend we attempted a sophisticated dinner party for over a dozen guests. Carol wasn't daft. We were the only girls there.

All the other diners were members of Headingley Rugby Union Club's first XV with whom Carol was very popular. While one star winger took snaps up Carol's black leather miniskirt as she attempted to make gravy, a scrum broke out over the duck she'd just dished up. It was bad. Scraggy in fact.

"We can't eat this!" bellowed a Boris Johnson lookalike. "This bird," (the duck, not Carol) "needs a meal more than we do!"

There were no further attempts at cooking. After all, Carol's popularity in the wine bars of Leeds on a Friday night when those same guys flocked round her was nothing to do with her domestic skills.

She lapped it up. But I hated those rugger buggers.

Perhaps that's the key to lasting friendship. Never go after the same blokes. Or jobs.

Whatever.

THE BIRD AND THE BEEB

It's amazing how that little clique struggling to survive in a suburb of Leeds somehow produced three media careers, so far spanning over 30 years. I certainly never imagined that I'd ever be on the radio. Or Our Andrew on the telly.

But, through a series of surprise events and a lot of good luck, our lives were soon about to change forever.

Chapter Six

OH YEAH (ON THE RADIO)

"You're a lively young gal. Do you know anything about pop music?"

Imagine Mr. Burns asking Lisa Simpson that and you'll get the picture. Here was an ancient BBC 'suit' (actually he was probably just nudging 50) bent over a desk, fixing his beady eye on me, and interrupting me full flow to enquire about my grasp of the Hit Parade. Just bizarre.

I'd invited myself into Radio Leeds to see the boss about his telecommunications needs.

Part of my job at BT was to get more revenue out of the telephone network by getting people to install more phones and to make more calls. It seems strange nowadays, when we all go round with a handset permanently glued to our heads, but back then phones were still seen as an expensive luxury. Not every home had one. And those that did only had one wired into their hall and used it sparingly as needs must.

Of course we advertised but I'd come up with a cunning plan to use the local media to do our publicity for us at no cost to us. If I could get the BBC and all the other broadcasters across the region from Sunderland down to Sheffield and from Huddersfield to Hull to make more of phone-ins and sell them the latest hi-tech digital equipment it would instantly increase traffic and revenue while promoting the whole idea of phoning. For free. Tidy.

So here I was in full flow to the BBC's top dog in West Yorkshire. But his mind was on other things.

He'd just had a directive from above to make the station 'younger' and just as he'd been pondering how to stop the ageing audience quite literally dying out, I'd walked in. It could have been any 20-something crossing his threshold for the first time in 20 years. But serendipitously it was me.

The right time.

The right place.

And yes. He'd found his 'gal'. I did know my 'pop'. I'd been drinking it in since childhood and at last that was about to pay off.

"Er... well, yes, I suppose I do," I replied. "I'm in a band. And I write a weekly music column for the Yorkshire Post. And I've done a bit of radio on..."

I didn't get another word in.

"Excellent. Excellent. Then you must do a voice test. I'm looking for a presenter for a new show for young people. Are you free next Wednesday?"

OH YEAH (ON THE RADIO)

That was it. The biggest break I'd had and it came about because the BBC needed someone like me quickly and I had walked through the door at exactly the right moment.

I was ushered out of the building and, blinking in disbelief, back into the late afternoon sunshine.

I'm not sure it's ever really sunk in.

As I smiled to myself, I remember thinking that it would take a bit of explaining back at BT's NETEL (North East Telecoms) House.

How was I to tell my bossy boss that the only thing I'd sold to the BBC was... er... me?

Meanwhile I was bursting to tell my brother and, ironically for a BT bod, I desperately needed a phone. In those days only the biggest bosses had mobiles – huge prototype grey plastic bricks – with ridiculous aerials that could be pompously extended in a display of one's corporate status, all attached to a shoulder bag containing a battery pack the size of a microwave oven (except no-one knew what they were yet. This was two years before Dire Straits sang that we all needed to install one of those).

Oh sod it. Looking up Woodhouse Lane I could see on the University's Parkinson Tower clock that it was nearly home time anyway so I jumped on the next bus to Headingley to use the phone, in the hall, at Shire Oak Road.

Our Andrew had recently moved out. When he got the push from Radio Aire he'd made a list of all the people he'd ever met in the music business during his time booking and putting on bands at the university. He must have sent out about 100 letters cheekily telling record companies and agents why he was the best thing that could ever happen to them.

Most of the recipients probably filed them under 'young

upstart from t'north' but eventually it paid off. He was taken on by Pete Jenner at Sincere Management. Pete was a real music svengali who'd managed Pink Floyd, produced Ian Dury and the Blockheads' first album and got them a deal with Stiff Records, and was now managing a little known troubadour by the name of Billy Bragg.

Pete remembered that Our Andrew had rescued Billy's debut album from the reject bin at Radio Aire and had invited Billy up to Leeds to be on his show. Billy and Our Andrew had bonded big time. And Pete was impressed by this young gun, who, like him since the '60s, knew a good thing when he heard it and was prepared to stick his neck out when he did. Billy wasn't making any money for Sincere yet and they couldn't afford to actually pay Our Andrew but he was offered a room and full board in the Jenner family home (the office was in the front room), a packet of fags a day and the promise of riches to come.

"You what? A radio show on the BBC? Yer jammy bugger!" Our Andrew blurted out when he heard my good news. He was between road trips with Billy Bragg and sitting feet up on the desk having a ciggie (one of the 20 a day he was 'paid') in Billy's management office. He wasn't to know that, just as suddenly and amazingly, he'd soon be snapped up by BBC TV. But for now he was just chuffed for me.

We've never been in competition with each other. Mainly because we've never had a plan – we've just been a two-member support group. He was also my biggest supporter when it came to the band I was in – Dawn Chorus and the Bluetits.

One night, while at a Billy Bragg gig, we had given a tape to the sound guy during the interval. "Hiya," big cheesy grin. "Can you play this for us please?" It was a demo tape of the band. Billy and Our Andrew were on tour, in town, and camping out at mine as they did whenever their criss-crossing of the country brought them through Yorkshire. Which, as it's kind of centrally placed in the UK, seemed to be about once a month.

Our flat was still a social hub but a bit quieter since Our Andrew had gone to work in London. So I'd love it when he and Billy would burst through the door, throwing their coats, bags and guitar cases across the hall and plonking pizzas and booze on the kitchen table. Then we'd all sit round as various old mates arrived to catch up with the prodigal brother and to meet Billy. I liked Billy. And so did my girlfriends. Dixon was so last year now.

Billy must have decided he needed to apologise to me one day, explaining "'Ere, Our Elizabeth. If you weren't Kersh's sister I'd shag you." Ah, thanks Billy. I don't feel so left out now. Was he pleased to see me or was that a huge wad of cash in his pocket? It was a big roll of used tenners. Hundreds of pounds he'd be paid for his gigs. More cash than I'd ever seen in my life.

"You shouldn't be carrying that round with you Billy. It's dangerous. You should put it in the bank."

"Yeah. But my bank's in Barking."

"OK, but which bank is it?"

"Barclays."

"Well there's one at the bottom of the road. We can go down now and pay it in."

"No. My bank's in Barking."

This naivety was as surprising as it was endearing. For the prophet of our generation he seemed to know very little, at that stage, about how the world worked.

I thought his politics were a bit naive too. And his solutions simplistic. But you couldn't argue with Billy. He'd hit a rich seam with the miners' strike. Oh well. We were all having a great time and doing rather well under the Thatcher government.

In exchange for bed and board, Billy would put me and a mate on the guest list for his gigs. A bargain. For both of us I suppose.

At this one, thanks to that grudging but understanding sound man, the crowd got to hear Dawn Chorus and the Bluetits before the top turn.

Amazingly someone in the crowd not only loved our demo but was working at Radio 1 at the time. Not in a paid capacity you understand but, as I came to understand a few years later, as one of the admiring young women that frequently wrote to Peel and was occasionally, if they took his fancy, invited to hang out and help out 'just for fun' on his show.

When Peel's intern went and asked the dude on the desk who the interval entertainment was from, he instantly donated our tape which had my name and number scribbled on it. So a few days later I got 'the call'. The call that every aspiring band dreamt of back then. An invitation to the BBC's Maida Vale studios in London. To record a Peel Session!

There was just one small problem. Dawn Chorus was now minus Bluetits. Carol's telly career had really taken off. Countdown had become a must-see show for a cult following so she was getting her fix of fame with that and Lindsey had become besotted with a BT executive she'd met at one of our parties so it wasn't pop stardom that now filled her dreams. Plus neither of them really wanted to sing.

So that just left me. Should I just give up, turn down Peel's invitation and call the whole thing off? Or grab the chance of a lifetime that people would kill for and have a go on my own? We'd always thought Dixon was just full of bullshit when he claimed he knew everybody. But apparently he did. God knows how, but he'd roped in John and Damian O'Neil from The Undertones to play guitars with us. And Dixons in the city centre had sold Uncle Al (Our Andrew's pal and self-appointed band manager) a state of the art (v.1985) drum machine. So we had a band!

The Peel Session was set for a Sunday and the M1 South was deserted and drenched with blindingly low sunshine when the band (Al and me with the drum machine on the back seat) left Leeds at daybreak in his Jag. Al was of private means (rich mum) and he liked a nice car. He'd got this one because Princess Di had one at the time. We arrived back just under 24 hours later, absolutely knackered but ecstatic.

What an experience. It was all very industrial. It had to be in the time available. Four tracks recorded and fully mixed in under eight hours. Me doing the three vocal parts. But it was also magical.

We were in awe of the place... thinking of the young hopefuls turned legends that had been there before over the (what now seems short) 17 years since Peel's Radio 1 programme, Night Ride, had first gone out. Icons like Pink Floyd, Marc Bolan, and The Faces etc, etc.

Our allocated producer/engineer was Dale Griffin who, only just over a decade earlier, had been a member of chart topping (well... no. 3 in 1972 with 'All the Young Dudes') Bowie favourites Mott The Hoople before joining the BBC. And then there were the two members of one of my all-time favourite bands who joined us for the day. Two 'ordinary' lads from Derry. The O'Neils. In the previous few years they'd had no less than seven Top 40 singles and toured and changed the world (of music, anyway). But they were just dead normal and helpful and didn't seem fazed to be part of Dixon's latest dodgy deal.

A few weeks later, in February, 1985, we gathered round the radio at Shire Oak Road with piles of pizzas and lashings of Lambrusco bought with the spoils of the session, a 200 quid Musicians' Union standard fee from the BBC. It was 10 o'clock. "Tonight in session, Jesus And Mary Chain and Dawn Chorus and The Bluetits," Peel told the world.

Bloody hell we were in good company! J&MC were brilliant. I've loved them and played them loads on the radio ever since. I wonder if they, and the many bands who've gone on to international success, still remember that moment when they first heard Peel speak their name. Obviously I never cluttered up the charts. Except with a mighty No. 43 four years later with a 'cherridee' single with me old mate Bruno Brookes. But I can always say "I once did a Peel Session!" and nothing (not even a 'cherridee' single with me old mate Bruno Brookes) can ever take that away.

Meanwhile Dixon capitalised on this kudos and got us a meeting with one of the founders of the coolest label in the world. Dave Robinson of Stiff Records. (I know. Amazing. Don't ask). By now Stiff had abandoned its tiny shop premises in Notting Hill and its indie status (due to financial pressures rather than a loss of ethics) and merged and moved in with Island Records down the road in a big posh glass building in Chiswick.

Our route to Robbo's office took us past a wall full of gold discs celebrating U2 album sales which had presumably, rather than those of Stiff's own Lena Lovich or Wreckless Eric, funded these swanky surroundings. Blimey. This was big time.

I remember what I was wearing (a very '80s double-breasted bright blue ankle length wool coat with massive shoulder pads teamed with a jaunty red beret, matching shoes and lacey tights. Straight off the set of 'Allo 'Allo!') but I don't remember the conversation at all. I don't think I was part of it.

Dave Robinson was loud and 'larger than life' and as far as I was concerned he could do the deal with Dixon. Dixon had paid for the recordings at a studio in Wakefield owned by another mate of his called Neil. Neil had bought it with the huge proceeds of all the enormous hits he'd had with another local band – Black Lace. And I mean huge and enormous. They may not have been cool or had any cred but since 1980 they'd sold bucketloads of vinyl to happy holiday makers returning from the Costas.

That amazing tale was told in a telly film a couple of years later when I interviewed them. My opening lines were "I'm surrounded by the trappings of wealth..." before the camera panned out from the cocktails by their kidney-shaped swimming pool, to the factory chimneys of Cleckheaton.

Whatever. Dixon pulled off a double whammy. Two 7" singles were released through Stiff Records but still promoted the 'Wonderful Musical World of Chris Dixon' branding on the centre sticker.

With a couple of plays from Peel, Mike Read (Dixon got him to agree to having his photo taken with me outside Radio 1 which was generous and exciting... at the time) and Janice Long, one of the singles hit the dizzy heights of No. 11 in the charts – albeit the Jumbo Records Shop, Leeds, Indie Chart.

When Our Andrew joined Radio 1 he was able to introduce Dixon to Janice, and Dixon was able to thank her in his own special way.

I remember doing my ironing listening to Janice when she played it. I always listened to her show. And music is so evocative that even now just saying 'Echo and the Bunnymen' or 'Orchestral Maneouvres In The Dark' on the radio brings back memories of the early '80s and Janice and that ironing board in that kitchen. I never imagined then that soon I'd meet her. Never mind be doing the same job as her in a couple of years' time.

Eventually the money (Dixon's – from his day job at YTV) ran out and I suppose so did our luck with people's sense of humour and good will. So our punt at pop stardom just petered out. But it wasn't all a waste of time. I'd like to think that foray into the music biz has helped me to support some of the thousands of unknown bands that have come my way since, understanding all the record company bollocks and knowing how important it is to get a break on the BBC.

And, just learning some of the recording processes in a studio has taught me to how to deconstruct tracks, to recognise the technical skill as well as the musicianship involved, and to appreciate just what it takes to make a great record... as well as simply loving the sounds obviously.

I don't remember the official voice test – whatever that was – at Radio Leeds. I'm quite sure it never happened. How would I ever have passed? I didn't have a 'BBC voice'. And, look love, any idiot from Leeds would have spotted straight away that I was frompt wrong side ert Pennines. Anyway, the following Wednesday I just turned up.

OH YEAH (ON THE RADIO)

It turned out that I was to be a sidekick on a show devised by the two youngest people who already worked there. Jan and Jeremy. Jan Baers was a big bear of a bloke (about 30?) who, like many Yorkshire lads (the more south you go in Yorkshire, the more heavy the metal for some reason) was well into his rock music and had an astounding collection of guitars and keyboards in his impressive home studio. He resembled a road-ie in his tatty jeans and t-shirts. Jeremy (about 24?) was posh and from no particular place because his was an army fam-ily. Whizzing around 'covering every corner of the county' (as one Radio Leeds slogan boasted) as a reporter in his VW Golf, stripey shirt, chinos and signature signet ring, he didn't strike me as much of a muso at all. But he was terribly enthusiastic and passionate about having fun and playing records. Anything for a bit of light relief from reporting on council squabbles, pot holes and un-neighbourly disputes over Leylandii trees.

Now the main thing to know about BBC radio, especially lo-cal, is that it's first and foremost a name game. Think up a title for a show and then fill in such details as: 'what's it all about? who's it for? what's in it? and who presents it?' later. Thus over the years I've found myself fronting such shows as Backchat, The Crunch and The Vibe. Details coming up later.

Meanwhile, here are some other examples of BBC manage-ment inspiration – some of them still running today. There's Chatback (for listeners who want to chat. Back), Trunk Of Funk (NB; all about funk music rather than a show for local ele-phants), Jail Mail (for men in prison – geddit?), Masala Matters (for people to whom curry eating is important?), Chinatown (have a guess who that's aimed at) and You Don't Have To Be Jewish (for people who clearly do).

And so 'On The Rocks' was born. Not 'With Liz Kershaw' but 'With Dawn Chorus'. I'd decided, for professional reasons (I didn't want my BT boss, Margaret Backhouse, to find out I was moonlighting on the radio) to use my showbiz name and I was assured that the programme's name was to reflect its musical content rather than the state of my burgeoning career.

I was given what I assumed at the time was the customary BBC induction tour. It included being introduced to the star of the station 'Petey' Levy, (who I already knew from Radio Aire before he'd shocked the city to its very core by defecting to the BBC); the host of mid-mornings Alvin Blossom; the coffee-making area "here's the bloody kettle. Good luck finding a clean mug lass" and the First Aid Room. This was a windowless cupboard with a wall mounted locker emblazoned with a green cross, a small sink, and a vinyl covered medical looking couch. "This is where yer come if yer fancy a shag love." Classy.

"Radio Leeds Where Others Follow!" boomed the station 'ident' in my headphones. (Yes honestly). It was 10pm. We were on. This BBC local station had been set up when promoting local culture (including live music) was still a big part of its remit and budget. So the heart of the old Methodist chapel that now housed the BBC had been converted to retain a cavernous two storey high central hall suitable for live audience events such as piano recitals, choirs, brass band concerts and that kind of cultural carry on. Every Wednesday we filled it with loud bands like The Mission, Sisters of Mercy, Red Lorry Yellow Lorry and The Cult along with their armies of eye-linered black clad fans.

On every other night of the week we'd be checking out the live scene at local venues. There were weekly fixtures like Snake

OH YEAH (ON THE RADIO)

Davis and His Alligator Shoes in a packed pub on Wellington Road near the City Square. Snake was a saxophonist who had us dancing on tables there long before he joined M People.

David Bowie (his real name) was another local lumineri. And Brendan Croker was a blues guitar protégé of Our Andrew's who tipped us off that there was a secret gig in a seedy pub near the canal basin one night. We turned up to find Leeds University Alumnus turned international superstar and by now stadium filler Mark Knopfler sitting on an old buffet, and strumming on a National steel guitar in the snug of this smoky pub to... oh, let's see... 20 of us!

Me, Jan and Jeremy became decent-sized fish in a medium-sized pond and quite an item round town, ligging our way onto guest lists for gigs and backstage parties. Jeremy was really getting into it and decided to host his own do in his very smart pad in a very 'safe' block of flats twixt (as estate agents say) ours and Chez Vorders. I think his parents may have chosen and paid for it. It was unconvincingly Georgian but very smart. Certainly above his pay grade. One of his neighbours being the BBC children's TV presenter Mark Curry. I remember arriving and being impressed about that and also how immaculate it was. It was all brand new and beige and Phil Collins was playing. Probably. And he'd arranged a lovely bowl of fresh fruit on his pristine pine coffee table. This was all a bit healthy and alien to us.

None of us would touch the stuff normally. The nanny state's five-a-day fascism had yet to be invented but we couldn't help noticing when the centrepiece, a sumptuous honeydew melon, mysteriously disappeared. As did one of the partygoers, who returned later and horrified our host by announcing that nobody should eat it now because he'd hollowed it out, taking care to remove the scratchy pips, and shagged it senseless in Jeremy's ensuite.

Our parties at Shire Oak Road were getting no less fruity but far more frequent and Dixon never failed to dress to impress. He was a stickler for colour co-ordination. So if he was wearing his blue lurex suit he'd smoke Rothmans and drink Foster's.

If he was sporting his Saturday Night Fever outfit of a white suit with red shirt he would bring matching Marlboro fags and Red Stripe beer. Every few weeks, much to the disgust of our refined neighbours, we'd clear out all the furniture, roll back the few carpets we had, and jack up the jukebox.

With all the bulbs in the flat removed, its pink neon lights, catching on its chrome trim, would blaze through the huge hall and pump out the scratchy sounds of the Dusty Springfield singles I'd amassed from junk shops.

When its dusty 20-year-old smelly valves overheated and threatened to self combust, we'd stick on a more contemporary LP while it all cooled down. ZZ Top's 'Eliminator', Frankie Goes To Hollywood's 'Welcome to the Pleasure Dome' and Tina Turner's 'Private Dancer' were useful buffers between those sounds of the '60s and a 999 call. Sadly, in some ways for us girls, the boys from Fire and Rescue never actually needed to attend. But the boys in blue were a bit of a fixture. In fact, if the West Yorkshire Constabulary didn't pitch up the do was deemed to have been a bit lame. And we soon learned that any zealous young visiting PC could be easily distracted from pursuing a neighbour's noise complaint with, as the song goes, cigarettes and whiskey and wild wild women. In other words, a fag, some booze and a snog with one of me mates.

OH YEAH (ON THE RADIO)

During one party a torch light was seen flickering in the stair-well as a young nervous copper picked his way gingerly up the steps. About 20 girls in short skirts and high heels were linked in a circle belting along to Cilla (big at the time on Blind Date) Black's 'You're My World'. All the usual noisy bastards, the rugger buggers, the fan club that Carol Vorderman always had in tow, were sitting meekly in the living room chatting and smoking cigars.

Imagine PC Crowther's (names have been changed to protect the rampant) conundrum when he was admitted by TV's own Countdown totty to find just a roomful of lovely young ladies. He was very lovely too. Big, broad, blond, blue-eyed and soon after (within about 20 minutes – tops) my boyfriend.

It didn't last. He was a bit kinky about his helmet and trun-cheon. And he had a thing about acting out Tudor history. And he liked his Alsatian dog to lick his buttocks while he was taking down my particulars. Anyway, my brother wouldn't come home while I had a copper there. And then there was the incident with the yogurt.

One night I was feeling the full force of the law and being very vocal in my appreciation when there was banging on the door. I pulled on my pants and top, left PC Crowther in bed covered in pineapple yogurt (he'd asked for plain but they only had one kind left at the late night corner shop and the superfluous fruity bits and sugar were making it all a bit sickly and a right sticky mess) and ventured out into the hall. It was dark. We often forgot to replace lightbulbs between parties. Oh here we go. A young nervous policeman was there waving his torch.

"Good evening Madam. We've had reports of screaming. It would seem someone is being attacked."

"No, everything is OK, officer. I'm fine."

"Well, I'm sorry miss but you could be being held under duress. In these cases we have to come in and check."

And with that he pushed past me and burst into the bedroom shining his torch straight onto Constable Crowther who'd had time to cover his modesty and the pineapple chunks stuck in his chest hair (etc) but not his face.

"Oh, hi Mike. Sorry to disturb you mate. Everything OK?"

He never got over his embarassment down the nick. And even my attempts to re-enact Elizabeth the First's 'I have the body of a weak and feeble woman' speech could not rouseth him in mine bed chamber anymore.

And anyway, by then, I'd been introduced to an ex-con with a penchant for robbing seaside bingo halls. He also had a love of soul music as well a soft spot for spotting a bargain antique. His collection of gorgeous art deco objet d'art soon adorned our MFI flat pack shelves and he added to it every time he came back from one of his trips where he scoured auction houses for a deal. He'd disappear for weeks on end around the country selling the stuff which he'd stashed and piled high in our garage, including things like cheese graters etc. Or so he told me.

Mysteriously, the massive and extremely lucrative and UK-wide demand for these kitchen gadgets suddenly dried up and after sitting skulking and sulking in our flat for a couple of months he packed his collectables, emptied the garage and went back to his mum. Maybe he left partly because I'd put on so much weight. He was vegetarian and I'd complied by eating only pasta and cheese sauce for months and had ballooned.

It was a relief to be back on bacon butties and I'd soon trimmed down and taken up with an insurance salesman who offered to be my ski instructor. There were no slopes in Headingley so I assumed it was a euphemism. That all went downhill very fast when he became resentful of the time I was spending at Radio Leeds and he slapped me hard across the face one night when I got home from the BBC.

He was full of remorse when he saw what he'd done. But that was it. I was always doling out advice to others about not putting up with domestic violence so I couldn't forgive and forget myself. I wasn't giving him a second chance. It was trickier than I'd thought to shake him off though. But then he was offered a job in Slough so I went with him to case the joint and told him I thought it was a lovely place to live. He moved down there expecting me to follow. But I didn't. Good riddance.

So, for the first time in years, I had no love interest in the Leeds area. And no real career plan either.

Because back at BT, Margaret Backhouse had found out about my double life. My moonlighting in the media.

"Come in. Sit down". She peered at me disdainfully over her glasses. It was hard not to laugh. Margaret was great. A really down-to-earth, honest, funny, straightforward Leeds lass born and bred and who liked a right good laugh in the nearby wine bars of a tea time as much as anybody. But she was management and right now playing her part and being very grown up and serious about it too.

"Alright Liz Kershaw. That's enough of this pop music malarkey. It might be alright now but yer gonna look very silly when yer 30." Oh 'eck. Bit ominous. Not long to go then. I was already 26.

I don't know how old Margaret was. Probably about 40. But she had very trim short hair, immaculate blouses and skirts, and loads of crap to put up with. I really admired and loved her but did I aspire to be her one day? Mmmm. A no-brainer. I decided it was time to find an exit strategy.

Clearly it wouldn't be through Radio Leeds. They were 'paying me' 20 quid a week. I never got it. My fault. I was so thrilled to be on the BBC and, as rock 'n' roll rebels should be, so ideologically averse to any form of bureaucracy, that I could never bring myself to fill in the necessary forms. I found them in a box recently when I was looking for photos for this book. So whoever's running the place now better brace yourself for a budget busting bill of, ooh, a few hundred quid, coming your way one day soon. Or, in the kind of language BBC management will surely understand, as much as 0.0001% of a Byford...

It was about this time that one or two things – or maybe three – happened to, as The Jacksons once sang, 'show me the way to go'.

Our Andrew got a 'proper job' in London and, for the first time in his life, was able to afford a place of his own. I was thrilled for him but sad too because clearly he wasn't coming back for good to live in Shire Oak Road.

He'd taken Billy Bragg to BBC TV Centre to appear on The Old Grey Whistle Test. While Billy was rehearsing his stuff my brother was waiting in the wings when a producer appeared at his side out of the shadows.

He might well have asked "I say. You're a lively young man. Do you know anything about pop music?" He didn't really have to. They got chatting about music and my brother's knowledge and enthusiasm was instantly evident. Trevor Dann was set on revamping the show and spotted Our Andrew's potential as a new presenter.

OH YEAH (ON THE RADIO)

Next thing you know, Our Andrew is on BBC TV. Amazing. How did that happen? I was so, so thrilled for him and never for a split-second thought I could follow that. How would I be able to? This happened in London, which might as well be on a different planet. All I could do was watch Our Andrew in wonder and be ecstatic for him as, on more than one occasion, the whole world hung onto his every word...

Chapter Seven

LONDON CALLING

"It's twelve noon in London. 7am in Philadelphia. And around the world it's time for: Live Aid."

Anybody who heard that at midday on July 13th, 1985, can remember exactly what they were doing as those words opened the biggest music event and most ambitious global television show ever attempted.

The satellites were set. The stars were waiting in the wings. The sun was shining. A hundred thousand music fans were packed together in the sweltering heat of Wembley Stadium. Millions of us all over the country had gathered for barbeques and parties arranged around our tellies, looking forward to the unprecedented experience of 12 solid hours of the nation's favourite bands back to back on the BBC.

At my mate's house in Headingley everyone was excited.

And I was also shitting myself.

There was my little brother on screen in a tiny makeshift commentary box up in the gods wearing his favourite Whistle Test shirt, with the look of a rabbit in the headlights, no idea what was coming next, the whole of the stadium behind him, and a billion viewers around the world watching him.

How was he going to cope? It was like watching Doctor Who as a child. You wanted to look at the screen but kept a cushion close to your face in case it all got too much. Apart from a few excruciating moments when he obviously hadn't got a clue who he was interviewing and when Bob Geldof grabbed the mic in exasperation to rant "give us yer fucking money," I needn't have worried.

He was his natural entertaining cheeky-chappie self. He was fine. The whole thing was a triumph. On that day 'Thatcher's Children' believed we were 'sticking it to the man', giving a V-sign to governments and changing the world order.

On that day we felt proud to be young and British.

And I was particularly proud of Our Andrew. And the BBC.

In hindsight I don't honestly know if Live Aid really changed anything for anybody but the bands. The likes of Queen and U2 were catapulted into a new super league and went on to shift millions more albums and tour tickets on the tide of this TV exposure while artists who decided to decline Geldof's 'invitation' now privately admit that they lost out forever on sales.

Meanwhile I doubt that Spandau Ballet strutting their stuff actually helped to eradicate the wars, corruption and economic globalisation that cause death from genocide, disease and starvation. It was all about aiding Africa. But with hardly any black faces on the bill wasn't this simply unwitting but well intentioned cultural colonialism?

And as for us fans, isn't it hypocritical and even obscene to enjoy a picnic during an anti-hunger event? In 2005, the 20th anniversary of Live Aid was marked by a cluster of concerts called Live 8. Ironic as '8' is the universally accepted texting abbreviation for 'ate'. That night, reflecting the day's events on Radio 2, I thought I'd get things going with the nation's truckers, shift workers and insomniacs by suggesting that anyone overweight (including me) should have been instantly turned away from these gigs. Isn't being fatter than you should be the embodiment of everything that's wrong? Of, quite literally, consuming more than you need? More than your fair share of the world's unevenly distributed food resources? At some other poor bugger's expense? Discuss.

Loads of listeners who apparently hardly eat anything and are only obese because of their glands queued up to come on air and tell me what a disgrace I was in no uncertain terms.

"Ok. Bit political there I know. Er... it's just coming up to 2am. Here's, er, Spandau Ballet!"

Back to the summer of '85. There were plenty of other big concerts in Leeds. Bruce Springsteen played Roundhay Park with the E Street Band and his biggest ever album 'Born In the USA'.

This was his seventh and, on the back of his first ever chart single 'Dancing In The Dark' a year earlier, his breakthrough album.

We had them all and had seen him in Birmingham in 1981 on 'The River' tour. Then he was still the best kept secret in rock. You could weigh up somebody and decide if they were your kinda guy (or girl) by whether they knew and liked Bruce. Now we diehard fans were sharing him with the rest of the world.

I got a job backstage at Roundhay Park as a washer-upper in the marquee where all the roadies and stage builders and other site workers took their breaks and had their meals. I reasoned that, as even Bruce had to eat and being just a regular blue collar guy, at some point he'd come in and chow down with his crew. And I'd get to meet him!

My hands were red raw but the atmosphere was so charged it was worth it. Even on just 20 quid for a 12-hour day spent swilling dirty plates and cutlery in a bowl of lukewarm water. I worked for five days around the show day itself and I got really good at working out who did what and how important, or in most cases, self-important, people were by the way they looked and sounded. So a wiry jovial chap in jeans, with dreadlocks, a roll-up stuck to his lip and a Brummie accent was likely to be a scaffolder building the stage. Whereas a loud mouth with attitude, a ponytail and a big gut hanging over his tight denim cut-offs with a walkie talkie welded to his head was likely to be an American promoter or management. A big knob.

On the day of the show, just as I was about to trek to the standpipe to get some fresh water, one big knob came in and threw what turned out to be a red shirt in my face.

"Hey you. Wash this."

"Sorry?"

"Wash this now. And get it dry. It's needed by seven."

"Why? Who does it belong to?" As I unfolded it and saw it was sleeveless with a winged collar my heart leapt a little and my attitude changed completely. As any true fan would have done, I recognised it instantly as the signature garment of one of the band. "Clarence. He wants to wear it tonight." Clarence Clemens was the saxophonist and, if I did as I was told, he'd be sporting this very shirt on stage later live in Leeds.

When showtime finally came, clutching the free ticket that was part of my pay, I found a spot as near as I could get to the stage. When The Big Man stepped out in that clean red shirt (I didn't have an iron but it was pulled smooth over his huge chest) there was a huge scream. From me. "I washed that. I washed that for him." I tried to tell anyone around over the roar of the crowd.

Then the band struck up 'Badlands' and watching, singing and dancing around I was ecstatic. This was what it's all about. I've never felt so alive.

The Boss never appeared in the catering tent so sadly we never met. And we never have. Even though I got the chance to be introduced to him a few years later. When, for reasons I will explain, I ran away.

That was my last stab at concert catering. There must be an easier way to meet my heroes. I'd rubbed shoulders with a few lesser known ones who came to 'On The Rocks' at Radio Leeds. But it was when I was just 'A Face In The Crowd', as the Tom Petty song goes, at an ABC concert that I decided to make a list of goals.

I like lists. I get teased about them.

This one went:

> *Move To London.*
> *Get fitted kitchen.*
> *Meet bands.*

And it could have sat on my kitchen table to this day. Except that's when someone walked into our office at BT and helped me tick off everything on it by making me an offer I couldn't refuse.

Phones have loomed large in my life. And not just in my seven years with BT. In more recent times at the BBC they've landed me in deep shit twice. But more of that later.

In 1986, phones were my friend and, in just over a year, got me onto Radio 1.

Remember Dial-a-Disc? It was very quaint. Basically you could sit bored at your desk and, by dialling a three-digit number, listen down a crackly line to a hit of the time.

However, you couldn't choose which one. As I said earlier, part of my brief at BT was to get telephone subscribers (as they were then called) to rack up bigger bills by using such services and also to come up with new ones.

So when a young executive hit town from a new branch of BT in London, charged with going round the country, spreading the word to the BT regions about the latest technology and getting us to exploit it by inventing new applications, it was me he came to see in its north-east HQ.

Not long into our chat about maybe getting more songs down the line, it must have dawned on him that he could exploit my passion for pop and understanding of how record companies and the music media worked.

As the Pet Shop Boys song goes 'you've got the looks. I've got the brains. Let's make lots of money'. We were made for each other and he offered me a job in his group. The carrot was a whacking big pay rise. The stick was an unwelcome move to London and the end of Radio Leeds for me.

His office was in the heart of London's fashionable West End but he put me in Dalston which was a dump back then. He explained that space with him in Covent Garden was at a premium and because of my need for studios and bulky digital exchange equipment, a grotty district the wrong side of Islington made more commercial sense.

It didn't really. All the people I needed to meet to get content for 'Livewire – the number one music station on the phone' were on his doorstep in showbizzy Soho. But, remote from anyone above my grade, and in a large airy office suite with free parking right outside and a fantastic shop round the corner that did the best ever egg mayonaise butties, it suited me.

And him. With me never seen in central London by management, all credit for developing the product and its profile, and an ever-growing bottom line, understandably went to him.

I arranged a big launch at the top of the Telecom Tower and invited anyone and everyone in record companies. They all came along because of the venue. The restaurant, 500 feet above London with views across the capital, had been closed to the public after the IRA had bombed the tower in 1971. So this was a very exclusive do and the hottest ticket in town.

The outer doughnut of the restaurant revolved around a central core. So it proved a bit tricky keeping your balance if, drink in hand, you unwittingly had one foot on one side of the divide in the floor and the other on the other side.

As your legs gradually moved in a different direction, it was easy to think you'd had too many already. But it was a PR triumph and quite literally a great platform for my new product.

So what was Livewire? Well it all seems a bit crude now what with the internet, MP3 players, smartphones, tablets etc but basically you could choose a song by changing the last two digits of the new 0898 Premium Rate number you dialed. And pay dearly for the privilege. To give customers more reasons to ring, I came up with lots of options and was given a huge budget to sign up big names to introduce them.

So, for example, we had a dance chart rundown with Radio London's DJ 'Young' Dave Pearce, an indie chart rundown with Janice Long and the same for heavy metal with Kerrang magazine's Dante Bonutto. (I rang him one day. Turned out he lived with his mum in Muswell Hill. "Just a minute dear. I think Christopher is in the bath".)

When it came to the Top 40 it made sense to hire Bruno Brookes. I didn't know him then but he was the voice of the official UK chart rundown on national Radio 1 – the chart we used and paid for.

However, for some reason I was usurped on this and my boss offered Radio 1 Breakfast Show host Mike Smith a whopping £1,000 a week to present this. I know by today's BBC standards that's only 0.001% of a Byford but back then it was a colossal amount to pay someone to pop round the corner once a week for an hour after his radio stint.

No, he wasn't expected to schlep out to Dalston, I had to hire another studio on Great Titchfield Street just around the corner from Broadcasting House in W1. It was run by a big bearded techie, Joss, with a big heart who was loads of fun. We'd sit there all ready and waiting for Mike and chewing the fat until he turned up in a suit clutching a briefcase, and delivered his lines without barely speaking a word to us. Rock 'n' roll.

We took out weekly ads in all the relevant music magazines like Smash Hits, Just 17 and Kerrang of course, to list the recordings on offer and the numbers. These included the big interviews I'd got from bothering the record companies and persuading them that if they couldn't get their artists on the radio we'd give them some exposure.

'Hey, remember filling your face at the top of the Tower? Come on you owe me one'.

My first big scoop was with Tony Hadley and Co. I was so excited to be given access to Spandau Ballet that I fell down stairs the night before. OK, so Our Andrew should have replaced the light bulb on the landing. Whatever. I'd, quite literally, got my big break and had to be hauled up to meet some of the most glamorous stars of the time (really) in a goods lift with a walking stick.

I knew damn well that bands like that didn't really need Livewire. But soon an unknown trio who did need a break crossed the threshold. They'd been sent in by the same guy. He represented all the top turns of the time and he was touting this lot as 'The Next Big Thing' and so we welcomed three plucky lads from London to Livewire. They seemed nice. And simple. And also very giggly and high spirited. I had to ask them to calm down, concentrate and stop whizzing across the office on our swivel chairs. Blond twins Matt and Luke and their little mate Craig also made their Radio 1 debut with me with their single 'When Will I Be Famous?'

Sooner than any of us expected actually. Because after that, Bros visits to Radio 1 resulted in mass hysteria and police cordons.

Meanwhile, I'd spotted another use for the 0898 computer. TV voting. We'd been sent a video from an American tele-comms company starring a big orange lobster. It was a demonstration of how TV could use 'televoting'. The live lobster was being held over a pan of boiling water and viewers were being asked to dial one of two numbers to decide its fate. One number meant it was saved. The other that it went in the pot. Mmm. Could this work with all those wannabees on talent shows?

I got a meeting at TV Centre with a fat cat in BBC Light Entertainment. I explained how 0898 numbers could be used to instantly canvass viewers' opinions and give results within the same show. I suggested it could be used on Opportunity Knocks.

That stopped him leering and sneering and my boss started to see the cash roll in. For some reason he decided that he, not me, would sit alone in Dalston on a Saturday night and monitor the calls as they came in and then personally communicate the scores on the doors to our BBC fat cat. There were no checks then as far as I know. So, if he'd wanted to, he could have changed the results. And if the BBC had wanted to, nobody else would ever have known. I'm not saying that happened and it certainly couldn't now could it? Not with all current BBC accountability and transparency eh?

There were millions of calls and big bucks at stake now. So it seemed it must be some sort of celebration when I was invited to a soiree in Clapham at a flat full of hoorays. Some of them were young BT bosses, mostly called Mark with MBAs, and all of them had cash swilling around. And they had an announcement to make. (It had to go on hold when, over nibbles and mingling, we saw the horrific TV pictures of The Herald of Free Enterprise keeled over on its side and reports of a massive loss of life. It was all rather distracting but they ploughed on). My boss and his cronies revealed that they intended to set up their own company, buy their own gear, and offer the same services to the BBC (and by now The Sun newspaper too) but cream off all the revenue themselves.

Did I want to defect? Not as a fellow director. As their employee. I thought it best to stay at BT even though they were leaving and taking all our media customers with them. Mmm. Bit of a blow.

But it was the game changer. The kick up the arse I needed.

While I was still in Leeds, a Radio 1 producer had come to see me. I thought he was interested in me because of my little radio show but it turned out he was a broken man who needed a shoulder to cry on.

Over a pint in a pub he confided that, though married, he'd been having a bit on the side with a friend of a friend of mine and she'd dumped him. Could I put in a good word? That's all he wanted to talk about.

Not my prospects at the BBC.

At Livewire I'd been keeping the cassettes of the interviews I'd been doing. Now it was time to capitalise on them. The BBC's own 'Jilted John' didn't return my calls. Perhaps he was still crying into his beer. Eventually he invited me to lunch. I took my tapes but it was hopeless.

This time he was blubbing into his bolognaise. But he did suggest, probably to get rid of me, that I teamed up with Ro Newton, my brother's sidekick on Whistle Test, who'd also been pestering him for a break in radio.

I put together a half hour demo. A megamix of my interviews and music news from Ro, linked by both of us. By now Our Andrew had got his own show on Radio 1 so I couldn't believe they'd take me on too. So Ro took our tape to Radio 1 with instructions to keep my identity secret until they'd bitten!

I thought 'they aren't going to want two Kershaws on the radio' and while I remained in the shadows, they got back to Ro and said they loved the show, they loved the idea and when could we start?

Fortunately history was repeating itself. Like my 'Mr. Burns' at Radio Leeds, Radio 1 management had just been told they really ought to get some younger presenters on the BBC's youth station. You know. Some under 30 maybe? It had also dawned on them that girls were embarrassingly thin on the ground. Well on the air anyway. Me and Ro ticked both boxes and we were snapped up. We'd present a weekly half-hour show, following exactly the same format as the demo tape. As the radio equivalent of Smash Hits, we suggested it would sit perfectly just before the Top 40 Show. And that's where they were going to put us. At 3.30pm. From Sunday, October 4th, 1987.

That was it. Oh my God. I'm going to be a Radio 1 DJ.

I'd never been in to see anyone.

I'd never been interviewed.

I'd got nothing in writing.

I thought the guys I had grown up listening to, like Tony Blackburn and Johnnie Walker, were grown in a special maternity unit for DJs and then transplanted onto the radio. Plus there was only one woman – Annie Nightingale – and she was fantastic, so glamorous and living the life in swinging London.

And next thing I know, I'm going to be rubbing shoulders with everyone. And Our Andrew was there too. It was going to be the most fab fun. Not in my wildest dreams could I have imagined that.

However, it was only on Sunday afternoons, so I wasn't going to give up my job at BT. I was still dead practical and I wasn't thinking this was the way in or I had a key into showbiz. To me it was just an amazing bonus.

It felt like only yesterday that I'd been rolling around listening to Johnnie Walker while it felt like I was dying with a burst appendix and the next thing I'm having my Christmas dinner with him. How? Why? I just couldn't get my head around it! I did know it was fabulous.

To be in the right place at the right time, again, was just too incredible to describe.

Chapter Eight

WELCOME TO
THE JUNGLE

So I found myself striding up Regent Street in the late summer sunshine with something of a spring in my step. This was mainly due to the exciting prospect of joining the country's top jocks – even if it was only part-time – but partly to do with my fancy new footwear, snakeskin cowboy boots, teamed with a checked Confederate bibbed shirt and a suede jacket, all topped off with a humongous Stetson. A recent trip to Texas had certainly paid off – I'd only given a few bucks for it in a San Antonio thrift store. But it was real rock chick stuff and made me feel a million dollars.

Yes, I was making my debut at Radio 1 dressed for a rodeo.

THE BIRD AND THE BEEB

I tipped my hat, narrowed my eyes and looked up in awe at the iconic stone art deco edifice of Broadcasting House.

Was I really joining Radio 1? The station I'd been hooked on for 20 years? Me? Oh well. Here goes. I sauntered into the rather less imposing but adjacent 1960s annexe that was home to 'The Nation's Favourite' – Egton House. The House of Fun. Complete Madness.

"'Ello Darlin'. Can I 'elp you lovey?" 26 years later, times have changed. The line-up has changed. Big names have come and gone. There have have been tears and tantrums. Blood on the carpet. But Radio 1's receptionist Clare has stood her ground and held the fort for over four decades. Nowadays no BBC focus group would ever put a cheery bespectacled little 'cockney sparrer' like her in the shop window of its 'coolest' network and to be honest, it was all a bit incongruous then.

But it did serve to bring big timers down to earth with a bump. It didn't matter if you were Bon Jovi or you had come to clean the bogs. If you didn't have good reason to get in, you didn't get past Clare.

During the first Gulf War, I was sitting in reception when six-figure-salaried Alan 'what's he for exactly?' Yentob tried to breeze in. "ID please Sir. Sorry Sir. No ID no entry. I'm sorry I don't know you from Adam. For all I know you could be a Shiite separatist." Yentob did his own Desert Storm from the building. It was only temporary though. He's a fixture. I think it's in the BBC Charter.

"I've come to see Head of Programmes, Doreen Davies."

"Is she expecting you sweedart?"

"I'm not sure. But I start here in two weeks. The name's Liz. Liz Kershaw."

"Ridey 'O. Hi Sylvia. Can you tell Doreen I've got Andy's liddle sister for her darlin'? Thanks sweedart."

Doreen Davies jumped up from behind her desk to hug me enthusiastically. Evidently, before joining the cast of Friends, Joey Tribbiani's agent, Estelle was helping to run Radio 1. Dumping the ciggie hanging with ash from her lip into the overflowing ashtray on her enormous empty desk, she planted a big waxy red kiss on my cheek. The luxuriant silk rose pinned to her lapel looked like it was ready to squirt water anytime. And I thought she must be hot in that rather obvious wig.

Luckily she was more taken with my get-up. "Jeff! Jeff! Get over here already," she barked down the phone having re-lit her fag. "I've got Liz Kershaw here. She looks fab-u-lous."

Jeff Simpson (Radio 1 press officer) duly and dutifully shimmied into the room. "This is Liz. She starts next week. Doesn't she look great Jeff! We have to do some pictures."

It was all style over content because I don't remember any helpful advice about my imminent show. Sadly, because she was lovely and fair and championed 'her girls' on the station, but inevitably, because she was a woman of a certain age, she was retired shortly after.

She was always delighted to come back for big anniversary parties and, in 2012, she was the first of the old Radio 1 management to speak out and to remind them of their concerns about Jimmy Savile back in the day. A thoroughly decent and honest old school BBC boss. Oh, and her hair was genuine too. Not a wig after all. The next time I met Jeff was for my first interview with a paper.

"And how old are you Liz?" I was in a nearby greasy spoon, adorned with fading black and white signed photos of DJs who'd dined there down the decades, being grilled by the Manchester Evening News.

"I've just turned 29."

"Oh that's weird."

"Er... is it?"

"Yes. I interviewed your brother recently and he said that he's 28 and that you are a year older."

"O... kay...?"

"But this press release says you're 25."

I didn't want to queer my pitch on my first outing so I looked to Jeff for help. "Oh it must be a typo then," he blurted, moving on.

No biggie. Just my first taste of the BBC press office.

Then it was time to meet our producer in a tiny cramped office just about big enough for him to squeeze behind his desk. Paul Williams was waiting for me and Ro with a cigarette in his mouth and another one on the go in the ash tray.

He had too much on his mind to worry about sequencing his smoking. With blond collar-length hair that would make Boris Johnson look kempt, a gold chain and white shirt open nearly to his waist, and with sweat pouring down his red face, he waved us in. "Come in! Come in! Sit down girls! Take a seat!" He was extremely bright, (probably Oxbridge) and was a brilliant pianist (hence his role as 'Willy On the Plonker' on Gary Davies's daily Bit In The Middle as well as accompanying international stars at The Albert Hall), and very nice.

But it wasn't only with smoking that he always seemed to have several things on the go. I suppose he was a quintessential English eccentric. He just seemed delightfully potty to us and rather nervous. I don't suppose he'd ever had to work with female presenters before. "Right, girls. How are we going to play this then?"

There hadn't been a format quite like ours before on Radio 1. So he seemed relieved to let us tell him how it would all work. Basically Ro and I would go out and about all week getting interviews – about seven – from artists in the charts or about to chart that Sunday, and, with him in a studio, we'd edit them and then link it all together with music to make a 30 minute pre-recorded show ready for Sunday afternoons.

So every Wednesday after that we took him our cassettes, told him which songs went with them, and spent the afternoon in the bowels of BH as he flapped about, while a cool, calm and collected studio manager called Brian sorted it all out.

If Paul was overwhelmed by all this, remember I was still working full-time at BT as well. I was constantly juggling the two roles, trying to keep BT happy while also pinching myself that this was happening. Am I complaining about how busy I was? No chance, I loved every minute of it.

Our interviews back then had to be transferred from cassette to reel to reel tape before they could be edited, using a chalky marker, a razor blade and thin white sticky tape. What a faff. But it was a skill I'm glad I learned in Leeds. It was often needed to save stuff from being cut up, thrown on the floor and lost forever and sometimes we had to be really inventive and practical to get the sound we wanted.

Now you just download recordings onto computer and move squiggly sound waves around on a screen. So if you want to delete, you just select and press. Or if you need more of something you just double it up by dragging a mouse around. One Wednesday we wanted about five minutes of an intro to a

George Michael record to lay his interview over. Inconveniently George had only made the intro about 30 seconds long. So we kept recording it over and over again from the vinyl onto tape and then joined the bits together to form a loop. We then hung this out of a fourth floor window and through a reel to reel machine in a studio there so that it could play 'endlessly' for as long as we needed and be recorded onto more tape while we mixed in George's chat. That was then put to one side until it was pieced together with the rest of the show. Then it all had to be timed and tweaked, one word at a time, to fit our 30-minute slot.

Some Wednesdays we'd use some of the studio time to record an interview on the phone with someone in, say, LA, that we wouldn't get otherwise. Donna Summer was one of those. We were in awe but she was just lovely. Yet characteristically our producer had matters other than music on his mind. "Is she a lesbian? What do you think girls?" He thought only we could hear him in our headphones. "I think so. How about you girls? Do you think she's a dyke?"

When Brian pointed out that she could hear it too and all this was going onto the tape she was a professional and gracious enough to start again. How Backchat (there had to be a catchy name for it) ever got on air I don't know.

Simon Bates was less, erm, understanding according to the Controller, Johnny Beerling, in his own book about life at Radio 1. He describes how, on one occasion, when Paul had been producing his show and lost part of his script, Bates had really gone for him, grabbing him round the throat, before being prised off Paul and storming out, vowing never to speak to him again. Maybe that's why we'd been lucky enough to get him. And we must have been light relief after working with Bates. I always thought that if Radio 1 had been Rugby School, I was like a nervous fourth-former to Bates' 'Flashman' and DJ Adrian Juste would have been his fag.

One Christmas, in October, 1988, the annual DJs lunch was upgraded to a black tie dinner. By now, Johnny Beerling had 'lost' Janice Long and dumped Ro after she'd made some remarks in Just 17 about our colleagues being a bit wrinkly. I don't think Annie Nightingale showed up, because I remember being the only jock in a frock.

A quick scan of the seating plan revealed I'd been put next to Bates. Oh no. I'd been warned by Our Andrew and Peel, who'd both had infamous run-ins with him at these do's, so I tried to discreetly shuffle the place cards. But 'Justey' noticed. "Simes, Simes, Liz Kershaw's swapping places." Coming back from the Ladies my heart sank. There was now only one empty seat. Opposite Bates, who was now regaling the guys with stories of breeding horses on the family farm. Details of effective artificial insemination techniques. That kind of thing. Hardly table talk. He continued with an anecdote about the equine-related antics of Catherine The Great. I can give as good as I get. But there was nothing good about this. Wanker.

Most Wednesdays on Backchat, we'd arrive at lunchtime and leave at midnight. Plus we'd each have spent about eight hours during the rest of the week setting up guests and buzzing round London to meet them. In the late '80s, if you were in the charts you were on Backchat. Me and Ro got to meet them all. From tiny Jon Bon Jovi with his little Cuban heels to Aerosmith's Steve Tyler with his mouth like the Mersey Tunnel.

And for that we were paid the not very celebrity sum of 75 quid a week each. But then we were girls just wanting to have fun. I don't know what our great male mates' hourly rates were but I had to wonder when I parked up my battered old Mini Metro in the car park next to Bruno's brand new blue Porsche Carerra or 'DLT 1' – a massive Mitsubishi 4x4 with all the extras our money couldn't buy.

OK, we weren't doing it for the money. We were fans who could now get away with asking nosey questions of our idols by sticking a BBC microphone under their noses. And we met them all.

The Good – Boy George was intelligent, interesting, funny, self-deprecating and charming. Alice Cooper, who me and my grandma used to enjoy together back in 1972, despite his scary stage persona of black eyeliner and snakes, was just a poppet.

The Bad – Gary Glitter (who was once the ultimate showman: I'd loved his gigs as well as his records) was dressed to impress but quite petite without his platforms, polite, softly spoken, and a gentleman. But then I suppose, at 29, I was well past my 'best before' date as far as he was concerned.

And The Ugly – another hero (and he really is, so I'm not going to embarrass him by saying who) bent over to pick something up. It looked like his head had been stamped on with a football boot. His hair was arranged like studs. But this was only temporary. He now has a full head of lush black locks.

Sometimes I had to chase a story. Or rather the stars. Even though this was for the mighty Radio 1, occasionally I just had to forget any dignity and grab 'em whenever and wherever I could. So I got an exclusive with A-ha by chatting up their bodyguard, who told me where to find them and while the rest of the pop pack waited in reception, I got an interview on the go by running through the hotel kitchens with my microphone under Morten Harket's lovely Norwegian nose.

At Top of the Pops, artists spent a lot of time just sitting around all day in their dressing rooms between endless rehearsals and the real thing. So I hung round there on show days. That's how I got the likes of Run DMC, who were lovely but scary. They couldn't find the keys for their dressing room so one of their posse just put his big size 17 Adidas to it. Gene Pitney and Marc Almond, who despite sharing a big hit, 'Something's Gotten Hold Of My Heart', sat back to back and could hardly bring themselves to look at or speak to each other.

And Tina Turner was the same with me. Her face lit up and she talked the talk with her huge smile when the microphone was on and then she just turned away back to her mirror and her make-up. Interview over. And not even a goodbye. I was dead upset.

You kind of think that having invested a lot of time and belief (not to mention money) in a performer they will at least make an effort to return the compliment. Or pretend to, even for five minutes. But no. Great records like 'River Deep Mountain High' lost a little bit of their shine after that.

There were other divas who didn't disappoint. I'd grown to love country music and its 'First Ladies', Tammy Wynette and Dolly Parton. (Tammy) Wynette Pugh had been born dirt poor and spent her early years cotton picking in the fields. Then, leaving her first abusive husband behind and piling her kids and guitar in her old banger, she headed for Nashville to pursue her dreams of being a singer.

When we met she'd just recorded 'Justified and Ancient' with

The KLF and was over to do some concerts. She was kind and gracious and friendly and we spent that afternoon shopping together for her spandex jeans in Kensington.

That night, after her show at the London Palladium, I was invited backstage. What a shocker. What a change in a few short hours. Tammy didn't recognise me now. She was coming down from the high she'd been given to get her through the show and was completely out of it. Addicted to prescription drugs and on her fifth marriage, she was still playing out her painful private life in the public glare when she died suddenly, and broke, in 1998.

Dolly couldn't be more different – she's still with the husband she married in 1966. You'll never see him and you'll never know what else Dolly might have been up to. Dolly is in charge. I've taken a few leaves out of her book. She was the epitome of Girl Power to me, long before those silly Spice Girls coined the phrase. One of 12 kids, hers was also a rags to riches story built on self-belief and sheer grit and determination.

Dolly knew what her best assets were and she damn well used them. But no-one else has exploited Dolly. She's had her head screwed on and has taken 'no shit from nobody', building a huge career, business empire and fortune. "Darlin'. It takes a lot of money to look this cheap." I've met her a few times now and she's funny and charming. She also seems to be getting younger!

George Michael on the other hand didn't measure up to my great expectations. I'd always thought that he was the music business's ultimate man-with-a-plan, a clever lad who'd kept control and seen it through. I was working for the BBC at the 1988 Free Nelson Mandela Concert at Wembley Stadium when

I grabbed him as he came off stage and asked him, on live TV, why he was supporting the cause.

"Hiya George. Can you tell us why you're here today?"

"I think that's obvious isn't it."

It just went downhill from there!

A taxi driver reminded me about this Great Moment In Broadcasting History not long ago, explaining why it had made such a lasting impression on him.

"That was the worst interview I've ever seen on the telly."

Mmmm. Thanks. Yes I still cringe a bit when 'I'm Your Man' comes on in the car.

All these examples explain why, when I got the chance to meet Bruce Springsteen in 1993, I chickened out. Terence Trent D'Arby had been on my Radio 5 show, The Vibe, and he mentioned he was off to Madison Square Gardens to support Bruce. I couldn't believe it. I was going over to see my mates in New York and to that very gig. He said he'd arrange for me to go back stage to meet my all-time hero.

So on the night, I went down to the stage door at the appointed time. But just as I raised my hand to knock I had a change of heart and ran back to my seat instead. What if Bruce did a Tina or George on me? What if I'd been wrong about him all along? What if he was a complete twat? I'm sure he's not. But it wasn't worth risking a life without my favourite music. Best leave well alone.

Obviously London provided rich pickings in pop stars. But being sent by Radio 1 to cover the Montreux Rock Festival in Switzerland (a must in the music calendar since the venue burned down in 1971, inspiring Deep Purple's 'Smoke On The Water') meant we'd have access to the international super league. Except Gary Davies went too and got the likes of Run DMC while we got Curiosity Killed the Cat.

Gary's superstar status meant he could always pull rank. Like once at Wembley when I was lined up to introduce the headliners INXS. At the time he played 'Need You Tonight' on every show, so took it upon himself to swap us over in the running order, leaving little me to introduce some old has-beens from the '70s.

After I'd brought them on stage, I spent their set standing to the side of the drums as the singer gyrated one buttock then the other out of her tight leather shorts. With a whip in hand, and fishnets she reminded me of a Beryl Cook greeting card character.

Thanks Gary. It was Blondie. Another heroine.

In Montreux I was happily hanging out with the platinum selling Eurythmics (who'd been near neighbours of mine and whose manager still was) when I hit gold. I was ordering some drinks and fumbling in my purse when someone came and stood next to me at the bar.

One glance and I froze on the spot, staring at the beautiful man in a stylish trilby and long beige raincoat. The Thin White Duke.

"Er... hello. You won't know me," I blabbed. "But I'd just like to say thank you for all the pleasure you've given me over the years. I think you're fab. I'm Liz."

"Well, thank you, Liz," he graciously replied, extending his hand. "I'm David Bowie. Have a nice evening."

And then, clutching his beers, he was gone.

Paul Williams wasn't so good at star spotting. Being a concert pianist he couldn't resist the hotel's Steinway and gathered us one evening for a sing song.

We were joined by a cluster of groups including Johnny Hates Jazz and a blonde mate of theirs who started crooning.

"Get her off. Get rid of her. She can't bloody sing. Go on. Tell her to bugger off."

It was Kim Wilde.

I was now rubbing shoulders with those I'd once admired from afar. I was really Living The Dream and loving every minute of it. Nothing could stop me now. Could it?

Chapter Nine

BECAUSE THE NIGHT (BELONGS TO US)

I was still trying to hold down my 'day job' at BT, promoting and expanding Livewire. Now that my boss had gone to set up his own version in direct competition, I was running it too and grabbed the chance to cut costs and change our Chart Rundown presenter.

And that's how I met Bruno Brookes.

It was in a greasy cafe near Radio 1. All the top jocks and visiting bands filled their faces there so no-one batted an eyelid at the odd couple tucking into a full fry-up. I was dressed like a World War One officer in khaki breeches, a heavy green ankle-length canvas coat with brass buttons and leather riding boots and matching shoulder bag – all from a flea market on a recent trip to Amsterdam. Bruno was dressed in a satin bomber jacket, tight denim jeans and shirt, and blindingly white trainers, topped off with a bouffant blond mullet, twinkly blue eyes, and lots of freckles. He was smaller than I'd expected. Dead dinky. And with all the attitude you'd expect from someone who'd been a star since he was 14 in the clubs and pubs of Stoke-on-Trent. His dad had set him up with a mobile disco from the proceeds of the family car wash business which boasted 'the best hand job in town for two quid'. Bruno always reckoned he'd pissed off Johnny Beerling by *arriving* at Radio 1 in a Porsche.

Anyway, never dreaming that one day we'd be a radio 'item' I signed him up. I don't suppose Mike Smith was very thrilled.

But it was a great move for Livewire and life at the BBC was also going remarkably well.

"Now then girls you've been nominated for a Sony," Paul Williams blurted across the studio. "Good news. Good news." We had no idea what he was talking about. "A Sony. A bloody radio award!"

Me and Ro had been on Radio 1 less than six months when suddenly we found ourselves at the Grosvenor House Hotel in Park Lane. We'd been nominated for an 'Oscar' in the Best Magazine Programme category at the annual Radio Academy Awards along with a couple of Radio 4 series on farming and medicine. Paul Williams was all suited and booted and very agitated throughout the long lunch which led up to all the gong giving. "Don't get excited girls. Don't get yer hopes up, you won't win." He was right. We didn't. Our little pop show was trumped by serious stuff on crops and cancer. Well. At least we'd come third and now 'The Girls' had been recognised by the radio industry. Time to strike while we were hot.

"I'd like to make a demo for a live late night programme," I told Stuart Grundy. Stuart was a Radio 1 'exec' with lush grey curls and a deep velvety voice who was not averse to booking himself to do shows. And, like lots of the guys, jumped at the chance to shove a couple of balloons up a skimpy jumper, don a mini skirt and a long wig, and run amok in the privacy of our parties as well as in public at Radio 1 'Fun' events. I often wondered "couldn't they just employ a few more real women?"

"OK. I'll book Studio B15. Bring me the tape," he replied. I knew if I didn't do this I'd never be considered for anything but our Sunday slot. This wasn't just a hobby anymore. I loved it. It was the future. I needed to show them I really could be one of the boys.

The singer Mari Wilson and comedian John Shuttleworth came in late one night for a couple of hours and with a pile of cool vinyl we recorded a 'lively blend of music and chat'. I gave the results to Stuart and resigned myself to rejection.

Again, serendipity was on my side.

In late 1987, the announcement by Janice Long that she was pregnant soon had Stuart rummaging through his drawers for those tapes.

Johnny Beerling had 'lost' Janice. In a ham-fisted attempt to do what's known as 'refresh the schedules' (getting rid of a presenter), he had kindly explained he was taking her off the Evening Show because she would be too busy with the new baby.

He offered her a weekly Saturday show but Janice was rightly insulted and walked. She also talked. The press loved it. Sacked for being a mum.

BECAUSE THE NIGHT (BELONGS TO US)

I can just imagine the morning management meeting in Beerling's office.

"What are the press saying Jeff?"

"Well, the Daily Mail says that you're a true guardian of the nation's morality and applauds you for protecting our young people from an unmarried mother. "

"Right. Good. And the other papers?"

"Er... they say you're a misogynistic old twat."

The Evening Show was now Simon Mayo's following Janice's departure.

Well, that is until Mike Smith went on holiday in the May and Simon filled in for him for a fortnight on Breakfast. Maybe someone had the bright idea of putting a woman back in the evening slot for PR purposes. Maybe they loved my demo. Maybe both.

"Hello Liz. What are you doing for the next couple of weeks between seven and 10?"

I'd never done a live show on Radio 1. I'd never done a radio show on my own. I'd never operated a studio desk. I had to learn fast. Just as I'd been terrified for Our Andrew on Live Aid, he was now petrified for me and hiding from view in the corridor outside the studio. About 10 minutes into my first show he was jumping up and down on the other side of the glass. During the next record he came bursting in. "You can do it! Bloody hell you're OK!" It may seem like faint praise but it was all I needed. I was OK. He was right. And anyway it was only for two weeks.

Sometime into that fortnight, there was another 'schedule refreshment' moment. I didn't know what had happened but suddenly Simon Mayo was staying on Breakfast. Mike Smith was going. Could I carry on? Beerling explained it was only until a bigger shake-up in the Autumn when he'd already got someone else signed up. But with Sunday's Backchat and Monday to Thursday evenings, I'd be doing five shows a week for a few months.

I was up for that. But how would my BT boss take it?

Not very well. For a couple of months I was working at Livewire until about 6pm then running up Regent Street to Egton House to be on air at 7pm. It was tricky but I thought I was pulling it off. I wasn't.

"I don't think your mind's really on this job anymore," my BT manager informed me. It was like being back in Leeds with Margaret Backhouse. "I won't put up with it. It's time to choose. BT or the BBC?" I had to think hard but not for long.

For the five shows on the radio I'd be paid £475 a week. By this time at BT, with promotions, annual increments and London weighting I was on more than that with a juicy pension scheme. But could I honestly live with myself if I turned down my big chance? If, in a few years' time, I was sitting at a desk watching the clock and thinking 'I could have been a Radio 1 DJ.' That was the end of the matter. I was delighted. My dad was less impressed.

"You've what?" he cried. "You've given up a proper job for that? What about your pension? How are you going to pay your mortgage?"

My dad had once said 'once you've got a degree you can do whatever you like.' We'd believed that ever since. Obviously he hadn't really meant it. To describe his dismay he took to borrowing from Lady Bracknell in The Importance of Being Earnest. 'To lose one child to Radio 1, Mr. Kershaw, may be regarded as a misfortune; to lose both looks like carelessness.'

BECAUSE THE NIGHT (BELONGS TO US)

I don't think he ever forgave us. Where had it all gone wrong? He thought Radio 1 and Top of the Pops were subversive. (He was ahead of his time there). He'd banned his children from listening or watching and now they'd taken us both. Occasionally he'd mention our forays onto Radio 4 with some pride. But generally he was a terminally embarrassed and disappointed man.

So, on with the Evening Show then. The producer Phil Ross's loyalties were being tested because he'd loved Janice since they'd worked together at Radio Merseyside and he'd just had a baby, too, but kept his job.

Obviously he didn't have to do the stuff that our controller had suggested would be so work-incompatible for Janice (like breast feeding) but after a full day in the office he did have to rush off just as the show was starting, leaving a very shaky new presenter unsupervised in a studio and in charge of a national BBC network.

In a couple of years, as a new mum, home alone for more than 12 hours a day with a baby, I realised why his wife was desperate to get him home. No wonder he was in a constant state of flux.

Good job 'Our Jane', another Liverpudlian, who booked all the guests for the show, kept me company most evenings, with good vibes. Phil had done all the fiddly bits. Nowadays these are taken care of by computers but back then each 7" single or album track had to be timed with a stopwatch, added up with a special mechanical hours-and-minutes-calibrated calculator and a list typed out by one of 'The Girls' in the main office. This was then put in a black programme box the size of about 30 LPs along with all the records in order, as well as any tapes of interviews to be played. When showtime came these tapes would be handed over to the T.O. – technical operator – who sat in an adjacent studio behind glass, waiting for a wave from the DJ when the tape needed to be played.

Some of those guys were really good company and loved being there. The best nights were when Ralph was on. He was lanky with long hair, loved the music and was full of good vibes. Just like the dude who drives the school bus in The Simpsons.

Jane was dead bright, big and beautiful with a thick Scouse accent, an enormous personality and an infectious belly laugh. She booked up-and-coming musicians like Tracy Chapman and comedians Harry Enfield and Julian Clary plus legends like Squeeze and The Ramones.

They were promoting their greatest hits, 'Ramones Mania'. I couldn't believe I was with the coolest guys on the planet whose records I'd bought ever since I'd discovered them at Leeds Uni in 1977.

Listening back to that interview recently I've cringed. I sounded so scared. I was still learning and in awe. I still am and that's OK. When a presenter starts to believe they're as big as their guests, it's, quite literally, a real turn-off.

I don't and that's why, I like to think, I'm still on after 30 years.

The amount of care Jane put into looking after some of the guests went way above and beyond her line of duty. In fact, to this day, she's still 'looking after' one of her 'bookings' every time he's in town.

After getting passed over time and time again for producer jobs, Jane gave up on the BBC and now works for Reuters in New York. Me and Jane are still 'bezzies' as they say in Liverpool.

BECAUSE THE NIGHT (BELONGS TO US)

One young guy who beat Jane to a producer's job had never worked in radio, had to be trained up and led by the hand by Jane (who could run rings round him because she knew the ropes inside out), and, hardly able to disguise his daily disdain and impatience, used it as a stepping stone to TV 'exec-dom'. Jane just had to accept that her gender was holding her back. So she cut her losses and left Radio 1.

There was only one female producer then. And everyone called her Our Brian. Otherwise women were doomed to type for the rest of their days for such poor pay that sharing bunk-beds in a nearby BBC hostel was, if you were single anyway, the only way of affording to work there.

When 'The Girls' went on strike for better conditions, the 'ringleader' was called in by one of the Radio 1 execs who laid out her career options.

"You're a pretty young girl. Why are you trying to be a man? Why don't you just wait and see who you meet. One day a nice pop star might walk in and ask you to marry him."

For someone who'd been brought up to believe you should make your own way in the world and that finding a nice man was the icing on the cake not a meal ticket, that made my blood boil.

The treatment of 'The Girls' made me join the picket line with a placard. The Radio 1 demarcation by gender was so dated, blatant, and obscene and many of them were my friends. I wasn't really 'one of them' in work just as I wasn't really 'one of the guys'.

I'd made a few real DJ mates like Peel, Johnnie Walker, Nicky Campbell and Bruno (as opposed to great mates which is DJ speak for someone who purports to be your good friend and colleague but is just waiting for you to take a holiday so they can grab your slot).

Apart from the four of us girl DJs – three after Janice had gone – all the other 25 or so jocks were blokes and after Doreen Davies departed, so were all the management. Being female and on air meant you didn't really fit in anywhere. You were a bit of an oddity.

I've always said that walking into that workplace was like stepping into a rugby club locker room. I got well and truly tackled by Mike Smith when I blew the whistle on that in 2012. I was really bruised but at least now the public know the score.

My great grandmother had run a business and so had my grandma. My dad and his family were all great socialists and trades unions activists. All of my female relatives had worked all their mothering lives. Both my parents had gone to college and become managers in the teaching profession and my mum was also a bit of a bigwig in local politics. Me and Our Andrew had been brought up and educated as equals and been encouraged and expected to do equally well in life.

So by the time I started work in the late '70s, I thought Women's Lib was not just positively passé but redundant. Gender was irrelevant and the world was my oyster. I was wrong. At least when it came to the BBC.

At Littlewoods and BT there were plenty of powerful women as well as men, and my peers were an equal measure, getting the same pay for the same job. Women weren't forced to leave work when they married or started a family and we could have mortgages and our own homes. We could vote and there were women running the country. One as the head of state and another in Number 10.

Born with
a smile on
my face?

Driving in
my car,
1960

Bridesmaid
duties, 1961

My dad, Jack Kershaw

My mum, the mayor. Councillor Eileen Kershaw with me,
Sam and Joe, 1996

Grandma Norah Acton, with supplies of pies, at the Southport Roadshow, 1989

Happy Birthday grandma! 1996

Cyril Smith, MP, supporting the scouts (with me in the background), opens a fete near Rochdale, 1981

Our favourite barmaid. Grandma and grandad Acton, with me and the loyal staff in their pub, The Green Gardens, 1979

The man who discovered The Kershaws. On the Martin Kelner show at Radio Aire, 1981

Hyde Park Road, Leeds, with Our Andrew, 1982

Carol, me and Lindsey.
Dawn Chorus and the
Bluetits, 1983

Billy Bragg,
left, with
Paul and me,
on one of his
regular visits
to Shire Oak
Road when
touring the
country,
1983

Still crazy
after all
these years.
(Chris) Dixon
modelling for
BT, 1982

Shire Oak Road. Home sweet home to
great parties and tons of happy memories

The infamous 1960s jukebox, from a junk
shop, takes pride of place in Shire Oak Road

Woodlands Studio, 1984, with (L-R) owner Neil, 'Uncle' Al, Dixon, Black Lace, John and Damian of The Undertones, and Our Andrew

London calling. My leaving party at BT, Leeds, 1986

Radio 1 new girls. With Ro Newton, 1987

I've got the Radio 1 Evening Show! 1988

Bruno and Liz wowing the Roadshow crowds. Mmm... Maybe not with our outfits! 1989

Hello Dolly. The Kershaws get to meet one of their heroines, in London, 1987

Another international superstar.
Tony Bennett joins me on 5 Live, 1997

Me and Jase, 1989. Jason Donovan was huge, and on Bruno and Liz nearly every week!

Hanging out with the Beards. Whistle Test's Andy Kershaw on the road in Atlanta, Georgia, with ZZ Top, and his driver (Our Elizabeth), 1986

The ultimate hair do – or don't. Oh come on...it was the '80s!

Stairway To Heaven. Robert Plant signs the album I've loved for 27 years, 2003

I Haven't Stopped Dancing Yet. Me and my bump (baby Sam) rock the Radio 1 crowd at an indoor Roadshow, 1990. Now co-host Gary Davies wasn't the only one with a bit in the middle!

BECAUSE THE NIGHT (BELONGS TO US)

But at Radio 1 it was still the swinging sixties. Or at least some of the swingers who'd been around since it started in 1967 seemed to think so.

Tucked away in our own building, our all-powerful Controller, Johnny Beerling, was rumoured to be shagging his secretary, Celia. One night, after a party she took a gang of us girls back to his office, put on his boxer shorts (he kept spare clothes in a cupboard), helped herself to the contents of his fridge and put her feet up on his desk swigging champagne from the bottle. Call me Miss Marple but this confirmed all my suspicions. Celia became the second of his three wives. Beerling came to remind me of Swiss Tony on The Fast Show. "Running a radio station, Liz, is like making love to a beautiful woman."

Sometimes it felt like we were on the set of 'Carry On Regardless.' I opened a broom cupboard once to startle another boss getting stuck into another 'secretary'. And I know at least one other exec was very 'close' to his personal assistant while several of the producers were 'seeing' members of staff.

Look, I was no nun. But I wasn't married. Or management. And I always remembered my old mate Sheena's mantra of 'never take your clothes off in front of somebody you might have to sit in a meeting with'. Wise words, mate. Wise words.

The Radio 1 culture of the time was captured brilliantly in the 1994 TV comedy 'Smashie and Nicey: The End of an Era'. It's 'only' a spoof, but genius because it's so spot on. No wonder Enfield and Whitehouse were blamed for the demise of the 'dinosaurs'.

Us Kershaws got off lightly...

"Hiya. I'm Simon Northerner and this is me sister!" That's how they portrayed us.

THE BIRD AND THE BEEB

When I first arrived at Radio 1 from BT, I was impressed by the comparative lack of managing. Without any signs of supervision everybody just seemed to get on with it. The suits were hardly ever seen on the shop floor. The only time Beerling came down to my show was when I had a Page 3 girl on one evening and he took the trouble to welcome luscious Linda Lusardi personally.

Pride in the output and fear of failure to come up with the goods on time (which would be very public) meant people did what they knew they had to do, ideally by lunchtime, and then went down the pub for the afternoon. The emphasis was on fun. Management seemed more like cheerleaders than leaders. That's not to say they weren't ever hands on. In some cases that was part of the problem.

And from across the street in Broadcasting House, the powers that be seemed happy to keep their distance. They'd only set up a pop station 20 years earlier because they'd been forced to by the popularity of the Pirates. They didn't understand it and they weren't going to ruddy well spoil a good thing by trying to.

Having said that, from time to time we'd be wheeled out to meet the Director General and the Board over a glass of red in the oak-panelled Governors' dining room. They'd ask us "and what do you do?" before glazing over, reaching for another canapé and making a beeline for a familiar face from Radio 4. Once again I was reminded of 'Are You Being Served?' and Young Mr. Grace. "Oh you're getting 20 million listeners a week are you? Jolly good. You're all doing very well. Carry on."

Back then, if the most senior BBC managers had claimed they didn't have a clue what Jimmy Savile was up to in the BBC, I think I would have believed them.

BECAUSE THE NIGHT (BELONGS TO US)

Anyway, life and the summer of 1988 rolled on. Radio all week and festivals every weekend. Reading festival was a roller-coaster. The highpoint was when The Ramones, two days after they'd been on my show, name-checked me as they started their set. "This one goes out to Liz Kershaw. One, two, three, four... let's go!" into 'Blitzkrieg Bop'. It was a downer when a scary girl threatened to beat me up afterwards. "I'm Joey Ramone's girlfriend. He bought me this watch. Just fucking back off!"

It was a real rush to be compering and introducing all the bands for three days. It was piss poor to dodge the bottles of wee as they were lobbed at every turn. It was impressive that Bonnie Tyler was... er... plucky enough to obliviously duck and dive and carry on. It was embarrassing that Meat Loaf behaved like a big girl and bottled out and it was a bummer that I never got a penny because the organisers went bust.

That summer was fantastic but soon it was dawning on me that October was approaching with Beerling's new line-up and I didn't know if I'd still have a show.

However, he knew I'd taken a risk by giving up my day job to help cover his summer schedule and, all credit to him, he'd found me a new role. I was going to be on daytime which meant that my days of solo presenting were over. Women couldn't expect a prime time slot on their own. It just didn't happen. The received wisdom was that the majority of listeners were housewives and they wanted a man (maybe with a few recipes) for company.

That thinking still prevails on BBC radio. In 2014, it's still back to back men from dawn until dusk on Radio 2. And on the BBC's 40 local radio stations there's only one woman trusted on her own at prime time – breakfast. After banging on about this to management and MPs for years, I'm pleased to say that's finally changing at last – slowly.

Thanks to Beerling's decision, I would spend the next four years (and most of the next decade) being paired up and playing sidekick to a succession of men, starting with Mark Goodier.

When you started on radio you weren't given much in the way of guidance. There was the sign on the wall of the Radio 1 studios: 'One thought. One link. Johnny Beerling 1985'. But nobody understood that. You were told to pretend you were talking to one person. If one of the biggest radio stars of the last three decades had bought into that one we'd never have had the magic and mayhem of Steve Wright in the Afternoon's 'zoo'. The other mantra was: 'Put a smile in your voice'.

Mark Goodier certainly bought into that last one. Every time he'd open his mic he'd stretch his face into what I can only describe as a disturbing grin as we sat opposite each other for four hours every Saturday and Sunday morning from October, 1988. It was only for a few months though. Every evening at 7pm that summer, I'd followed Bruno's tea time show and during our matey DJ handovers, I'd relentlessly but affectionately taken the piss.

When Goodier applied for a holiday in February, 1989, I was asked who should 'dep'. I'd had such a laugh with Bruno that I suggested him. He loved the banter too and so did Beerling & Co. Goodier got back from his break to find he was gone for good on Weekend Breakfast. The Bruno and Liz Weekend Breakfast Show was born.

Chapter Ten

IT TAKES TWO

"I haven't a clue what's going on," Our Andrew once admitted after listening to it. "But I never stopped laughing."

I didn't either and Beerling said the same. It was chaotic and entirely on the hoof apart from bits of stuff I'd script for the two of us. Bruno, being the bigger star of course (I owed everything to him!) and, as he loved to remind me constantly, being on twice as much per show as I was, would just breeze in with seconds to go.

Usually he'd have driven overnight 'fresh' from a gig, maybe in Glasgow, and after the show he'd be off to open a kitchen showroom in somewhere like Cleethorpes.

So why was this odd couple such a smash hit with the audience? Well deconstructing it now I'd say they heard a big-time little bloke who was used to getting his own way (in every sense) with the ladies, trying to put down a feisty bird who wouldn't take any shit and always got the last word. And like Morecambe and Wise, one of us thought they were clever and the other one actually was. One of us thought they were in charge but the listeners could hear it was the other one. One of them thought they were funny and the other was actually setting up all the gags.

Mix that up, throw in the essence of Les Dawson – you've actually got to be really good (on the piano) to be that bad – and the fact that we were laughing at ourselves, Rochdale and Stoke style, and you've got real radio comedy.

OK, this was an entertainment show. But the music still mattered to me. I soon found which bands weren't seen as suitable though. "We're not playing that." Bruno was at the controls and could veto my favourites. "R.E.M? I'm not playing that woolly jumper shite."

I only took exception to one band. To my cost. Wet Wet Wet had stood up their fans at 'Gary's Winter Warmers'. I'd been Gary Davies' sidekick for that week of February half-term Roadshows in school sports halls. So I was there to witness him coming out of his bedroom when the hotel fire alarm went off in a pair of old man's pyjamas his mother must have packed for him. By the time we were assembled outside he'd slipped back and was posing in a slinky wrap in the car park. I also saw how gutted all the girls had been who'd travelled across the country just for Marty Pellow and Co. not to turn up. So when Bruno put their new single on I wasn't having any of it. To this day I can't imagine why a piece of 2x2 timber was lying around in the studio. But I grabbed it and smashed the 7" disc to smithereens live on air. Sadly, for me (although apparently it was hilarious if you were listening) the turntable also came a cropper. Beerling hauled me in and outlined his repayment plan. I was docked 50 quid a week from my wages until I'd paid for his sensitive state-of-the-art studio gear. A snip at £1,000.

Me and Bruno did agree on some bands such as the Bee Gees. And we were absolutely gobsmacked to find out it was mutual. The biggest 'boy band' in the world ever loved us too and specified that, when they did a live concert on Radio 1 and round the globe via the World Service, they wanted Bruno and Liz to introduce them live on stage and on air.

They had been on our show and were amazingly unspoiled by their massive fame and wealth. Barry was living in Florida and I asked him what he missed most about Manchester. His response was amazing. He missed Holland's meat pies. They're a 'northern delicacy' made in deepest Lancashire and the staple of any chippy supper. They're the first thing I grab when I go home and he said he had a supply driven down to London whenever he came over.

So there we were, me and Bruno at Wembley live in front of a capacity crowd and 500 million BBC listeners around the world, about to introduce the Bee Gees. There was an army of radio engineers and producers and a massive Outside Broadcast unit round the back as well. No pressure there then.

We played the crowd, whipping them into a frenzy until we got the signal from the side of the stage that the boys were ready to go. At least that's what we thought.

"And now... won't you give a big Wembley welcome to Barry, Robin and Maurice... the Bee Gees!" The roar from the crowd was deafening. It kept going for a while and then kind of petered out. No show. No Bee Gees. Where the hell were they? (Was Barry still finishing off his pies?)

So we filled and filled and blathered and bluffed for what seemed like an age. We reflected on their career and reeled off their hits. I just wanted the stage to open up and put us out of our misery.

"Does anyone know the words to 'Tragedy?'" Bruno quipped.

Another roar from the crowd and howling laughter as they were finally spotted strolling on behind us bumbling idiots. Backstage we got a right bollocking from the head BBC honcho.

Oh well. The Bee Gees forgave and never forgot us and always sent Christmas presents. Very un-rock 'n' roll ones I have to say. I've still got the crystal glasses and decanter they sent one year.

An even more unlikely supporter was the keeper of the nation's morality and defender of its youth. Mary Whitehouse. I'd been to interview her for a TV series I did about the wisdom of our elders. After that she took to writing very warm letters to me. Apparently her granddaughter was a fan and that was good enough for her. I assume she never actually heard the show. And I'm guessing she didn't hear that I'd had a child out of wedlock!

Other famous fans included our heroes from Coronation Street, Jack and Vera Duckworth. Bill Tarmey and Liz Dawn listened every weekend as they were driven to Granada Studios and got in touch. Forget Michael Jackson or Madonna. Simon Bates could fawn over them. We knew our market.

"Eh kid," said Vera as she installed herself by spreading her fags, lighter and ashtray across the desk.

"We bloody love you and Bruno. Don't we Jack?"

"Yes love." There was no greater compliment.

"I don't know 'ow' yer do it. Der yoo Jack?"

"No Vera Love."

"No script. I can't even remember the lines they give me. I 'ave to 'ave 'em written in felt pen on a bloody frozen chicken. I 'ave to bend over't deep freeze in Betterbuy to read 'em".

Staff in real supermarkets still remind me about that.

This kind of stuff (the antidote to DLT drooling over muzak makers) was our trademark. We had cheesy features like 'Just Chucked' (dedications for the newly dumped – in contrast to DLT's worthy 'Wedding Spot') and tacky quizzes. Bruno would play the tacky quiz show host, asking my daft multiple choice questions as I played the sequined hostess describing deliberately naff prizes (taking the piss out of DLT's 'Snooker On The Radio').

As was 'It's Not Dave's House'. This came about because I'd gone to LA for a holiday and was taken round to Dave Stewart's new superstar pad in the hills by his manager, who was my neighbour in Crouch End. Dave and Annie Lennox had lived over a shop in Crouch End as a couple when they first arrived in London as struggling unknowns. I'd been to Annie's beautifully elegant home in London and later I'd bump into her wearing an old raincoat and a pair of specs in the park when she'd be, like me, on the swings with her kids. But now Dave was a megastar he was living the life with Siobhan of Bananarama. So I'd spent the day by his pool with a load of glamorous but vacuous record company execs.

When I got back I was full of it. And Bruno started bringing it up all the time.

"Oh has Liz mentioned yet today that she went to Dave's house?"

So from that came a cross between Through The Keyhole and Desert Island Discs in which I took an imaginary tour of a musician's home just checking out their record collection while the audience guessed who it was. Then came the reveal when the celebrity joined us on air. It became a standing joke that everyone owned Fleetwood Mac's 'Rumours', Phil Collins' 'But Seriously' and the 'Grease' album.

Whenever we had a male guest of any age, Bruno of course insisted that I fancied them and he took the piss accordingly. Except I didn't. But it made good banter and a lot of fun and not, ultimately, at my expense. I think the subtle suggestion was that little Bruno fancied me himself and was jealous. Which he really wasn't.

We had become interdependent professionally and got to know each other inside out. And even though we were very different people with almost opposing values and goals, there was an unspoken mutual fascination and respect. We genuinely liked each other and enjoyed being together.

And that's why it worked.

Bruno just lived in a different world. Before online shopping and home delivery, if I had wanted something from town I'd have just gone and got it. But not Bruno. Having ordered an electrical lead over the phone and, naturally, negotiated a knockdown price from a shop on the Tottenham Court Road, he then booked a taxi firm to go and collect it. The controller recognised the name and decided not to send a dodgy cab. Best send something more befitting such a celebrity customer, eh? A stretch limo. Unfortunately when the guy got back to the house with the tiny package on the back seats, Bruno had fallen into a post-show stupor and couldn't be roused. So he sat outside for several hours with the meter running. In the end Bruno had to cough up about five hundred quid to get his bargain £5.99 cable.

Oh how we laughed at that one. And, to be fair, so did he. Eventually.

I'll admit that we kept the listeners guessing. Will they, won't they? And I know there was genuine disappointment when it dawned on them that reports in all the tabloids that we'd got married weren't true. It was April the 1st. Even my grandma read that in The News of the World and was taken in.

"How the bloody hell can you do that and not invite me?"

"Grandma... look at the top of the paper. What date is it?"

Radio 1 was so big then, and so were we, that we ended up in the papers almost every day it seemed. You couldn't go anywhere then without having a lens shoved into your face.

I was loving my new 'celebrity status' in so far as it got you on the guest list for every gig and party that was going but I really didn't want to be recognised in the street. I soon learned that you can't have it both ways.

I thought Bruno was just being his famous tight self when he said he couldn't go shopping to buy me a birthday present. But halfway down Oxford Street I realised he wasn't fibbing. It was hopeless. You couldn't walk a few steps without being stopped. But he kept his word on my gift. The next day a gleaming pearly white drum kit was delivered to our door.

Everybody instantly recognised Bruno. He'd been on Radio 1 for years now and every few weeks presented Top of the Pops. I'd been on the show with Ro Newton when we first started on

Radio 1 and apart from that me and Bruno only did Top of the Pops once together. It was terrifying.

The thought of the huge audience at home. The sheer size of the operation in the studio. All the technicians had been setting up all week. The crowd were all staring up at you. Everything was timed down to the second and now the moment had come to do your bit. To introduce the next band. If you fluffed it everything would have to be reset. Everyone would have to go back to their places. Valuable time would be lost and someone would be screaming at you from the gallery out of sight and high up in the gods.

I felt like a rabbit in the headlights. Oh why couldn't I just introduce a nice act like Jason Donovan or Sinita? Why did it have to be one of the biggest, most fearsome heavy metal bands in the world? The mighty Iron Maiden. Try doing that when you're terrified and the song is the testosterone-packed 'The Evil That Men Do'!

I was never asked back. But I don't think it was anything to do with any flakiness on my part. Bruno and I were having a whale of a time but someone in our circle had their reasons for resenting that. They were very thick with the producer, Paul Ciani, and I suspect had a quiet word.

And if your face didn't fit with him you were Top of the Pops toast.

Our Andrew had a taste of it when he was already a big name on Whistle Test. When he'd just started on Radio 1 he was invited to the TV Centre bar by Paul Ciani. Over a few drinks it was explained to him that he could join the roster of TOTPs DJ presenters if he went round to Ciani's house one night wearing a little kilt.

Our Andrew made his excuses and left. He never presented the show.

In hindsight I don't think that did either of us any harm. And anyway, there was another visual spectacular to get under my belt. It was time to take the Bruno and Liz show on the road!

As a Radio 1 novice I'd been sent on a Roadshow induction course in 1988 and been introduced to its foibles by Steve Wright on a grassy knoll in Windermere. My protégés Bros were top of the bill but couldn't make it. My first taste of how bonkers it all was, was when 'Wrighty' told me to put on the instantly recognisable red leather jacket Matt Goss had donated as a prize and to shimmy on stage with my back to the crowd wiggling my bum. The screaming, which could have caused a landslide in the Lakes, was just surreal.

But the masterclass in hysteria was yet to come. In Bournemouth. With the biggest crowd pleaser of them all: 'Oooh Gary Davies'.

"Where's Gary? Where's Gary? Has anyone seen Gary?"

Willy On The Plonker was running about like a headless chicken. The fun had started at 10 and by now the crowd were loud and whipped up into a frenzy. We were live on air at 11, it was ten-to and the star of the show was nowhere to be seen. "His back's gone. He's gone to see someone," Willy was informed.

"Right. Well, if he doesn't get here quick she'll have to start," he said, looking at me.

'She' was shitting herself. I'd never seen anything like it.

Peering round the red velvet curtain (classy) and across the Roadshow stage I could see a seething mass of humanity in the sunshine. They were on rooftops along the pier. They were hanging off lampposts. They were wanting and chanting for Gary. Nobody had come to see me. Somebody ring Gary!

"Hello, mate. Don't worry. If you don't get here on time Liz Kershaw can kick things off." What a miracle cure.

With seconds to spare Gary appeared, wheels screeching along the Prom. He was wearing a support garment. A kind of corset I suppose, tucked under his t-shirt around his 'bit in the middle'.

"Oh, Liz Kershaw. You're so white," he noted, checking me over as his perma-tanned bare legs hobbled up the steps. "Where's yer shorts?"

Anyway it was time for the show.

"Today. Live from Bournemouth. With Gary Davies. The Radio 1 Roadshow."

"OK gang. Let's do it," he said.

"I can't Gary. I can't. I'm scared."

"Liz Kershaw. You're a Radio 1 DJ now. A celebrity. Kindly behave like one," said the bloke in the surgical basque shoving me onto the stage.

And with that, Snap's (I've got) 'The Power' blasted across the beach, Gary wiggled his white shorts and the place erupted.

When Johnny Beerling invented the Roadshow in the early '70s, it was a low-key affair off the back of a trailer, supplied and driven by Tony (Smiley Miley) Miles through a company run by his brother John, near Bristol. Beerling came to an arrangement with the Miles brothers that, while he was busy producing the broadcasts, they could take care of selling a few souvenirs.

Beerling had no idea that the Roadshow would become the massive success it was but as the popularity grew, and with custom-made Radio 1 branded Goodymobiles in tow, complete with BBC presenters directed to get behind the counter quick post-show, millions of pounds were made through the increase in merchandise sales.

Beerling loved the Roadshow. In his autobiography he openly recalls his arrangement with the Miles brothers and recounts the deals and pranks he and his boys (the DJs and crew) got up to.

From 1973 it was his baby and even when he'd moved up from actually running it, he'd pop along to the coast throughout the summer months until he retired in 1993.

Still, following all the Savile-related revelations recently, he was quick to assure the public that he witnessed nothing untoward when Radio 1 was on the road.

After I'd got over the Roadshow fear, I was hooked. Even though I'd really never signed up for this. I'd just wanted to play records and interview musicians. I'd never dreamt of standing in front of a baying crowd and having to look into the whites of their eyes. Or at a row of OAPs – including my grandma beaming proudly in a deckchair, showing her bloomers and clutching a pile of homemade pies she'd brought us at Happy Mount Park, Morecambe.

But for one week a year it was like being a rock star. Getting ready, listening to the build up on the radio in the hotel room. Being driven into the site with a police escort. Introducing the likes of Status Quo and Kylie Minogue to the stage. Rolling into town, riding high in the cab of the massive articulated truck with rock music blaring. Flying in by helicopter. Chugging home in an ice cream van.

Phillip Schofield flew me to his Roadshow when I was still shadowing. We were airlifted in like James Bond and the Queen but it was back down to earth with a bump when I had to cadge a lift home with one of 'The Girls' in her old banger. Two hours later on the hard shoulder of the M1 a passing Mr. Whippy spotted us, took pity and delivered us back to the BBC 100 miles away at a giddying 30mph, to the jingly jangly sounds of that all-time favourite, 'Greensleeves'.

But it was a live rendition of 'The Green Green Grass Of Home', one of my mum's old 45s, that really brought home to me how far I'd come from my little record player in our front room to fronting all this. My mum had drooled over Tom Jones. But this little 'mother of two' in Rochdale couldn't have any expectations of meeting her heart-throb. Now, as he joined us on the Roadshow stage and launched into 'Help Yourself' I... er... did just that.

My conspirator Bruno had introduced him live on air while I took my place in the audience. Tee hee. As the Voice of the Valleys let rip, I leapt up as though I was just one of the crowd, tugging at those trademark tight trousers. The crowd went wild and so did he, shaking his leg as if a rabid dog was trying to get its jaws into him. And, through gritted teeth, shouting off-mic "get security, get her off!"

"What?" mouthed Bruno all innocent. "She's our presenter."

My mum, like millions of his female fans, had invested a lot in this 'Sex Bomb'. Now I was getting their money's worth!

The Roadshow of 1989 was like a homecoming tour for me and Bruno. They gave us the north-west coast leg. All my northern family (including my dad who lived in Blackpool) and friends joined the tens of thousands of Radio 1 listeners welcoming us to the familiar places I'd holidayed in as a kid.

Little did I know I would be soon having a child of my own.

Chapter Eleven

BORN TO RUN

When I'd first moved from Leeds to London to work on Livewire, I couldn't afford to buy a flat. The cheapest I spotted was £58,000. More than four times what I was paid and nearly twice what my flat in Leeds had been valued at. I tried to rent and scoured the Evening Standard but found myself queueing for viewings with dozens of other hopefuls. This was pre-internet and buy-to-let landlords. So I camped on Our Andrew's couch, the cheapest, flimsiest sofa bed you could buy. But that wasn't what kept me awake.

"Oh, don't worry. You can sleep with Our Elizabeth." He was very accommodating.

So I'd spend most nights surrounded by visiting American bands or various mates.

Janice Long slept over once and we woke up to the sight of a line of black scanties on the radiator.

"Is that your gear Janice?" I asked.

"Fuck off. I thought it was yours," she cackled

They were claimed later by the LA chick Our Andrew had tapped off with at a film premier the night before when we'd got stuck with a loud spotty wannabe called Courtney Love and her mates.

Janice had her car brought round. She couldn't drive but she owned a Ford Escort. We could but didn't have a car. So together we were off on one of our Sunday runs to the seaside or, on this occasion, Peel Acres. The sight of John and Sheila, by the fire and surrounded by their four adoring children, made Janice all broody and weepy. "Oh God. Your life's so lovely and mine's just crap," she wailed.

Our Andrew used to make cassettes for the car and on one of these road trips in 1986 we first heard 'I Believe' by an unknown band from Athens, Georgia. R.E.M. That led us to drive across the southern states to track them down. After that, whenever they came to London we'd hang out. I even bought the beer one time because they had no money. And spent a pretentious afternoon going round galleries with Michael Stipe in Soho. And then there was our bust-up in the Mean Fiddler. I'd been excited and wittering on so I suppose I was annoying him. He certainly seemed quite irritated.

"Shut up! Shut the fuck up!" I left him at the table.

"What's up Our Elizabeth?"

"Oh Michael Stipe's just bawled at me."

"Oy! Stipe. Over here. You may be the front man of the world's most innovative rock band on the brink of international super stardom. But nobody... but NOBODY talks to Our Eliza-beth like that." He was humbled and mumbled his apologies. We never stopped loving the band.

Record companies were awash with cash then. They'd fly you anywhere to see a gig. Simple Minds in Pompeii was a top trip. Being taken round LA in a stretch limo was the best. And there were lavish parties in London most nights. Mainly at the Kensington Roof Gardens. That's where we rescued Prince with half a lager and lime when he was so famous nobody else dared talk to him at his own do. Mind you, he did stand me up a couple of years later.

"I'm sorry Liz," said his plugger. "He won't be doing the interview on your show. He's got two interests in life. Making music and shagging. At the moment he won't come out of his hotel room because of the latter."

That plugger had seen everything. When a famous American long-haired rocker with a reputation for the ladies hit town I was dead excited I was going to meet him. "Mmm. You do realise all those chicks on his arm are hired in from an agency don't you." No!

Pete Wylie was part of Janice's Liverpool ex-pat posse and was always around. It was his set on Top of the Pops with 'It's Sinful' that got Peel in trouble in 1986. "If that doesn't get to number one I'm going to come round and break wind in your kitchen."

John Cooper Clark was another one who popped round one afternoon and as he stood in the kitchen, a tooth fell out of his mouth – just like that. "Oh fuckin' 'ell not another one," he moaned before bending over and picking it up. As you can tell, life was anything but routine.

Billy Bragg was a bit of a fixture at this flat too. One night, U2's 'The Joshua Tree' was put on repeat as he and Our Andrew cried into their beer. They'd both been unlucky in love and spent the evening drowning their sorrows to 'With Or Without You'.

I'd had a big rise at BT so I'd found a flat I could now afford with my brother as guarantor. Andrew was now on Radio 1 as well as Whistle Test and the good times rolled. Just before I moved out the phone rang. "Hi. Is Andy there please?"

"No sorry can I ask who's calling please?"

"Yes, it's Robert Plant."

"Oh yeah, sure. Fuck off. You'll be singing 'Stairway To Heaven' next."

"There's a laydee who's shooer all that glitters is gold and she's buying a..." 'Percy' obliged.

This was the sex god I'd loved since 1975. We didn't meet until 2002 but he didn't disappoint.

When I first moved down I was often home alone in Our Andrew's flat. I'd been a big fish in Leeds but now I was a minnow in the big city and it took time to make new friends. But I soon found I had plenty of suitors. "Bloody hell Our Elizabeth, some people play squash to keep fit..."

Our Andrew was one to talk.

Then his mate from Uni, Paul came to stay. We'd always been rather fond of each other but after an idyllic sunny day spent picnicking and rowing in Regent's Park and a party where a girl was after him, I realised it was something more. So I threw myself at him at a Motorhead gig pretending to have been pushed in the mosh pit. It could have gone either way. He could have simply pushed me away. But he didn't. He grabbed his chance and grabbed hold of me. A few weeks later he moved into my new flat which was a bit of a comedown after the leafy luxury of Shire Oak Road.

My new London pad was in a tatty Victorian terraced house on a busy bus route, but with four bedrooms it was huge (and dark and shabby with woodchip paper painted brown on every wall). However, for a price I could afford and I'd soon stripped the walls and hired a decorator. He'd been recommended to me by his sister who worked for a record company. At 6'4" and with stylishly cut blond hair, he did seem unusually glamorous.

As he was hanging paper one day it all came out. He was only the drummer from the Boomtown Rats who had found himself on his uppers after splitting up with Bob Geldof for reasons he was only too happy to go into. Crikey!

The gossip alone was worth every penny of the premium prices this celebrity tradesman was charging me.

I wish I'd known then (I found this out recently from reading his book) that Frankie Goes To Hollywood guitarist Nasher turned his hand to plumbing about that time. Then all I'd have needed was a member of Kajagoogoo to sort out my electrics.

The remaining money left over from the sale of Shire Oak Road meant I could go out for the first time in my life and buy new sofas. Big squashy comfy luxury ones from no less than Heals. And my first curtains!

But whatever I did it was still a dump. Acccording to Bruno. "They live like students," he'd tell people. "There are empty beer cans and fag ends all over the place!" That wasn't entirely true. But it was a lot different to his 'ideal home'. That was right on the banks of the Thames in Wapping and all of a four storey Georgian house on a square overlooking Tower Bridge.

No expense had been spared. From the pristine glossy designer kitchen untainted by food to the sunken bath set in shag-pile carpet to the tented ceilings over the beds. Antiques and mirrors adorned the many reception rooms. And then there were all the leather bound books and oil paintings, none of which he'd read or bothered to look at.

"I don't really read much mate, I bought them by the crate load at a bankruptcy auction," he told Paul one day.

"As for the art, they're alright aren't they. I just told the gallery I wanted some stuff in gilt frames."

I thought it took years to make a baby. You'd have thought so from all the articles in women's magazine on IVF, adoption and surrogacy. I know it does for some couples and it's heartbreaking but not me and my amazingly fertile fanny!

One night of 'trying' and I was pregnant. And in shock. I'd only been in the Radio 1 job two years and I'd just signed my own P45. My GP couldn't understand why I was so miserable.

"I'll get sacked," I snivelled.

"Don't be silly. That doesn't happen anymore. It's 1990 for goodness sake!"

When I outlined my employer's track record she tentatively suggested an abortion. I went home and cried. Livelihood or motherhood? I'm ashamed of myself and angry that the Radio 1 culture at the time made me consider, even for a second, murdering my first child.

I didn't want people to treat me differently and for pregnancy to become the only topic of conversation. So I kept my bump a secret for as long as I could by wearing bigger, baggier jumpers until at five months, in May, 1990, I had to tell everyone, including the BBC, why I was turning into a bit of a porker.

"Are you mad?" My dad certainly was. "Do you know what you're doing bringing a child into today's world?" War, hunger, poverty blah, blah, blah. I was sure fathers had been saying this for donkeys' years.

"You can't be. You're one of the lads. How did this happen?" My brother couldn't take it in either.

"Oh that's OK. Congratulations. I'm sure we'll manage to fit things around it".

Bloody hell. That from Beerling.

"But... Janice... when she had a baby...?"

"Oh that was different. You're doing great business. I don't want to get rid of you. Of course you won't want to do the Roadshow now. Best to stay in the studio and take it easy, eh?"

What a relief.

But hang on. I did still want to do the Roadshow. Why not? Pregnancy wasn't an illness. I hadn't been a bit poorly. I was in rude health. The days of being sent away to the country for confinement were long gone. We had listeners who got pregnant didn't we? Sod that. If he just wanted me to be heard but not seen he'd have to say so.

And now it was all out in the open I was going to let it all hang out. (A couple of pop stars have told me that when they were pregnant I was their inspiration to boldly show off their bumps on stage). I went shopping for size XL stretchy lycra wear. But first I shopped around for a hospital. I'd been to the local NHS unit. What a dump. It was dirty, the wallpaper was peeling off and the staff were so take it or leave it, I did. This was a special occasion. I was going to treat myself. Like a luxury holiday in a posh hotel with Pampers as well as pampering.

THE BIRD AND THE BEEB

In 1988, while my show was being broadcast, the Duchess of York had her first baby. That was nice and a contrast to all the people who've since pegged out during my programme.

On such occasions it's customary to follow the announcement with a 'relevant' song. (Indeed for departing A-listers there was a black box kept in the corner of the studio with appropriate music.)

So we scrambled around and stuck on Fleetwood Mac's 'Sarah'. It stuck in my mind that Fergie had delivered at The Portland Hospital just round the corner. That would be handy if I went into labour at the BBC so I booked myself in. It was worth every penny as soon as the consultant proudly informed me that his instrument had last been down the Duchess's drawers and that everything was AOK.

So back to work – which meant a trip to Northern Ireland.

I was worried. About my safety. Not as a mother-to-be but as a mouthpiece of the 'Bruddish'. The Troubles were brewing again. Even Bruno, who gave scant regard to current affairs, apart from news of his shares on the FTSE 100, had insisted that the BBC really needed to think about it this year.

They have since with reams of risk assessment forms to fill in. Before one trip in 1995 in the section headed 'Worst Possible Scenario', my producer scribbled 'presenter may die.' On this one back in 1990, we were simply allocated a bodyguard each. Grudgingly. What could possibly go wrong? This was the Radio 1 Roadshow. It was all about 'F.U.N.'

My bodyguard was positioned stage left, he was about 70, had no top set and his toupe was gently lifting in the summer breeze as he scanned Londonderry/Derry's civic square. (We'd been instructed to keep both factions in the crowd happy by referring to the venue in alternative ways in alternate links). On the ramparts above us, squaddies clutching automatic weapons were watching our every move.

"It's time for the 'Yes/No Challenge'. You can't say 'yes', 'no' or 'I don't know'. Remember that and you'll win a Radio 1 Fun Goody Bag!"– Bruno was in full flow as I beckoned an enthusiastic contestant onto the stage.

"Hi, mate. What's yer name?"

"Free the Birmingham Six! Free the Birmingham Six!"

The crowd went wild. But not in a good way. The soldiers on the walls readied their weapons. "Free the Birmingham Six!"

"Alrighty. There you go mate. You've done it! Give the guy his Goody Bag Liz. Well done. Thank you. Just fantastic. Here's Aztec Camera!"

Back in England, not even Noel Edmonds could shock me into labour with one of his 'Gotchas' in the basement of Broadcasting House. The plot was that our show had been moved to a makeshift studio because of building work. After constant banging finally caused Bruno to lose it on air, Noel, dressed as a workman, burst in as the false wall behind me came crashing down.

"Right that's enough, mate. I've got a heavily pregnant woman here," Bruno raged. So he did care! He laid in to the fella in the flat cap until he ripped off his false beard and glasses. It was only his all-time idol 'Noelly'! Bruno was gobsmacked. Just hilarious. Anyway, it's on YouTube.

In fact nothing shifted baby Sam. He must have been happy where he was. By early September he was way past his due date and a scan showed he now weighed a whopping 10 pounds.

"You're a big girl. But you have an androgynous pelvis. So you can either wait, struggle with labour for hours and end up having an emergency caesarean, or you can book in for Saturday morning and get it over with." A posh voice is very persuasive.

I worked until the previous Sunday morning and on the Friday night, after checking into a lovely room at The Portland, we went for a Mexican meal.

"Here's your margarita. Oh... when's it due?"

"Tomorrow at 8.30." Hasta La Vista, baby.

I was excited but also thinking this was a kind of Last Supper. Tomorrow my life would change forever. I couldn't just please myself any more. I'd never be able to put 'me' first again.

But I had no regrets. I wouldn't be sitting at home thinking 'what if?' I'd never feel like I'd somehow missed out. I'd had my fair share of glamour with a good run of travelling the world and partying hard.

A song I'd heard on Radio 1 as a teenager, doing my home-work one Sunday afternoon in my bedroom in Rochdale, had inspired and stayed with me ever since. Dr. Hook's 'The Ballad of Lucy Jordan':

> 'At the age of 37,
> She realised she'd never ride,
> Through Paris in a sports car,
> With the warm wind in her hair.'

I'd made sure I'd been there, done that and got the t-shirt. And now I was ready to be a parent.

We already knew it was a boy and that he was massive.

The big surprise was his mop of ginger hair. And that he looked so cross.

"Oh he's brilliant. He's the best baby ever. All the other babies are crap." I was deliriously happy and weeping buckets. I was high on drugs.

"Bloody hell," said Uncle Andrew (as he was known from that moment) arriving in full leathers, much to the delight of one of the nursing staff, and pointing at my drip. "Our Elizabeth is mainlining on heroin." It was morphine but, hey.

Uncle Bruno was soldiering on with our Saturday show and as soon as he got word he played my request for Sam: Gladys Knight's 'You're The Best Thing That Ever Happened To Me' but just in case it was all getting a bit too sentimental he then stuck on something just for me: 'Born To Run'!

After the show he shot up to The Portland to meet Sam. With other mates popping round all week (maybe it was a bit too handy for the BBC after all) the bed and board – a huge ensuite room and endless champagne and sandwiches – cost nearly as much as the medical care. The number of bouquets, cards and cuddly toys that arrived from complete strangers was amazing. But then, in more than 20 years, Sam was the first baby ever to be born to a Radio 1 mum one who didn't suddenly disappear. He was a sensation that was sweeping the nation.

Photos were taken of me looking completely out of it, but I was relieved I hadn't tried to attempt anything natural, clutching a newborn with freaky feet sticking out of his blanket. I could never buy him baby shoes. His first pair were meant for a three-year-old. I have to get him size 14s online now.

The consultant asked if I had any questions before I went home. It was like a sketch from a saucy seaside postcard.

"Yes doctor. When you do think we can have sex?"

"That's awfully kind of you Miss. But I'm playing golf in half an hour..."

Five weeks later I was back at the BBC.

They'd only keep the job open for so long and weren't paying me while I was off. I needed to pay the mortgage and the four grand for that week in a posh hospital. It meant leaving Sam for five hours every Saturday and Sunday morning. That was painful. He was a big lad and needed constant feeding. So the rest of the time we were literally inseparable. Sitting in the studio I could feel my chest swelling and by the time I got home I was in agony and bursting to see my baby. "Where is he? Give him to me quick!" I'd rip off my soggy bra and the milk would squirt across the room like two water pistols before I could get hold of him.

When I was asked to voice a documentary for Radio 4 I knew it would take a full day so I told them I could only do it if I could bring my baby with me. Sam slept in his carrycot in the corner of the studio but when I needed to break off to feed him the producer got very shirty. "Oh how long is this going to go on?" he barked. "About nine months actually". It was a mistake. I couldn't do that again.

As the Christmas of 1990 approached, I was asked to go to a lunch with the Board of Governors. I was worried about how I'd cope but I couldn't be seen to be letting motherhood get in the way. I was placed next to a peer of the realm and was wearing a festive stretchy gold lamé top which was quite adequate when they brought our starters.

By the time coffee and mints were served I'd gone up a cup size per course and was bursting out all over.

Lord Lennox was new to the Board and trying to understand its pop music service. He was charming. If he'd been told Radio 1 was a bit end of the pier it certainly was now with 'DJ Liz and her amazing inflatable chest!'

By Spring, things were easing off, Sam was about eight months old, and after a lot of soul searching we decided we could all cope if I went away for a few days to cover the Eurovision Song Contest in Rome.

I didn't dare to say to Radio 1 "actually, I can't leave my child. I can't go." I dreaded being written off because work didn't always come first.

But who would look after Sam? Paul was also at work so it was impossible for him too. Bruno's wife-to-be had volunteered a couple of times. She'd also volunteered that she loved kids but the thought of growing a baby was just gross.

Sam Fox and her sister were happy to mind Sam for a couple of hours. Not many men can say they were babysat by Britain's biggest topless model. I loved Sam (Fox) but I had a problem with Page 3. There is a place for tits and bums in print (magazines – that's sex) but not in a paper (that's sexist). But if Sam could make a mint out of the Murdochs, who was exploiting whom? I thought the fact that her dad was her manager and cashing in on his daughter's impressive knockers was a bit rum though. I had a go at it once for my show (keeping my frock on) to see what the girls went through. "Chin up, eyes wide open, chest out, tummy in, knee up. That's it. Fantastic. Just hold it there."

That posing episode was painful but it meant Nicky Campbell invited me onto his Central Weekend Live TV show one Friday night to debate the pros and cons of glamour modelling and cosmetic surgery. I was sent home with a silicone implant as a souvenir. Twenty years later that was to land me before a judge in Court No. 1 at The Old Bailey. I'll explain later.

Meanwhile, The Sun's editor, Kelvin McKenzie, decided to even things out for a while with Page 7 Fella. One of the first to make a tit of himself was Bruno.

By now Mo, the cleaner we shared with the Eurythmics manager round the corner, had taken on some babysitting as well. Sam had taken to a bottle and to Mo. They really seemed to love each other, and I knew I could completely trust her so, finally, after eight months, I thought I'd pulled off the working mum malarkey.

Until I got back from that first time of leaving him for a few days. I'll never forget Sam's face. The shock when I walked back in – as though he'd given up on me. As though he thought he'd never see his mamma again. He just looked completely heartbroken and betrayed. We hugged and hugged. Occasionally he'd pull away just to look at my face as if to check that it was really me. That I really was back. And he gripped onto me like he'd never let me go again.

I felt just awful. Especially a week later when I nearly lost him forever after he was struck down with meningitis.

"I don't think Sam's very well," Mo said as I emerged up the stairs into the flat.

I'd only been out for a couple of hours this time filming in central London. He was bright red, hot and limp with a pathetic little whiney cry. I instinctively knew this was something a dose of Calpol couldn't cure so I rang our GP. It was after five and the out of hours service was rubbish.

"Look I'm not trying to order a pizza here. My baby's really poorly." We waited but nobody came so we took Sam up to A&E. A junior doctor diagnosed constipation and sent us home with a prescription.

We were up and down all night and by early morning were starting to really panic and at the front of the queue to see our GP. She saved his life. She took one look at him, shot him full of penicillin and told us to go back to the hospital but this time not to bother with A&E, go straight to the children's ward.

We walked in as the paediatric consultant was doing her round. She knew what it was straight away and she ordered a lumbar puncture.

Sam was soon laid out on a bed with wires everywhere and several drips feeding a huge plastic tap punched into his tiny hand. You know it's serious when the doctor pulls up a chair and puts a hand on yours. She was telling us that he might be permanently damaged, or worse, he could die.

He looked like he was sleeping and it seemed cruel when, every so often they raised his lids and shone a torch into his eyes. What was that for? "We just want to check for response. To see if he's gone into a coma."

The consultant came back. The good news was the penicillin had worked. The bad news was it had made it impossible to grow a decent culture from the spinal fluid that had been taken so she couldn't tell us what kind of meningitis this was. Now all we could do was sit by Sam and wait.

We spent the rest of the week there, night and day. By Saturday Sam was on the mend. I was minging and supposed to go to work.

I was hoping that Radio 1 would say "Liz, your baby is very ill. Take some time off." But no.

So in I went for a few hours, put on a brave face and a complete act and then ran back to the children's ward.

A few weeks later we bumped into Dr. Heather Mackinnon in a cafe in Crouch End. She greeted Sam so warmly that I burst into tears and hugged and thanked her profusely. Years later she was named in press reports of the Baby P scandal. I knew how caring and competent she was so I wrote to support her at the hospital and sent her a picture of Big Sam.

She took the time to reply saying she was delighted that he'd grown into such a fine, healthy young man. All credit to her.

When the Roadshow came round again in the summer of 1991 I wasn't for going unless we could go as a family. So Paul took time off work, packed Sam and his pram into the car, and we headed off for the south coast.

I thought I'd done well losing my baby weight but all week I got digs about looking lumpy. After Bournemouth, Exmouth and Weymouth the finale was in Torquay. "I don't know how you've got the nerve to wear that," one colleague sneered just before I leapt on stage in head-to-toe lycra.

By now we'd been joined by a new 'suit'. He was extremely tall and clean cut. That was it for John Walters. John Peel's legendary producer said he knew it was time he left Radio 1 when the new boss arrived looking like he'd just won the Silver Whistle at the Hendon Police College. Sam was at the side of the stage in his buggy. When the crowd started chanting "we want Sam, we want Sam," I looked towards him but saw the face of our new exec.

I knew I was fucked.

Although Beerling had assured me everything was OK, I guess that, really, a woman with a pushchair and a pot belly was just too mumsy. Not the young, free and single image they wanted. But I was paid a compliment after one show. "You did OK for a mum!"

By December, 1991, a decent amount of time had passed and I was called in.

"Hi, Liz. Jo here from Johnny's office."

Jo had replaced Celia, the secretary Beerling had been shagging and since married.

"Can you pop down this afternoon?"

"Er... not really. I don't have any childcare arranged."

"Oh, don't worry. Just bring Sam with you. OK?"

It was four days before Christmas and I had a 14-month-old baby on my knee.

"I'm sorry to say Liz that I've decided to refresh the schedule from March and I'm putting Gary Davies on the Weekend Breakfast Show so it's the end of the road for Bruno and Liz."

I couldn't cry. I couldn't argue. I had to keep calm for Sam.

How handy. How cruel.

So this was the infamous courtesy three months' notice being served then? Hence the crap timing. I rang Bruno but he apparently already knew.

He was getting the weekday Early Breakfast Show. Commonly know as a graveyard shift. But he'd been promised that it was just a warm up for promotion to his dream slot, Breakfast. What a con. He trustingly did that horrible shift for a couple of years until they showed him the door too.

I had to drive home thinking my world had come to an end. I'd given up a job at BT for this. And less than five years later I was out on my ear.

What a failure. How was I going to give Sam the life I'd hoped for now? Elton John and George Michael were summing it all up on the car stereo. 'Don't Let The Sun Go Down On Me.' It felt like it just had.

Going in there week-in, week-out for three months knowing that everybody knew I was for the chop was like being on radio's very own death row but in the end I didn't have to serve my time. I got rescued by Radio 5.

And anyway, being sacked shouldn't have been such a shock. Walter's 'exec with the silver whistle' had tried to show me the writing on the wall (or rather a load of printouts on a clip board) at the annual DJs Christmas Party which was recorded as usual in October. "You see, Liz, the Bruno and Liz show is on the slide," he said festively. "The figures show it's just not what it was." Did they? A mole told me that when the Bruno and Liz show was scrapped there were celebrations at Capital Radio as ours was the only show that beat them in London.

Whatever, on February 9th, 1992, I left Egton House for the last time. No embarrassing 20-minute rants on air about 'resigning' from me. I went quietly, slipping as I walked down the ramp in the rain to my car, ripping my favourite trousers and grazing my knee.

That just about summed things up and gave me an excuse for tears as I drove past a cluster of well-wishers waving me off.

When the end comes it can take many forms. Janice Long told me how she didn't even know that she'd done her last show. "As far as I was concerned I was going on maternity leave. I was packing all my stuff when my producer shuffled in with a bottle of champagne in his hand. I said to my partner Paul 'I've got a funny feeling about this'. I should have married Peter Stringfellow. They would have liked that."

Bruno's own, eventual, leaving do was arranged by a load of truckers. "They'd arranged everything including a live band, and they cooked me a fry-up on the pavement outside," he told me. "It was like Death Row. Anything you want mate: bacon, eggs, booze, fags. But there was no management. A commissionaire came to say 'well done mate' and a cleaner just coming in gave me a wave. As I walked away I just thought 'bollocks to the lot of 'em'."

Top tip. Don't moan to the press. I didn't. So the good thing was nobody seemed to notice I was gone for a while. I got booked for all sorts of stuff as a Radio 1 DJ. Well, if they didn't listen, I wasn't going to tell them. So stuff just kept on coming.

As well as Radio 5, Radio 4's Saturday morning travel show Breakaway still wanted me. I'd presented Pick of the Week and was still doing documentaries and appearing on various discussion programmes.

Woman's Hour had banned me but I was proud of that. 'That Liz Kershaw is a poor man's Julie Burchill!' was their verdict on my full page in the Guardian about why the whole concept of radio for ladies was archaic and should be scrapped. Why this ghetto for female listeners? Were women still housebound, darning hubby's socks and polishing the lino? Weren't they welcome to listen to Midweek? Couldn't they get their pretty little heads round The World At One? Was the Today programme too much? (To present – obviously).

Also, following our Gotcha and a good 'gunging' (which was awful, imagine being sacked and then being very publicly humiliated by your own company with its smuggest employee in charge) me and Bruno were signed up for two series of Noel's House Party.

THE BIRD AND THE BEEB

Our role in the show was simple, if not tedious. We had to hide behind a wall of Crinkly Bottom, and on cue, fling open our panels and shout. "I've got a question Noel!" That was it. We had to be there all day Saturday to rehearse it, which meant hanging out with Frank Carson who never stopped for breath, relentlessly reeling off corny old gags. And the ultimate lounge lizard actor Leslie Phillips. "Oh Leslie, I wish I could be as calm as you," I told him once. "Mmm... nonsense, darling. Why do you think I always wear brown trousers?" came the reply.

Noel's Garden Party was his telly equivalent of the Radio 1 Roadshow and it took us on the road round the country every weekend in the summer of 1993. It also led to several interesting moments.

"You dirty fucking bitch."

"I beg your pardon! Who is this?"

"You want me don't you? You dirty fucking bitch."

The phone had rung next to the shower in my hotel room. Bruno had written a note. He'd signed my name and even sealed it with red lipstick and then slipped it under fellow guest John Leslie's door.

Apparently, I'd left John in no doubt exactly what I'd do for a Blue Peter badge. I thought the world of John, I really really liked the guy – we always had good times together and Bruno's prank had us rolling around. With laughter.

I didn't blame John for thinking he was on a promise and I felt so, so sorry for him a few years later when his career was effectively ended by rumours about his private life. It was so unfair. I had seen girls literally queueing up, one by one, to try their luck with him. He was hot. And single. So why would he throw anyone out of bed who was throwing themselves at him?

Later, in 1996, we presented a weekly show together in Manchester. When we'd go out afterwards the local lovelies would be round him like bees round a honey pot.

My mate pleaded with me to take her to the studios one week. As soon as I'd introduced her to John they both disappeared. She spent the time between rehearsals and showtime holed up with him in his dressing room. She spent the entire train journey home with a big grin on her face. Of course there were tears and tantrums when he never got in touch again. I wasn't surprised. He was living the life and loving it.

There was no end to thrills and spills and some odd couplings at Noelly's events. Like the game where me and Jeremy Irons had to hook up buckets of water, in full flying suits, hanging out of a low hovering helicopter. How he kept his fag lit and stuck to his lip was a feat in itself.

I never, ever felt like Noel Edmonds actually saw any of us as equals. Sure, he was the consummate pro who realised our appeal and was only too happy to exploit it. And I was grateful for the work. But he always kept his distance.

He was the boss and we must never forget we worked for him. And we'd only enjoy this patronage as long as it suited him.

One Saturday during a run of Noel's House Party, I caught the train to go to TV Centre. As it pulled out of the station I spotted a bag on the platform. It was mine and had all my clothes in it for the show. Too late. I had to fess up when I got there that I had nothing to wear. Some sort of ghastly blouse was loaned to me by the wardrobe department and I could see that Noel was none too pleased.

"Sorry, Noel. I'll try to be more professional I promise," I said. I was half-joking but he was dead serious when he replied stone faced "yes, please do that." I guess he didn't get where he was by being anything other than completely focused and flawless. And ruthless I suspect.

Chris Evans then made me a good offer. "If you get this job I'll buy you a classic Mercedes sports car," he promised. We were standing by the canal at The Big Breakfast house and I'd been auditioning for weeks to be his sidekick. It was now down to just me and Gaby Roslin. I really wanted that job. I wonder what life would have been like if I had got it. Apparently me and Chris were 'too alike'. I can't really comment. After meeting him several times I think I've only got to see his public persona. I wonder if that applies even to those he works with every day.

I did go on The Big Breakfast later as a guest. Sam went with me once and played with Fifi Trixibelle and her pony while I did my stuff with her mum. I liked Paula Yates. She was dead glamorous, and true to herself, never acting the dumb blonde or little woman to get on and never apologising for her sex drive.

A great role model and a dedicated mother but I guess it's hard to get good press when you're a 'sinner' married to a 'saint'.

Janet Street Porter was disgusted with the blokes running Radio 1 and the way I had been treated and she sent for me at TV Centre. How could she help? How about a role in a new show she was putting together? For the audition, I had to jump out of a dustbin and describe what I'd found.

Contestants then had to guess which celebrity's bin I was in. It was rubbish and I was secretly relieved when it was dumped. Never mind, thanks for the effort Janet. You're a top bird.

And for the next 15 years or so it was top birds and gay men who kept me going at the BBC.

Chapter Twelve

FIVE YEARS

Jane and Alison, two producers at Radio 5, threw me a lifeline when I needed it most by signing me up to present The Vibe when they heard I was about to leave Radio 1.

Brit Pop was breaking big and every Thursday night, from May, 1992, to November, 1993, we showcased little-known bands called Blur, Pulp, Oasis, and Suede.

It was a hotbed of talent with contributors like Caitlin Moran, Miranda Sawyer, Mark Lamarr and our telly critic, up and coming 'comedienne' and Liverpudlian loudmouth Lily Savage (now Radio 2's Paul O'Grady).

The backroom boys went stellar too. Producer John Yorke went on to run EastEnders. Barbara Windsor's agent had to beg him to sign Babs up as Peggy the landlady. Having resurrected her career he went on to run BBC Drama. And Phil Critchlow, another producer, now owns one of the biggest suppliers of radio programmes to the BBC. I'm glad they got out. These guys were henpecked by all the 'wimmin' who worked there. The tables had been turned but a bit too far for my liking.

Then came The Crunch. A team at BBC North were putting together the first nationwide daily topical phone-in to go out on Radio 5 at lunchtimes between the Johnnie Walker and John Inverdale shows and producers Lynn and Gabby asked me to present. Great, it was a regular income again, even if it meant being in Manchester every weekday.

When I'd been 'let go' by Radio 1 I didn't see how I'd be able to pay a mortgage so I panicked and sold our lovely London flat, leaving us temporarily homeless. We camped out in Crouch End above Banner's Restaurant which was owned by my brother's girlfriend. All our worldly goods and me, Paul and Sam were piled up in one room for eight months. To get out we had to climb down a ladder and go through the restaurant past all Our Andrew's rock 'n' roll posters and paraphernalia to the sounds and smells of the world's music and menus that he'd picked up on his travels. Sam loved sitting at the bar chatting to customers. One of his mates and biggest spenders was Martin Chambers who'd been the drummer in the Pretenders but now had a lot of time on his hands. We were sitting listening to his stories one day when he got handed the phone. It was a call from some 'Chrissie' woman to say she was putting the band back together. Trebles all round!

The 'Kershaw' connection (Andy) gave the place a certain kudos and you'd have been hard pressed to find a customer who wasn't some kind of celeb – or media type.

FIVE YEARS

Actors would 'rest' at the bar. Newspaper columnists would scribe at the tables. Editors would camp out with their kids. Bands would tuck into breakfast on a break from recording nearby. Bob Dylan got bounced for ordering a beer.

The staff had been told not to serve customers who didn't order food. One waitress was too young to know to make an exception for the two scruffy Americans who just wanted booze. When Our Andrew found out that 'Baaarb' had been refused service she was made to study an old Dylan poster on the wall right next to the table while a plaque was put up to mark the spot forever.

Sundays were good for passing star spotters. Peel would regularly hold court at the big table in the front window, with a rapidly growing collection of empty Russian 'champagne' bottles and a motley crew of musos.

Living above a funky bar full of 'faces' was really great and we were grateful. But it wasn't a place to bring up a kid. A child psychologist who was a regular customer said that Sam had the most extensive vocabulary he'd ever found in a three-year-old. This came as no surprise. On his first birthday we'd counted how many words he knew. It was 60. His nursery school loved their 'little eccentric', the little old man who walked in everyday with his lunchbox held aloft like the Chancellor on budget day making his statement, "it's cheese today everyone!" It hit me that it wasn't healthy that most of his friends were over 30.

In May, 1992, we'd been visiting my mate Sheena's new house and spotted a bloke sitting in a car outside the old cottage next door. It had been home to a right Flash Harry with a big Merc who used to roll off his luxury sun lounger to pee in the large leafy garden.

Now he'd done a bunk it belonged to the bank.

"How much are they asking?"

"Er... it's £62,000" said the estate agent in the motor.

"I'll take it"

"Don't you want to see inside?"

"No need thanks. It's a lovely spot. I can see it's a wreck."

Over a year later it still was. Before Flash Harry had left he'd turned on all the taps. Huge mushrooms were growing out of the sodden stone walls. He'd taken everything he could. Including the kitchen sink. However, presenting The Crunch was going to pay me £200 a show so a grand a week was plenty to make it habitable again.

We couldn't have afforded one in Crouch End but we were going to have a whole house! With a garden. In a chocolate box village. With a little school. And at a price that wouldn't keep us awake at night. Paul was happy to commute the 60 miles to London and if I never worked again, we reckoned it was easier to be poor in the country. And we'd still have a roof over our heads. And a really nice one too.

In order to be in place for The Crunch, me and Sam had to take the train to Manchester every Sunday evening. I've still got all the drawings and writings we did on the journeys. We stayed at my mum's. She'd said she'd look after him but after a couple of weeks she decided he was too demanding. So every morning, on the way to work, before she got up, I'd have to get him ready and get him to nursery. I hated it and so did Sam. We'd both be in tears when I left him. But for six months I saved every penny I could and we moved in to our country home just before Christmas, 1993.

It was very rustic in a distressed Tuscany kind of way. We had bare plaster walls, no carpets, the old cooker from Shire Oak Road and a few bits of second hand furniture. But we had a big log fire, two tatty comfy sofas, and it was home.

The Crunch was housed in a couple of portakabins in the car park behind the BBC's Oxford Road Manchester HQ, packed with really bright, hard working journalists. The star reporter was a brilliant Brummy called Adrian Goldberg who's still a beacon in broadcasting on the BBC in Birmingham. And Julian Worricker, who now presents on the BBC News Channel, was very welcoming. The whole team was great, and balanced. A 50/50 mix of men and women.

We were proud of our two-hour topical debates. Especially the final segment when a celebrity guest asked a question for the listeners to answer. Some of the more surreal offerings were "what colour is Monday?" The consensus was purple. And "how can you be sure that the light's gone off in your fridge when you shut the door?" Sorry. Can't remember the answer to that.

It was a ratings winner and a really happy place to work. But we'd been warned that the BBC was going to shut down Radio 5 and replace it with a rolling news and sport station so I'd known The Crunch would only last a few months. And, to be honest, it was hard camping out at my mum's and seeing Sam cry every morning when I left him.

Radio 5 Live was launched in April, 1994. I couldn't believe I was offered a free transfer.

I celebrated by getting pregnant again. This time the NHS branded me an old mum (I was 35) and insisted on testing for Down's Syndrome and Spina Bifida even though sticking a big needle in my belly might cause a miscarriage. While I waited for the results of the test the futility of it dawned on me. What was I supposed to do if I was told that my baby wasn't perfect? By now it was really making its presence felt by wriggling around.

Whenever I felt a foot poking into my ribs, I could actually grab its big toe. We'd bonded. Was I supposed to kill it? I knew that whatever the news I just couldn't. It was too small yet to be perfectly formed but big enough to be a force to be reckoned with. It was alive and kicking. The envelope dropped on the mat. It was all OK. And it was a boy. I was pleased and relieved. And, ever since, against abortions after 12 weeks. If you don't know you're pregnant or can't get your act together in three months, tough.

The BBC accommodated this baby's arrival with another short unpaid break. Little Joe (so called to this day because he was a couple of weeks early and only weighed eight and a half pounds) was born at the end of August, 1994. This time I couldn't go private. I wasn't as flush as I'd been on Radio 1 and surely a new NHS hospital in the leafy Shires would be better than an over-subscribed, under-funded Victorian pile in North London. Er... no.

My experience left me believing that the difference between private and public sector isn't the building, it's the culture.

When a patient is running up an actual bill for the service they're treated as they should be. As a customer. As someone who has a choice. With courtesy and respect. When you are getting it 'for free', (except it's not if you're paying your 'stamp') from a government-run monopoly with staff who think they've got a job for life, you're treated as a bloody nuisance with a self-inflicted condition who should be grateful for whatever they throw at you.

FIVE YEARS

A scary caesarean by a junior surgeon sent me into shock and I had to lie wrapped in tin foil while they took my new bundle away. I developed an infection and with a drain and several drips holding me back I was left to fend for my crying baby for hours on end when staff ignored my calls for help.

At least I could look after myself. I was 36, fit and healthy and could speak up for myself. Within a year I'd found out what it was like to be 87, feeble, and dying in the 'care' of the NHS, and discovered that we should all 'be afraid. Be very afraid'.

Back home, our happy and definitely complete little family would have to overcome the the same problems with boobs and being parted, because just five weeks later I was back on the train to Broadcasting House.

During four years on 5 Live (1994 to 1998) I was teamed up with two male co-presenters starting with Radio 1 Newsbeat's Mark Whittaker. I loved Mark. He was a sharp cookie, a real lad with a brilliant sense of the ridiculous and a good laugh.

This combo worked well for over two years under the wing of our matriarchal Controller, Jenny Abramsky, but the moment it was announced that Roger Mosey was replacing her, a news-reader – a household name at the time – took the trouble to cross the newsroom floor to whisper "well, that's you out then. He won't want you will he? He'll want proper journalists."

Lovely. I was shocked but not really surprised.

I'd watched the way the 'best journalism' in the world had rid itself of another 'jumped-up' DJ, Our Andrew. He'd visited dozens of countries recording their bands but he wasn't blink-ered and he was a news junkie too, so he started covering news. Like when he was on a rare romantic trip and the Montserrat volcano blew the island apart.

He was straight on the phone to the BBC and, as their invaluable on-the-spot eye-witness reporter, brought the story to the world. And he went several times to places the BBC's intrepid staff reporters had yet dared to set foot, risking his life, dodging landmines and militia, to report to the 'Today' programme and 'Newsnight'.

He made some remarkable documentaries, winning awards for the BBC but, crucially, he was never accepted by the chino-clad correspondents club and was eventually and inevitably put in his place – packed off back to exploring the world's music rather than its politics.

I was now told I was leaving the studio to cover big weekend events as the roving reporter for The Adrian Chiles Show as 'our' slot was now billed. He was the rising star of the BBC and they ousted Mark to give Adrian his own show. He had a really generous spirit and became a good friend to me. So with him as an ally and the fierce support of the two producers, Beth and Stephanie, I was kept on for another year or so, criss-crossing the country covering everything from the Eurovision Song Contest to the FA Cup.

By now, me and my microphone had grabbed hundreds of interesting interviewees for the BBC.

But getting football features for 5 Live was a whole new ball game.

Long before a glitzy TV drama put the spotlight on them, footballers' wives fascinated me so I interviewed a few and wasn't disappointed. These beautiful people were far more interesting than the beautiful game. Or their husbands.

What was wrong with footballers? The rock stars on Radio 1 could be full of shit and of themselves but at least they could string a sentence together. When a club signed a new star did they send them for a frontal lobotomy? Or were their brains just in their boots? Or were they trained to trot out stock phrases to avoid dropping themselves and the team in it?

What was striking was that social skills varied from club to club.

"Hiya I'm Liz from 5 Live," I said. I was on a press pass at a posh dinner in a stadium up north.

"Yeah?"

"I wondered if you'd come on my show sometime."

"Nope."

"Oh why's that?"

"Why should I?"

"Well, er... all the Liverpool lads have been on."

"Well they're just easy aren't they."

'As opposed to a charmless little fucker like you,' I noted silently.

I'd say who this was and how I caught him at it in the Ladies at the Lowry Hotel, Manchester, with a TV presenter in a cubicle later that night, but he'd only take out a super injunction.

On the same night I'd already spotted that Eric Cantona probably didn't want to mix. He and his wife were on a table on their own with all the other chairs tipped up to signal not to try and sit there. However, I did get to 'chat' to Eric just before the FA Cup final in 1996. I'd been sent to the Man United training camp. Not to interview the team you understand but to interview their long serving (and maybe suffering) kit man Norman. I'd hired a car and wasn't told anything about heated seats. Or how to switch them off. At first I liked the feeling of my bottom getting warmer. After 60 miles, it felt like my arse was on fire. By the time I pulled up by the training pitch I just had to jump out quick.

The sight of me fanning my burning buttocks (I hadn't spotted the team were out there) was met by whooping and hollering from the Reds. Not Cantona though. He was too cool and like God at the time.

"Excuse me please," I said trying to compose myself like a true pro. "Do you know where I can find Norman?"

That was it but back at base the sports reporters were agog.

"Oh my God. You spoke to Cantona! What did he say? What did he say?"

"He said..."

"Yes... yes...

"He said: 'Norman is on zee bus'."

"Oh my God! That's so amazing!"

Was it? Norman was on the bus and dead normal. We talked washing machines and tumble dryers. But Cantona had spoken. And he never normally did. I dined out on this exclusive for weeks.

Earlier in that year's FA Cup campaign I'd also been given access to the Liverpool training ground. They were due to play Rochdale, my home team, in the third round. We hadn't a hope in hell and it made a good David and Goliath story. "Eh, Rochdale! Over here!" Jamie Redknapp seemed pleased to see a new face. An excited Ian Rush enjoyed taunting me about our inevitable thrashing. "She's a spy! She's a spy! Eh, lads. She's from Rochdale!"

And John Scales thoughtfully asked if I'd like to see the game. Sitting in the players' seats. Next to an injured Neil Ruddock. And with drinks after in the Players' Lounge. David James was the first in, scrubbed up from the showers and John Barnes (the rapper on England's 1990 World Cup hit 'World In Motion') was a picture in his suit.

He explained that he'd designed it himself as he highlighted the motif on the jacket. Each edge had an appliquéd hand. One black. One white. When the garment was buttoned the hands interlocked as a symbol of racial harmony. What a bobby dazzler.

I was invited back regularly after that and always got a 'yes' from Liverpool's manager Roy Evans if I needed a footballer on a show.

My mate Binksy had a season ticket so was glad to hob nob and he was delighted when Adrian Chiles asked if he could use his Liverpool home to cook for rising star Steve McManaman and record it for the radio.

Binksy had designed and built his own footballer-style gaff. He'd bought an old Victorian villa, demolished it, selling all the architectural features over the wall, and built a modern mansion on its prime site overlooking the park.

Of course, none of our listeners would see it but at least it wouldn't be too shabby for this multi-million pound midfielder. Adrian grilled Steve about rumours of him wanting to move to Spain while I served the fancy chicken dish he'd created. "Alright, Steve?" I asked, watching him push it round the plate with his fork. "Er... yeah, great. Er... it's OK, like. But ter be 'onest witcha Liz, I'd rather 'ave 'ad McDonald's." Binksy was back in minutes with a Big Mac.

Despite his denials, McManaman left Liverpool a couple of years later. Presumably after his agent had confirmed that he'd get a proper meal at Real Madrid.

When Binksy was made an offer he couldn't refuse for that house by another player, he took the cash and moved into the top floor of one of the blocks of flats (sorry apartments) he'd built on the other side of the park.

They proved to be dead popular with foreign signings while they found their feet and a place to buy. And not just players. One morning I was up first and sitting out on the balcony sipping coffee when I accidentally got an eyeful from the opposite block.

"Oh God, you should have seen it Binksy. Some fat, dirty old bastard was standing across there in his dressing gown, stretching and scratching his bollocks," I told him.

"Are you sure?" Binksy asked. "That's Gerard Houllier's place Elizabeth." Obviously I wasn't.

I'd had even more awkward situations with footballers before then. In 1989, when I wouldn't have recognised anyone in football, a famous player tried to cop off with me at Buckingham Palace. In the presence of Her Majesty the Queen.

A charity had asked me to DJ at a big outdoor event and she was its patron. Everybody at this drinks reception was a name who'd helped in their own field with fundraising. I was chatting to Radio 2's Derek Jameson and his wife when suddenly a hush fell on the room and the crowd parted to allow the Queen, black patent bag over her arm (who carries their own handbag round the house, eh? Perhaps she doesn't like leaving her purse lying around) to move among us, mingling, smiling and chatting. She stopped at Derek who salivated more visibly than usual throughout their brief exchange. I was trying not to laugh at the sovereign being sprayed with spit, so fixed my gaze above the heads of the other guests opposite.

One of them towered above the rest and was bobbing about waving and winking and trying to catch my eye. When the monarch had moved on, he came and said hello. I can't say he introduced himself. He assumed I knew who he was. I didn't and I think he actually found the challenge of a blonde not instantly falling into his arms quite erotic.

That and the prospect of scoring in such a right royal setting.

He asked me if I had a car and could he have a lift. I said it was parked outside the BBC and I was going home. He shared a taxi with me and told me how great we'd be together. He could invite me to matches and I could get him tickets to see... oh... Simply Red. It sounded just peachy. First thing's first, though. Like, was he single?

"Will your wife not mind then?" I asked.

"Er, er, how did you know I was married?"

"I didn't. But I do now."

Just think. If it hadn't been for that and the other hitch – I didn't fancy him – I might have been a Footballer's Wife myself.

Going from presenter on The Crunch to reporter on the Adrian Chiles show had, effectively, been a demotion, a loss of status. But I soon got over it. Sitting in the same windowless studio week-in, week-out just couldn't compare to careering up and down the country, 'access all areas'. My mission? To bring hordes of fascinating voices, from all walks of life, onto the wireless and into people's homes.

I was set up with stars from every sport who were currently at the top of their game – Tim Henman on court at The Queen's Tennis Club, Damon Hill and David Coulthard in the pits at Silverstone, Lawrence Dallaglio at Twickers, and shopping with rugby league's Shaun Edwards (captain of Wigan and current baby daddy to M People's Heather Small). That was a revelation. Rugby league had always been the poor relation, now he was earning so much he didn't even bother to try stuff on.

It was a lot of fun and I got to meet legends like Barry Sheen, who I'd been in love with since Our Andrew took me to watch him race at Oulton Park in 1975. He showed me round the NEC Bike Show while another bike-racing superstar Giacomo Agostini locked himself out of his nearby B&B. As a teenager I'd had a poster of him on my wall. Now I was giving him a leg up to his bathroom window.

The Food and Drink Show had me mixing it with unbearably boorish celebrity chefs. (You can cook. Get over it.) I got to bounce on beds with male models at the Ideal Home Exhibition, wax lyrical about luxury yachts at Olympia's Boat Show and, at the NEC's Caravan and Camping show, find the latest fuck-off motor homes. (One of them had a car stashed under the bed!)

But one event was beyond belief. And description. The BBC's own Top Gear Live. The most baffling show – In The World.

Best catch up with Clarkson.

"So Jeremy. You've got guys in black tie flying in on high wires. You've got girls in swimsuits draped over sports cars. You've got massive explosions and pounding rock music. Can you tell me what this is all about?"

"I'll tell you what it's all about Kershaw. It's about TOTTY. It's about shifting up to fifth. When you're not even in the car."

Righty ho.

The Eurovision Song Contest needed no explanation. Nobody was better qualified to cover that. I'd been studying it since I was seven, had already been twice, and had even spent a whole night in a 'threesome' with Simon Cowell.

In 1991, Radio 1 had sent me and Bruno all the way to Rome to follow the fortunes of Samantha Janus. The best the UK music industry could offer. Or rather the one chosen by the Great British Public using the system I'd 'sold' to the BBC. Head of Light Entertainment, Jim Moir, was now working closely with my old BT boss and his new company. It was early days for tele-voting but even so, half a million viewers picked up the phone that year to choose our entry. I can't remember how much those premium rate calls cost back then but even if it only raised 10p a pop, somebody made 50 grand that night. Oh well. I was actually there. And that was priceless.

We went to eat first. Bruno sent back his pizza. It wasn't right.

"'Ere mate. Can you sort this out? I ordered ham," he said.

"But it eez 'am."

"Yer joking aren't you?"

"Is proscuitto Signor."

"Look mate. I don't care what is is. I want proper ham. Er... avez vous Le Mattessons?"

Meanwhile, our guide was giving me a taste of the local culture. "I show you how to enjoy wine. Like a true Italian." He rubbed some behind each ear (mine) and then took his time licking it off. Oh, well. When in Rome...

Then, on a driving tour of the city of romance, he took us on a detour down one of the Roman Empire's most important routes. The Appian Way. Each side of the narrow stony road was lined with ancient columns and arches and nose-to-tail stationary cars. With the windows completely covered in newspapers.

"What's going on here then, mate?" Bruno asked our guide. Even idiots abroad can't help but be curious.

"It's, 'ow you say, parking," he replied.

"I can see that, mate. But what's with all the papers?"

"Well they are... parking."

"Yeah but when I park I don't stick The Sun all over the wind-screen!"

"How to explain. In Italy young people live at home until they marry. If they have nice girlfriend and want to... 'ow to say... love her... they come parking on Saturday afternoons," he said.

"Right. I get it. So they're all... 'ow to say... shagging. Right that's enough mate. Take us back to the hotel."

On the morning of the contest, our Saturday Breakfast Show brought all the excitement of the build up, with interviews we'd recorded in two days roaming around Rome. It was a good job we'd seen the city because our view now, from a scruffy little rented studio up a backstreet, was obscured by some massive Italian pants strung on a washing line across the only window. No problemo. There'd be plenty of glamour to report tomorrow. All we had to do now was scrub up for the stadium spectacular tonight.

I was just taking my new tights out of the packet when the bedside phone rang.

"Hi Liz. Right. It's Ruffle here." Our new producer.

"Bit of a cock up lovey. Don't bother getting dressed up. You won't get in. We haven't got tickets. I thought I had it sorted. Turns out I only got us passes for the rehearsal."

We sat in the hotel restaurant frozen. It was deserted. Every-one staying there had gone to the Contest so they'd turned the heating off.

We were also frozen in terror, sitting in silence wondering what Beerling would say.

All the way to Rome and a no show.

What were we going to do on the radio tomorrow? What we did was come clean and laugh at ourselves. We got 'douze points' from everybody listening. Samantha Janus came 10th.

In 1993, the people's choice was little Scouse songbird and Bruno and Liz Show staple, Sonia. By now, I'd been sacked but Beerling agreed to send me to Ireland for Radio 1. Top bosses may get a big bung for leaving the BBC. To soften the blow for me, he coughed up just enough to get to Cork and this time I made sure I'd get in too.

I'd got full access behind the scenes to record the whole selection process, rehearsals, costume fittings, the lot, for an exclusive Eurovision documentary. Jim Moir had decided to embrace me and I was now part of his posse. So along with Terry Wogan, Ken Bruce and an entourage of their agents, family and friends, I was an official member of the mighty Moir-led UK delegation.

"Oh my God. Oh my God. I'm just gutted." Sonia was beside herself getting back on the bus. She'd come second.

"Honest to God, Liz. I couldn't have done any better."

"Yes you bloody well could! You could have bloody well won," barked our portly patron from the backseat.

"Come here, Kershaw. Come and sit on my lap!"

"Oh come on Jim!" Wogan piped up. "She a bit old fer a bouncy castle!"

Everyone at our after-show party was either from Bosnia, Israel or the UK. There were Gardai at every door with machine guns.

"Jim," we were on first name terms by now. "Why are we in this room?"

"Because young Kershaw," I was 34, "we are all a security risk."

The Irish are famous for their cheery hospitality but there wasn't much at this do. The Bosnians decided to make their own entertainment so they kicked off their shoes, linked arms in a circle, and danced their socks off, spinning as they sang. This was met by massive applause. I can't remember the Israeli 'entry'. By now our BBC chief, who'd suffered second place once already this evening, was plotting the UK's next move. Wogan and Ken Bruce were clearly not keen on making a show of themselves and Sonia was still sobbing.

"Right, Kershaw. What can you do?"

"Er, well, I know all the words to 'Puppet On A String'." We'd won with that one. 26 years earlier.

"Marvellous. Marvellous. Well? Off you go."

To get the full Sandy Shaw effect I kicked off my shoes too. 'Love is just like a merry go round. With all the fun of the fair'. It was a surefire Euro crowd pleaser. We'd restored national pride with a right 'Royaume-Uni' two fingers to the rest of the room.

Sonia was being comforted by her escort for the evening. The man from BMG records, AKA Simon Cowell. She was signed to him and he'd flown her over in a private jet.

"Can we go to bed now Sonia?" That was me, not Mr. Syco.

"No. Stay up a bit longer will yer Liz? I wanna gerroff with him."

"Really?"

"Yeah. He's gorgeous. Don't you think so Liz?"

FIVE YEARS

I eyed up the slick guy in the big black trousers.

"Erm... well. I suppose he is charming. And very presentable. But Sonia love. Seriously. I think you're wasting your time."

At 5am I left them in the bar convinced she was barking up the wrong tree.

A couple of hours later she was back on the jet.

A couple of years later she was out on her ear.

By 1997, the UK held a Eurovision record. For coming second more than any other country. But the times they were a changin'. We now had Cool Britannia and New Labour. Tony Blair was in charge with his Third Way and a new vision. Surely Katrina and the Waves could win Eurovision! I went to find out for 5 Live.

Shine A Light! She did it! Our new cool PM showed he really did have his finger firmly on the pulse of popular culture by being first on the phone. Land of Hope and Glory. Was he going to give Katrina a knighthood? No. She wasn't actually British. An American had saved our bacon. But she was rightly and richly rewarded for restoring the UK's standing abroad. Jim Moir, who was now running Radio 2, gave her a late night show for a couple of years.

Ireland really put out the red carpet this time. Us Brits (and Katrina) were the toast of the town and could enjoy the Dublin craic with the best of them because... hey... we were the best. At last. We were swept into the proper party this time. Security was still tight. A little blond lad in a long leather coat (odd outfit for a kiddy I thought) was stopped in his tracks trying to get in. "Oym Ronan feckin' Keating yer feckin' eejit!"

The Independent sent me to Stockholm for Eurovision 1999. I did the sights on a boat tour of the harbour, filled my sunburnt face with herrings and got shut in a hut with Ken Bruce. The BBC had booked commentary facilities at the venue. Two boxes to separate the simultaneous sounds of Terry and Ken for TV and radio. But only one could be found with a British flag on its door. A makeshift 'booth', bought in from the Swedish equivalent of B&Q, was hastily erected in the corner. I've always argued that the BBC's senior service should not be treated like the poor relation to TV. Mmm... Wogan had his sumptuous suite while Ken had his new garden shed.

It was a similar set up back at The Grand where Terry had rooms that had just been vacated by Madonna. His suite was one of a kind, located in the turret at the top of Stockholm's swankiest hotel.

Posing as a travel agent, I got to check it out as soon as Mr. and Mrs. Wogan had checked out. Bloody hell. A spiral staircase linked two floors with huge glass windows affording harbour views. Could the likes of me, (or even our Ken) afford this? Not at the equivalent of £3,000 a night in Krona we couldn't. I'm sure the BBC had done a deal. And anyway, wasn't it money well spent? Wasn't it essential that the main man enjoyed this level of total privacy and luxury for a few days so that he was suitably relaxed and ready for a full four hours on air?

When showtime finally came I was glad I was allowed to sit next to Terry to see for myself why he's so smooth. An ice bucket and a bottle of Baileys was brought in just before showtime. While he enjoyed a glass or two, I was glad to be able to contribute to the coverage.

"Have you noticed that all the Baltic states are voting as a block and that we're being blanked by the Balkans?" I told him.

"Bejasus. You're right!"

FIVE YEARS

I'd earned my place at his side by spotting this emerging Euro-skullduggery. Over the next few years it came to routinely ruin any chance we ever had and Wogan hung up his headphones in disgust.

At our house we still have our annual Eurovision party. Everyone has to wear a national costume and support that country. One year, Nicky Campbell represented Scotland (I know) dressed in a silky tartan dressing gown which kept slipping apart. And a producer once came supporting Germany in an SS officer's uniform.

His responsibilities now include upholding BBC standards.

The show will go on, though, because its huge audience in that slot puts all the piffle for the rest of the year into the shade. And our place in the final is forever guaranteed because of the millions the licence payers put into the Eurovision pot. These days Jim Moir's successor would kill for that shabby second place. But sadly, it looks like BBC Light Entertainment will never see the dizzying success of Sandy, Katrina, or even Sonia ever again.

Radio 5 Live, and Radio 4's Breakaway programme gave me loads of opportunities to check out far-flung places as part of 'we-scratch-your-back' deals with various travel companies.

So the BBC got 'free' content while the PR company got a 'free' plug for their client. It all seemed OK at the time but apparently it's totally unacceptable to Ofcom now.

I never actually got paid a penny. I mean I'd get paid my usual fee for doing the regular Saturday show. But not for the days I was away or the time spent editing my report together. So these armchair adventures weren't costing the licence payer anything.

All that globetrotting was a privilege and I'm still grateful for that. Because without a BBC pass I'd never have got all those stamps in my passport.

It was all so simple.

"Er... anybody fancy going to the Cayman Islands? Just had a trip come in from Blag PR. A week at the Hyatt Regency. One adult and one child over five?"

"Is that the Caribbean? I'll go!"

"OK. It's in two weeks. No fee obviously. Just bring back the goods Liz."

So me and Sam packed our cozzies and boarded that west bound plane. Joe was too young at two and was left with his grannies. "You went to the Cayman Islands and didn't take me Mamma," he reminded me for the next 17 years. Unfortunately when we arrived at the poshest hotel on Grand Cayman, our cozzies didn't. Neither did our clean pants or toothbrushes for a couple of days.

We lingered in our room in our complimentary fluffy white dressing gowns looking down enviously at the pool and surviving on complimentary star fruit and room service until our cases finally caught up with us.

Should we just jump in the pool in our filthy undies? I didn't think so. Lost luggage found, it was microphone out and we did our report. And I mean 'we'. Sam was born to broadcast. With all the other media mums' kids he swam with stingrays and turtles and saw the seabed from a submarine and I captured it all on tape. Job done.

We saw the Caribbean from a cruise ship too. But I hated that. It was just racist. The officers were all white Europeans. Filipinos served drinks. Goans waited tables. Chinese did the laundry. Black guys mopped floors. They got paid peanuts and relied on the obligatory tips that skew the real cost and keep brochure prices down. And the American clientele were just gross. "I hope you've brought your stretch pants darlin'. I call this cruise 'The Ten Pounder'."

When Sam was younger we'd been across Texas on a train together, boarding in New Orleans and heading for LA.

We were all sealed in and air conditioned so our senses were deprived by the time we got to El Paso where we were allowed off for a few minutes. It was smelly and like stepping in front of a hot hair dryer. Otherwise we sat together for nearly three days sightseeing and chatting, his little legs sticking out on the seat.

"Oh he's so cute honey. What's your name liddle guy?"

"I'm called Sam. This is my mummy and she works for the BBC."

"Oh my lord. How old is he?"

"I'm 14 months old."

I'd experienced the searing heat of the arid African bush on a 'real' holiday and now it was time to explore the arctic snow fields of Finland. Nothing can prepare you for the tranquility and beauty of those vast natural plains unspoilt by man.

In the half light of the afternoon I snowmobiled across the ice field with a little sledge in tow. Sam and Joe were covered by reindeer skins and we were going to meet Father Christmas. We found him in a log cabin lit by hundreds of twinkling tea lights. On another day huskies hauled us to a kirtle, a conical tent made of skins, with a smoking log fire burning inside and hot sandwiches waiting.

At the star studded opening of Disneyland Paris I queued up for the pay phone behind a short guy in a sharp suit and flip flops. Crikey, it was only Kevin Costner! He was tiny.

On the 'It's A Small World' ride, we shared a boat with a familiar looking bloke. It was Peter Gabriel.

I was sent to Majorca to have a go at being a tour rep. It was August and sweltering and not the place for a polyester uniform. My clients behaved like dependant kids. I couldn't be doing with their neediness and dumb questions. I wasn't cut out for this. But I got stuck into the Karaoke night with gusto. "You can't sing. Your attitude's all wrong and your hair's a mess." The on-air final appraisal didn't throw up any surprises.

All four of us went caravanning in Ireland, with a genuine gypsy rig and shire horse, and a map of single track roads and pubs willing to let us stay in their car parks.

It was an amazing way to get away from the 20th Century, its internal combustion engines and all they've got to answer for. Like two filthy urchins, Sam and Joe sat on the front, downwind of the horse, giggling at his big farts coming their way.

Leading the horse, we walked miles every day and by the time we'd rubbed him down, cleaned out his hooves and fed and watered him, we were ready to tuck into big steaks and fall into our bunks.

"Oy've got yer address and if I don't like what oy hear oy'll have a feckin' bomb shoved tru yer feckin' letter box," said the owner, as we returned the horse.

"We've had a good holiday and that will be accurately reflected in my BBC report, thank you," I replied. I was braving it out but I was quietly bricking it.

I did honestly report that it was a brilliant experience for a young family. But it just went to show... that really, there's no such thing as a free lunch.

Chapter Thirteen

THE REVOLUTION WILL NOT BE TELEVISED

"Mamma. Teletubbies has been cancelled." Joe was just three and very cross.

"And all because Princess Diana has died."

What? It was Sunday morning, I was just waking up, and sitting on the toilet bog-eyed with my pants round my ankles when the bathroom door burst open. Had Joe just had a nightmare? No. He'd woken up early and toddled down stairs, to find that rolling news of a royal tragedy had replaced his favourite telly.

Sam joined us on the sofa. What hell must Diana's boys have woken to this morning? Who'd had the horrendous job of breaking it to them that they'd never see their mummy again?

THE BIRD AND THE BEEB

How could a healthy mother, just a couple of years younger than me, be dead?

How could someone so full of life and so central to British life, not exist anymore? How had the world's biggest superstar died in such an ignominious way? How horrific that she'd had the life brutally battered out of her in the back of a car. How could the death of a beautiful princess be so ugly?

While we, like millions more, quietly sat trying to get our heads round all this, morbid TV reports and pictures suggested that mass hysteria was sweeping the country. We were all glued to the box for the rest of the day.

The next day I went to TV Centre to start a new job as a reporter on BBC 1's Watchdog with Anne Robinson.

Only by leaving our TV in a sleepy village, and venturing out in to the big wide world of the capital, did I realise that life was still going on as normal. Yes people were making pilgrimages and leaving flowers which were starting to spread like a deep carpet outside the gates of what had been Diana's home, but away from Kensington Palace and the nation's newsrooms, it seemed like business as usual. In London W12 anyway.

I was told to get on with a story about trains. That summer, conditions on the old rolling stock Richard Branson had recently inherited from British Rail were appalling. The privatisation of the railways had gone through earlier in the year, and so far, it seemed to me, as a daily commuter, that Virgin had repainted but not yet replaced anything. Virgin logos had been stuck on carriages and staff had smart new red uniforms. But that was all promotion and PR.

A classic case of what my grandma would have called 'all fur coat and no knickers' because us passengers were still suffering stifling heat and long dealys. Surely Richard Branson thought this was unacceptable under his brand and would want to share his plans urgently. We set about requesting interviews, bought a couple of tickets at Euston station and boarded a packed inter-city service with a thermometer and a camera.

We recorded on-board temperatures in the 90s and interviews with passengers who were very hot under the collar and only too happy to talk about their suffering in airless accommodation. Until we got clocked by a guard and nearly thrown off. Around a week later we got our audience with the Virgin boss after an invitation to his luxury home in Holland Park.

I got the impression it was all carefully staged. Well you wouldn't expect anything else really from the UK's ultimate PR supremo would you? I was led into an airy reception room overlooking the garden, and left to wait just long enough to start doubting myself, when the bearded, blond Adonis swept into the room.

It seemed he'd showered specially as his thin light coloured summer clothes were clinging slightly to his damp body and he shook his long locks as if to dry them in the sun streaming in through the huge sash windows. It was impressive. But his flies were undone. Pointing that out evened things up a bit.

I thought the interview went well. We established that the Virgin brand actually stood for something. He explained he couldn't transform his crappy trains overnight and set out his plans to replace the carriages and revolutionise the railways. To his credit he's done just that and I recently signed a petition to keep it Virgin on the West Coast mainline. The trains are now comfortable, clean, roughly on time and, if you book a year in advance, very reasonably priced.

But back in 1997 it was time for round two. Reliability.

We were waiting, as arranged, on Euston station when Branson suddenly swept down the platform with his entourage, waving at bewildered customers and shaking hands with surprised staff. He knew our cameras were rolling. His train wasn't by the time we got to the Midlands. An overhead line failure in the Birmingham International area meant we came to a halt mid-interview. After an awkward 40 minutes he decided to get off. As he left, a member of his entourage quietly suggested that my parents weren't married and that me and Richard wouldn't be seeing each other again anytime soon.

The Virgin press office complained that, after he'd left, I'd filmed my questions and changed them from what I'd asked him. There were no changes.

Meanwhile, Diana's funeral was looming large.

Her brother, Charles Spencer, announced that after a service at Westminster Abbey and a procession up the M1, she would be buried at their ancestral home, Althorp, in Northamptonshire. The world's media arranged for TV and radio crews to follow the progress of the hearse all along the route, from bridges across the motorway, at Long Buckby station to view her husband and children arrive, and outside the gates of the family estate, through which Diana had passed throughout her life, to catch her coffin crawl by for the final time.

I'd been there once. We live nearby and one Sunday decided to have a run out for a nosey around. In the room slept in by Winston Churchill, once the most famous of the Spencer clan, a selection of paperbacks had been thoughtfully placed on the bedside table. Apparently, preferred bedtime reading for the greatest wartime leader this country has ever known, was

'Fascination In France', 'Love Wins In Berlin' and 'A Kiss In The Desert' by Barbara Cartland. But then, her daughter Raine, was the current Countess Spencer and the business brain cashing in on Althorp's royal, and literary, connections.

Diana's wedding dress and other famous frocks were put on display at Althorp after her death. I was allowed a sneak preview of the collection in a converted stable block. On my own. Headless body doubles of Diana, dressed in instantly recognisable outfits, stood motionless against black walls, each mannequin lit by one downlighter. It was shadowy and spooky and slightly disturbing. Outside in the sunshine a tall toff was issuing orders.

I'd always understood that Diana and her siblings had objected to Raine's commercialisation of their family home. But with her packed off to a town house in Mayfair, brother Charles was preparing to open the gates for business as usual.

Raine's old mum, Barbara Cartland, was a scream. I was welcomed into her home many times for 'Encounters With The Pink Dame' (that's what I called my Radio 4 documentary about her life) first by the author herself and then by her son, Ian, who all these years after her death, still thinks to send me a Christmas card.

I've never met such an enigma. Barbara Cartland was a silly old snob, but also one of the most well-meaning women I've ever met, berating anyone who didn't know how to set a table correctly but fighting for the rights of gypsies to set up site and live as they liked on greenbelt nearby. She was obsessed by sex but always took the moral high ground. And her only career advice to us 'gels' was 'marry well' yet she was an ardent feminist. Her brother had been an MP but she'd been 'discouraged' from entering politics because she was a young woman. It just wasn't the done thing and she'd had to wait until she was in her 50s to enter public life as a county councillor. She urged me not to let my feminine wiles cramp my style in any way.

And yet...

When I once turned up in jeans. "My darling girl," she despaired "you'll never bag a duke in those trousers!" And when I left the room on another visit "you know she's a very pretty gel but you must get her to do something with her hair," she instructed my friend. By now hers was thinning and her false lashes were all over the place but she was always resplendent in diamonds and chiffon.

We'd be seated at the dining table and her faithful old retainer would hobble in with a silver pot and a selection of fancies which she'd break up and feed to her yappy Pekingese. That's when it wasn't shaggin' my leg, which it tended to do while she was lecturing me on manners.

"Do you have children my dear?"

"I do Dame Barbara" I was desperately hoping she wouldn't clock the absence of a wedding ring.

"Boys or girls?"

"Oh, two boys actually."

"My darling you're so clever. Girls are so useless."

When she died, the woman whose home was a shrine to chintzy excess and rococo bad taste, stipulated that no money should be wasted on a fancy coffin. Plus she was an ardent environmentalist. Way ahead of her time. So, under an old tree in the presence of a few close family and friends, the Queen of Romance was buried in a cardboard box.

Back to Diana. It was so sad that her funeral was the biggest 'event' that weekend in 1997. The only event. Radio 5 Live told me to get down to South Wales where my job this Saturday would be to report the reactions of patients and staff at a hospital. Why there? Simple. Because it bore her name. 'The Princess of Wales' in Bridgend. I offered to stay in the Althorp area and talk to locals who'd known Diana but they booked me on a Virgin train to Cardiff.

The CrossCountry train was severely delayed (surprise surprise) and finally lurched into the station at around 2am – chucking out time for the clubs. The place was buzzing and the streets ablaze with the lights of kebab shops, taxis and police vans. There were gangs of scantily-clad girls and loud lads holding each other up as they staggered home. And others, who were even past that, keeled over in gutters. It could have been any city centre on any Friday night.

But not this Friday surely. The whole nation was in mourning. Wasn't it?

"I thought it would have been quiet tonight."

"Why's that then?" asked the chirpy cabbie.

"Well you know. With the big funeral tomorrow and everything."

"Oh, yeah... oh, well. Life goes on see."

Perhaps they'd been drowning their sorrows. Perhaps they didn't give a fuck.

Next morning at eight o'clock, in complete contrast, the hospital was eerily quiet. The staff were expecting me and showed me into a ward. A young man was rolling around. His covers fell off and his bare bottom stuck out of the bed. I felt for him. He was obviously suffering some considerable pain and now a lack of dignity too. I turned away.

Nobody else seemed in a fit state to 'chat' about death either. I didn't think it was right to intrude any longer. It was too early for any able-bodied visitors to be around so after a fruit-less search for anybody remotely interested in being on the radio, I got a senior nurse by the plaque Diana had unveiled when she'd opened the hospital 12 years earlier.

"I don't really know what to say. I never met her. She only came here once as far as I know. I'll have to get back to my rounds now. Sorry."

Someone back in Broadcasting House was screaming in my headphones.

"What the hell are you playing at down there? You're in the bloody Princess of Wales aren't you? Get some bloody Welsh people to tell you why they're upset!"

"I can't. There aren't any. I mean there's hardly anybody around and they're all poorly or busy."

Another voice came on the phone and I was told that what I was telling them – the truth, that is – was not what they wanted to hear. Back at Broadcasting House, they wanted a sense of how upset people were. The problem was, those people didn't appear to exist.

"I know that you want devastated people but from where I'm standing they're not," I responded. "They've got other things to worry about. If I came on air and said anything different I'd be lying."

"I know," the voice on the phone said. "But do what you can. Just try. Please."

I had the idea that if I went to the hospital's chapel and looked through the book of condolences, someone might pour their heart out about their very own Princess and when

I got there, a woman and a girl were just making an entry.

"Hello. Can I ask your names please."

"I'm Gwen and this is my daughter Stacy."

"Gwen and Stacy. Could I please ask you for your thoughts on today's funeral of Diana, Princess of Wales?"

The woman's eyes filled with hate and tears as she bared her teeth at me. "My son has just died," she sobbed. "He was only 18. How dare you? Now just piss off and leave us alone!"

"I can't do this," I informed London. "It's wrong. It's obscene. Nobody here gives a toss about Diana's funeral. People here are trying not to bloody die themselves for God's sake!"

"Liz, I have to warn you. They say that if you don't come up with the goods you might as well not bother coming back."

I spent the entire journey home in disbelief.

BBC News had basically asked me to make stuff up to fit a predetermined agenda. I hadn't and now I was in deep shit.

I wondered if I should have done things differently. Just done as I was told. Obviously they cared less about truth than titillation. Could I have sensationalised it? Talked about how the people of Bridgend were devastated by Diana's death?

Sure.

But I hadn't met any who were so I couldn't report that as fact. They certainly weren't to be found in Cardiff city centre or here in her hospital. Should I have faked emotion in my voice as I relayed back to London how moved I was by the deep sense of sorrow I'd found? Should I have basically lied about what I'd witnessed in Wales? Apparently. Better that than failing to fit in with the rest of the BBC's reportage of wailing and gnashing of teeth across the land.

I had a little cry. Not for my career at 5 Live. Clearly that was down the pan. Stuff it. I had zero respect now for those lazy, bullying bastards. Those proper journalists. No, I was mourning a lifelong belief in the BBC.

Why should I unquestionably trust its news reports any more?

What I can truthfully report, is that some of what I've seen in its newsrooms since has done little to convince me I should.

On the Monday, it was back to Watchdog. I'd got my first assignment there a few months earlier after Adrian Chiles had recommended me to an editor who wanted to know if I'd ever been to Butlins. I told him how I went as a child and always loved it. He didn't think I would now. They'd had loads of letters from viewers complaining about how dirty and decrepit it was. Would I go to Pwllheli, with a producer called Kate, posing as holidaymakers and see what I made of it? Yes. Who wouldn't jump at the chance to sleep in a chalet and ride the chairlifts again?

It was scary because we'd be undercover with hidden cameras on private property. But we were fuming and fired up when we saw how shabby it all was for the poor families there. So for three days non-stop, we filmed the crumbling concrete, mouldy bathrooms, murky pools, threadbare carpets and dirty dining rooms. It was sad. A lot of it was exactly as I'd remembered fondly since the 1960s. That was the problem. Nothing had changed. Just got worn out. Before we left we had to summon the courage to confront the management.

At the end of the film Anne Robinson turned to the camera and announced to the viewers that Butlins were bulldozing Pwllheli. "Result," she declared with her trademark wink. Then, during the end credits, she turned and fixed her beady eyes on me. "Will you do more for us?" Phew. I didn't know it then, but she wasn't only the presenter. She was running the show.

The programme went out on Thursday evenings. We'd all run round researching, filming and editing in time for Wednesday afternoons. That was 'viewing day'. The tension would be mounting in the office as a huge BBC Mercedes swept into the forecourt. As the uniformed chauffeur opened a door, a black leather-clad leg would swing out, then another, then a black-gloved hand clutching a black handbag, followed by a black coat and finally that little ginger bob.

I reckon Annie had been paid so much for so long she didn't know anything other than Armani. In any colour as long as it was black.

"Is that an Armani jacket Liz?"

"Er. No."

"It's black. It's Armani isn't it?"

"It's not." She really didn't need to know.

"Armani? Yes?"

"It's from Topshop."

She looked horrified. One of her reporters in high street pret-a-porter?

You'd have worked a full week on a film with a producer. The original story and treatment would have been commissioned by the editor and the finished film passed and even praised by him. But if Annie came in and didn't like it, that was that. No support. No arguments. Binned.

We'd all watch his office door as each reporter came out.

"Yes! It's in!" would be welcomed with muted applause.

"Everything OK?"

"Nope. It's dropped."

"Sorry mate. It was good too."

I had a good run. But then one week: "No. No. No. I'm not having it," said Anne. We'd carefully done the research on the story and our film had been 'legalled'. But that was that.

On programme day she'd rehearse her interviews and lines from the autocue over and over again. Between rehearsals she'd retire to her dressing room which was filled with fruit. If you were in favour you might be invited in and offered a few grapes and pearls of wisdom to pass the time, otherwise it was the tea bar for hours on end.

She talked fondly about her husband 'Penrose' and he seemed a decent old cove. But he didn't last. I only met him once at the Watchdog Christmas party where she flirted with the hunk I'd brought along from another BBC show. And when James Dyson came on to the programme to be grilled about his unique, patented, suctionless system, she giggled like a giddy schoolgirl.

And one Guardian hack, who went to her home in 2000, wrote that he didn't know if she thought he was a journalist or a gynaecologist because of the way she sprawled on the sofa during the interview.

She was spunky and seemed ruthless. I was scared of her but admired her nevertheless. Her name was on the tin and so 'good on yer, girl' for making sure there was no shit in it. And for taking the BBC to the cleaners. Did they have to pay her so much? I wonder if she would've done it for less. Young Anne had helped change her family's fortunes by gutting chickens on their Liverpool market stall and with the proceeds she was sent to finishing school and set up with a sports car and fur coat. In those days she'd stalked the Beatles and bagged an exclusive on Brian Epstein. She lost her first husband and custody of her child because of her addiction to alcohol, and I could see that for all her bluster, this tiny, bony little bird was strangely vulnerable and not as hard and tough as her public persona suggested.

On a Weakest Link 'DJs Special' when she saw I was under attack she stuck up for me as one of her own.

"Tony (Blackburn). Why are you voting off Liz? Is it because she got more questions right than you?" "Why Liz, Lisa (I'Anson)? Is it because she gets more work than you?"

Anne Robinson is definitely someone to have on your side.

Television is seen as a step up from radio and I'm often asked "don't you wish you'd done more TV Liz?" Well no and I'll tell you why. Firstly I can still walk down the street without being clocked. Until I open my big mouth.

And secondly, in TV you have no control over the end product. It can take a week to make three minutes of content and working full time as a TV reporter was a complete bloody nightmare. Plus it's not just about the words. You're seen on screen so you can't just get up and put a paper bag over your head in the mornings. Keeping up with grooming and clothing was nearly a full-time job. And we were expected to be totally flexible and always on call to go anywhere, any time.

I carried a toothbrush and knickers in my handbag for six months. It was a hell of a job for anybody with kids. Apart from me, in an office of 40, I think only the top boss had any. Family life had to be organised with military precision even if the extra money was welcome. I stashed the cash and after five months had the £20,000 for the extension we needed at home.

"Result," as my old mate Annie would say. Without a trace of Scouse.

Bizarrely, after four years at 5 Live, I was now told there was a problem with my accent.

Our editor explained that because Adrian Chiles was so audibly from the Black Country, and what, with my flat northern vowels, it was just too much to expect listeners to cope with us together on a BBC news channel.

Bollocks! Maybe management would have stuck with the odd couple if the awkward one hadn't refused to doctor the facts from that hospital.

Anyway, whatever, I was out.

It all ended on a high at The Boat Race with Olympic gold medallists Steve Redgrave and Matthew Pinsent presenting me with a lovely bouquet on the banks of the Thames in the spring of 1998. It was bye bye BBC. Or so I thought.

Chapter Fourteen

COMMON PEOPLE

Here's the chip (butty) on my shoulder chapter...

"Now tell me Liz and Andy. How exactly did you get on to the radio? I mean. It's not like either of you have got very nice voices is it?"

We hadn't seen that coming and were rolling around on the sofa. It was a killer question that only a dear little old lady with a blue rinse in a disarming flowery frock and a twinkle behind her spectacles could get away with.

It was our 'now tell me Debbie, just what was it that first attracted you to millionaire magician Paul Daniels?' moment. In 2006 that came second in a poll of the best comedy one-liners of all time. But when Mrs. Merton ambushed us, she was yet to floor legions of celebrities on her weekly TV chat show. In

1992, comedienne Caroline Aherne was just making her pilot and me and Our Andrew, along with the founder of Viz, Chris Donald, were her guinea pigs.

Just as nobody had ever asked Debbie McGee what she was doing with a wrinkly little squirt, nobody had ever put it like that before. But come to think of it. Yes. What *were* we doing on the BBC with accents like ours?

Had people been thinking that for years? All the clues were there.

Before we'd moved to London most people we knew talked like us. Or broader. We'd been judged for what we had to say not how we sounded and neither of us had known what we'd be in for.

One Radio 1 jock loved to tell everyone, including the press, that I sounded thick and so The Sun said I needed subtitles because people in the south couldn't understand me. There are laws against racism but how do you legislate against that kind of crap?

I've now had donkeys' years to think about this and in the meantime I'm pleased to say progress has been made. I'm over it. Well... getting there. But here's the 'science'. It's all just down to human nature. People need pecking orders. We instantly and maybe subconsciously rank ourselves against each other on the grounds of race, colour, weight, height, looks, physical per-fection, age, gender, intelligence, education, job, car, address, clothes, mobile phone, etc, etc, etc.

But sounding posh is the trump card. Like it or not, class still counts. And unfortunately, any northerner (or Brummie or Bris-tolian etc), who actually sounds like one, must be rough trade.

Of course we're welcome to make winning comedy, albums,

or goals. Or help sell Hovis, Tesco or 'good honest broadband' and any other brand that wants to seem simple, homely and good value in an ad. Even better if there's a brass band involved. The likes of Peter Kay, Liam Gallagher, and Wayne Rooney, may be the toast of the nation. And the UK can now wake up laughing with Chris Evans and Nick Grimshaw. Ricky Gervais and Stephen Merchant have gone global, Frank Skinner has a chucklesome chat show and Adrian Chiles is hosting Drivetime once a week on Radio 5 Live.

But when did you last see anybody sounding like them marrying a Royal or reading the nightly news?

Where are the people from Newcastle or Liverpool or Hull who pay the licence fee? Meanwhile, why are there so many Scots on the radio? Because it's an 'acceptable' accent along with Welsh, Irish and 'received pronunciation' English. And by acceptable I mean 'classless'.

In 1991, I was asked on a show hosted by Leeds lad Jeremy Paxman (yes, really – he's from Leeds). Maybe somebody had spotted that this Radio 1 DJ had something up there. Something sensible to say. Paxman was my hero. Clever. Courageous. Candid. Maybe conceited. But charming and highly amused when challenged by someone like me, cheeky enough not to kowtow to him or treat him with kid gloves. So imagine my delight when I walked into the green room at TV Centre and found my host laughing and locked in conversation with another bit of thinking girl's crumpet, Angus Deayton.

"What's so funny then?"

"Oh you wouldn't understand Kershaw," Paxman (St. Catherine's, Cambridge) announced.

"Go on try me," I replied.

"Well we were just discussing our Oxbridge colleges," Deayton (New College, Oxford) informed me.

"And? How do you know I didn't go to Oxbridge?" Kershaw (University of Leeds).

"Oh Kershaw. You're so obviously Red Brick," Paxman retorted. Fondly. But nevertheless.

Elitism is endemic in the BBC but to be fair to Paxman, Newsnight is just about the most 'inclusive' programme in the News Division. They may not let oiks loose on the main bulletins but Paxo's posse has included Lancashire lad and Economics Editor Paul Mason (University of Sheffield) and Sheffield's Tim Whewell (Oxford). And Paxman's has more than redeemed himself since. In 2007, when management were singling me out for fixing competitions, he emailed 'how typical of the suits to blame the talent' and he's spoken out about the BBC's duplicity over presenters' service companies and tax arrangements. That's before the Newsnight/Savile fiasco. I could go on. He's still my hero.

And, even with a beard, the sexiest 60-something on telly.

I hadn't lived in London long when a member of the aristocracy took a shine to me. We'd met at the home of a Radio 3 presenter and we'd both been invited because we loved music and she was putting on a buffet and an African band.

I was fascinated by his stories of family shenanigans in Kenya's Happy Valley, school holidays at the ancestral pile, swimming in its infamous pool or picking out the diamonds his grandmother had hidden in his birthday jelly. I made him laugh. He invited me for supper. NB. Never say dinner. Or serviette, toilet or dessert. As I quickly learned, any etymological hint of French is a dead giveaway that your stock is rather nouveau. (Oops. Sorry.)

He invited me to a soiree (there, I go again) at his Cheyne Walk house in Chelsea. As he served up the rather stodgy plain dishes (I later learned these were amusing public school staples), it was slightly intimidating to find myself surrounded by super confident writers, film producers and politicians. The superficial small talk turned to the beauty of Istanbul. I spoke up for the first time.

"Well, I think it's a dump. Absolutely filthy and the abject poverty in the streets is obscene."

That killed the conversation. You could have heard a jaw drop. After a few embarrassing seconds of silence the guest at my side rounded on me. "Have you actually been?"

Of course I had. Why would I comment otherwise? He, though, seemed aghast that I could have. And that I was jumped up enough to question their pretentious world view. I couldn't stomach staying for 'pudding'. I knew my place.

In 1997, I was making films for a BBC2 series called 'Just One Chance'. It ran for two series and was presented by my old mate Carol Vorderman. The reporters were me and Princess Di's confidante, Martin Bashir. It was a consumer programme like Watchdog but for parents and all about education. For one report I was sent to a public school to see why some families spend so much on private education.

One mother told me it was because it had such an international intake and she wanted her children to mix with people from all over the world. Sorry, love, but that's baloney. They could go to most local comps and do that. No. This was an exclusive club. Once you joined and learned its nuances you were a member for life. Plus the teaching and facilities were fantastic. Yes. I could see how anybody would want those for their child.

I was even more envious when, years later I went to a Christmas craft fair at a stately home. I was less taken by the endless pot-pourri and candles on offer than by the breathtaking interiors and idyllic setting of the mansion. Wandering away from the stalls to find the Ladies, I stumbled across the signs of this being a school. Fading portraits of famous old boys down the decades. Photos of the First XV and the new swimming pool. Notices about jazz clubs, theatre groups and forthcoming concerts and balls. Anything and everything that our local high school didn't have to offer.

Out on the front lawn I had my Scarlet O'Hara in front of Tara moment. "As God is my witness. I'm gonna make sure my family never goes without again!"

Working seven days a week, I'd be able to afford this now. All Sam had to do was pass the entrance exam and get at least six A grades in his GCSEs. Not that every public schoolboy is that academic. If you've got the cash and connections you can be 'Tim Nice But Dim' and still find yourself in the fourth form. But independent schools like to bump up their grade averages by harvesting the brightest from the state sector. So they throw in a few bursaries. This way they can also claim charitable status and get all their VAT back.

Sam smashed it. They really wanted him. He was offered an amazing scholarship. This was my kind of bargain. Designer education TK Maxx style. With 60% off.

I didn't want my kids to have my accent, and that hurdle to overcome before they could get anywhere, so I jumped at the chance of Sam going there. It was like Hogwarts, it was so beautiful and he had every opportunity and facility he could dream of. You can't tell now that he's my child and that makes it sound like I'm ashamed of myself but I'm not. I just didn't want him to have the troubles I had. I'm not going to betray my roots but life will be easier for him without my accent.

He had a wonderful sixth form there. And I loved its staff, its teaching, its values and its ethos. His experience was as amazing as the setting. For me it was a mixed bag. I was always treated with courtesy and respect by the staff. (Well I suppose I was paying, like at The Portland). And the headmaster seemed positively relieved to have someone to enthuse with about the school's pop memorabilia. In 1963, a pupil had written to Brian Epstein and amazingly the Beatles turned up and played for the boys. He also loved a chat about his favourite bands and how he'd once been on my show. (I didn't remember!) And to boast about the rock stars' kids who'd been on his books. (I never did bump into the Jaggers). Some of the parents were another matter.

I had one mother nearly reaching for the smelling salts when she learnt our country place was too titchy to warrant a permanent gardener – or any other staff – and that we didn't have another address in London's SWs. Or own an Aga. Apparently I had the right clothes and car but as soon as I opened my mouth I was in trouble.

Still. I could always redeem myself by mentioning that I worked for the BBC. But then again, when I explained just exactly what I did there I felt like George Cole's character Flash Harry turning up at St. Trinians.

When the Queen landed on the lawn in her helicopter to open a new dorm, all parents were invited. As the young girl on the door took my name she was very apologetic.

"Oh I'm sooo sorry Madam. You don't appear to be on the list."

"Oh well," I smiled, scanning it, and pointing to a name at random. "I'll be Lady Olivio Spread then." (Some names have been changed).

A big fat moustached military "gentleman" next to me guffawed.

"That's highly unlikely," he said.

"I'm sorry?"

"Well. A Lady? Speaking like that?"

Best not disappoint him then.

"Perhaps," I suggested in his ear. "I am a Lady because I married an old codger like you and am shagging him just for his cash." I left him standing in silence as I was graciously waved into the reception.

Sam is proud to be an old boy and it wouldn't be fair to him or to his school to get any more gossipy. But, just to say, I found that public school culture really is riddled with all the ridiculous idiosyncracies of St. Cake's in Private Eye.

All in all though, I think it's very sad that every child can't be given that kind of start in life by our state schools. Including my Joe a few years later. He got more A grades at GCSE than Sam but I couldn't afford public school any more since becoming resigned to just one show a week by the BBC.

Happily, he wanted to stay with his friends at the comp and I was relieved to accept that one school doesn't fit all.

Several radio colleagues wanted to know if I thought it was all worth it. At least two of them have taken the plunge. One of them is now putting his four children through a school that's been the choice of princesses and has quite recently produced at least one comedian and a Royal bride. And he's working seven days a week to fund it. I saw him looking knackered on TV recently and had to text to see if he was alright. Like me he was brought up to believe that giving your kids a leg up in life is worth paying any price and going without anything yourself. Including sleep.

My headmaster dad always preached social mobility through education. His parents worked in a cotton mill and he might have done too if he hadn't won a scholarship to grammar school. Social mobility was delayed for a generation on my mum's side. My grandma won a scholarship but had to start work spinning cotton instead because her family desperately needed the money. My dad lived just long enough to finally see one of us – his grandson – get a place at Cambridge.

But Sam protested. "You only want me to go to Cambridge because you didn't." Too right. My old mucker Carol Vorderman is the first to admit that the 'B Eng Cantab' handle has helped make her fortune. So yes. I have always wished I had that 'branding'.

Maybe one day the BBC will get over accents. Maybe one day it will dawn on the BBC why Radio 4 has such piss-poor audiences outside of the Home Counties.

I'll tell you why.

It's because it sounds smug, exclusive and like it couldn't care less about anybody north of Watford.

In 2013, the BBC's Director General, Tony Hall, told the House of Commons Culture, Media and Sport Committee: "I think it doesn't matter what people sound like in terms of their accents. I happen to think Merseyside accents are great. I would like to hear more. It is an important point that we reflect the diversity of the UK outside London. I do worry about this. We have to guard against the metropolitan bias."

Crikey. Well he is from Merseyside, like.

So... it's been a long time coming... but a change is gonna come.

That wasn't soon enough for me though back in 1998.

Chapter Fifteen

(WHAT'S THE STORY) MORNING GLORY?

I missed being on the radio. I missed interviewing interesting people all over the country. There really is nothing in the world to match the BBC's flagship radio stations. OK, so some of the management might be lamentable and doing their best to ruin a good thing (by even trying to scrap it altogether in the case of 6 Music in 2010) but BBC radio is unique. To listen to and to work at.

Commercial Radio is ok if you're happy, as a presenter, to be used as a 'larynx on legs' or 'gob on a stick' (as I've heard bosses refer to DJs), linking ads for soap powder and car insurance. After all, Radio Aire in Leeds had given me and a host of other future BBC voices a break. But I'd never needed to look back. Until now, when fortunately, my break from radio was over before it had really begun.

Bruno called me in the summer of 1998 when I was almost on my uppers. I was surviving by doing a few films for a Watchdog spin-off with Vanessa Feltz but that was it. Bruno then made me an offer I couldn't refuse. The Magic group wanted to get us back together for a syndicated show on all their stations across the country. Including Radio Aire.

OK. Where from though? By now he'd built his own studio in a uPVC conservatory stuck on his medieval mansion. Could I get there for nine every Saturday morning?

So, once a week for a year, I drove the 70 miles to Newbury, arriving just in time to wake him up and make his first coffee.

Wow. The house and setting were stunning. Worthy of any '70s prog rock star. To get to the huge oak front doors you had to park up on the gravel drive and then, through the early morning mist, cross a little bridge over the 'private' river for which he had exclusive fishing rights. He'd always said that by the time he was 35 he wanted a big country home with loads of kids. Once inside I'd find Bruno, 39, on his own, slumped on a sofa in the huge central hall where he'd fallen asleep the night before watching telly in front of the fire.

His wife was hardly ever there. "Oh she went out early to her horses." He'd just bought her a 20 grand horse box. "I never see her Liz. Do you think something might be wrong?"

They'd got married in 1994, two weeks after Joe was born. I couldn't go. For a start, for some reason the bride had specifically stipulated 'no babies' which meant leaving my new one for a whole weekend. No way. Plus I couldn't afford two days in a five star hotel. My BBC 'maternity leave' meant I had no income. And, 'for the couple who have everything', guests were asked to stump up towards a £25,000 grand piano from Harrods. I felt like sending a cheque for a tenner and asking the store to stick 'all the best and good luck from Liz,' on one of the keys. Maybe 'F'. Maybe not. But most of all, with Bruno's best interests at heart, I'd never been able to buy into this match made in heaven. Eventually, after no kids and a very agreeable divorce settlement, Bruno's better half upgraded and took off with a bloke with a private jet.

After a few months 'Bruno and Liz on Magic' moved into the new suite of studios he'd installed in a local office block. His business of making in-store radio for the likes of Top Shop and Burberry was booming and he'd become quite the media mogul. I think he'd decided that nobody was ever going to sack him again. He was going to be managing director of his own life. I took a leaf out of that book not long after.

It was a regular income again and I was grateful for that but part of me fretted about whether this was the right thing to do. I was proud of what I'd done on Radio 5 and Radio 5 Live. I'd proved that I was more than a DJ – I found stories, I proved I knew and understood the big issues of the day and that I was informed and confident enough to be let loose on any subject.

And then, all of a sudden, I am back playing Bruno's side-kick. Although it was great fun to be together again, part of me thought that it was a backwards step. I'd spent the best part of six years proving I could do an intelligent show, and a show on my own. But now I was back making his coffee and being the butt of his jokes.

That is no criticism of him at all. And working with him

again was a really good laugh. And I soon realised it was never going to last. I think if we'd been reunited on the BBC we'd have been back in business, but with the rigidity of at least four strictly-timed commercial breaks in every hour and the other crucial 'junctions' for news, weather and travel, which we had to hit spot on to ensure a dozen or more stations were in sync, it wasn't the free wheeling format we'd enjoyed at Radio 1. We used to just go with the flow. Nobody knew what was coming next, including us.

Now we had to be 'tight', disciplined and professional. Us two together? That was never going to work. And it didn't. But it lasted a year. And tided me over until another surprising career opportunity came along.

Our Andrew had been writing a column for The Independent but with all his other stuff he was finding the weekly deadline too hard to meet. "Our Elizabeth will do it for you," he declared. They were happy with that. So was I.

The first deadline coincided with Johnny Walker's return to Radio 2 after a cocaine sting. I knew some of my colleagues in Broadcasting House thrived on Bolivian marching powder. Our Andrew once told me about being offered a snort in the men's toilets by someone about to go on air.

"Fancy a line, mate?"

"No thanks. I'm more of a herbal man myself."

Blimey. And we thought we were living dangerously when octogenarian broadcaster David Jacobs ticked us off like two naughty school kids for smoking fags in a studio – when that was still legal.

In April, 1999, Johnny Walker was accused by the News of the World of a range of naughtiness involving rolled-up fivers and totty by the hour. There were whispers that a rival jock had set him up to see him off and pinch his slot. That seemed entirely plausible to me. The BBC immediately suspended him for eight months.

Nobody who knew him was shocked by the claims but we were dismayed at the prospect of losing one of our best broadcasters.

So I wrote about how, when I arrived at the Fun Factory, I'd been a listener since day one and couldn't wait to meet all those Great Mates. I'd imagined them rolling up in their open top sports cars, leaping over the side and dashing to their turntables clutching the latest pile of hot vinyl.

What confronted me was a bunch of portly blokes with briefcases who would use the time when records were playing to ring their accountants. Only one guy lived the life. Only one guy failed to disappoint. He was the one I'd see at gigs and getting off on the music he was sharing with his listeners. He was the one with a Harley and tight leathers. Johnnie Walker was the real rock 'n' roll article.

He was fined a couple of grand for possessing cocaine worth a tenner and hardly enough to get a hamster high. As soon as the allegations were proved and he was properly convicted, the BBC put him back on air.

And why not? He'd single-handedly done more to rid Radio 2 of its 'Radio Cardigan' image than a whole host of management consultants ever could. And at no cost to the licence payer.

Did he sound sheepish? No. He flirted outrageously with Sally Traffic as she reeled off calls from the likes of Love Muscle and Mattress Man. There was more sexual chemistry between those two than in a viagra factory. It wasn't PC. But it was funny.

He once told me that I was 'good for women'. That meant a lot. So was he. And he'd provided the content for my first column. Just another couple of hundred or so to go.

In many ways this was the ideal job. On 5 Live, I'd once said 'cottaging' was working from home with a computer. Well that's what I was doing now. In a cottage. So hey. It fitted in with taking Sam and Joe to school and picking them up again and it wasn't much of a chore spending all week listening to the radio. Sometimes, simply surfing through the stations provided ample inspiration. Sometimes it would come from the dozens of cassettes BBC Radio Publicity sent every week. Sometimes I wondered if they'd actually listened to them first.

I'd picked out Jim Bowen because 'Mr. Bullseye' had once come on The Crunch, and, after the show, he'd taken me to the underground car park to give me something special in his Jag. A rubber Bully to treasure.

And Jon Gaunt had won three gold gongs in a year at the Sony Awards but was also no stranger to the Broadcasting Standards Commission. Three complaints had been upheld, including one when he'd threatened to visit a listener's house brandishing a baseball bat. So I thought he was interesting.

Now I heard him asking a woman on his morning phone-in if she'd ever gone out without knickers, discussing split-crotch panties, and telling another "we're gonna have to whip you. Bend over."

And Jim Bowen, in an interview about his Radio Lancashire show, told me all about name-checking his dog Sambo, and using what he called "terms of endearment" like tart and trollop. He resigned six months later after referring to another woman as a "nig nog."

(WHAT'S THE STORY) MORNING GLORY?

I felt really proud, seeing my name in print in a national broadsheet. And unlike in the Yorkshire Post, it was my real name as well! Agonising over every word and phrase and then seeing a well-argued, rattling good read printed up – just as I'd written it – was really satisfying. I loved the response I got from my media colleagues too. I was once on the beach in Majorca when a guy who ran MTV Europe came up to me and said he loved my column and read it every week.

However, I hated sitting there on my own – getting the kids ready for school then sitting there for three days, listening to tapes and then writing the column. I would turn people away from my door and I never answered the phone.

Sometimes I would realise I was frozen stiff and numb with cold because the heating had gone off and I hadn't noticed. It was a very isolating experience and I wouldn't repeat it in a hurry. I am very sociable and love talking to people, so to sit and hide yourself away in order to write instead was testing.

The radio column did get me out and about as well though and gave me a glimpse into a BBC I never knew existed. I went to endless parties as gilt-edged invitations fell through the letterbox at regular intervals. My column clearly had some impact in the industry as I was invited to the Today summer party as well as receptions at St. James's Palace and Downing Street. That do was a real shocker.

'The Director General of the BBC requests the pleasure of your company at a reception to be hosted at No. 10 Downing St by The Prime Minister of the United Kingdom, The Right Honourable Tony Blair MP.'

As soon as the PM walked in the room, radio industry executives started jostling for his attention. It was all a bit sickening seeing grown men turn so sycophantic. He probably just saw a sea of grey suits. Apart from me. And anyway, Tony seemed to know 'my work' so we talked for eight minutes. Precisely. Apparently. That's what was reported the next day in the gossip columns.

Someone there had been jealous enough to time it. And bitch about it.

"Does he not realise that Kershaw, a disc jockey, and being a close personal friend of Charles Kennedy, is a Lib Dem viper in his bosom?" Bloody hell. We were only having a chat about great albums. Power, eh? It hit me that if you fly too close to the flame, there'll be those who can't wait to see you burn. Anyway, the next time the PM and me had a pow-wow at No. 10 none of them were there to spy. And after what Tony told me, I never bothered to turn my telly or house lights off again...

Meanwhile, I now spent time quaffing champagne with the great and the good of the BBC while those on the shop floor got on with the daily grind of producing its output.

And, before long, I was back on the radio myself after a chap called John Ryan brought me back into the BBC fold, completely out of the blue.

"Hello Liz. This is Northampton calling." Lord Haw Haw himself couldn't have sounded more po-faced or ominous. "Our new managing editor, John Ryan, has heard you live locally and has asked me to try and contact you. He'd like a chat with you about his new schedule for the station."

It was only about nine o'clock in the morning. I'd just walked Sam and Joe to school and the phone had been ringing as I'd put my key in the front door. It had been the usual rush getting two boys out of bed, washed, dressed, fed and loaded up with lunch boxes, homework and the clean P.E. kit. So there I was, still in my tatty, greying trackie bottoms desperate for a shower and a coffee before settling down to plough through hours of radio tapes for my Independent work.

Strolling back through the village, I'd been wrestling with what to feature in this week's column and 'looking forward' to another solitary day, sitting for the next six hours, getting colder and stiffer at the computer.

So, preoccupied with that, I immediately assumed that this new bloke was just after publicity. A chancer trying to promote himself and plug his plans for his station in a national newspaper.

I couldn't have been more wrong.

The newsman who'd been told to call me, (it became quite clear very quickly after I joined that I would not have been his breakfast presenter of choice) went on to say that John Ryan wanted to offer me a job and could I meet him that lunchtime? Crikey. Within three hours I was scrubbed up and chugging into a car park by the Grand Union Canal in my now 12-year-old backfiring banger that I'd got new and eked life out of ever since the good times rolled at Radio 1.

John Ryan turned out to be a jolly, round, young chap who was already tucking in at the pub in Stoke Bruerne, a picturesque lockside spot halfway between Northampton and my home. He hadn't wanted us to be seen at his office. His interest in me was his big idea and still supposed to be his big secret. The clandestine nature of our meeting only seemed to fuel his excitement. Good job we weren't clocked by the other clientele then, all enjoying the two-for-one pensioners' specials.

I liked him immediately. He was warm and smiley and his blue eyes twinkled like an excited boy with a new train set who'd now got his very own station. His enthusiasm was infectious, he obviously loved radio and he also clearly loved me.

He wanted to boot BBC local radio into the 21st Century and to widen its appeal to an aspirational population in a thriving county with an expanding population.

And he wanted me to present the flagship Breakfast Show and make it sound BIG.

I was gobsmacked and very flattered. And absolutely bloody thrilled when he offered to pay me £200 a show. This was exactly the same as I'd been paid eight years earlier on Radio 1 but this was local radio so I couldn't expect inflation-busting network rates here. And, anyway, when I instantly did the maths I calculated that I'd be on a whacking 50 grand a year.

Being a freelancer is all about feast and famine. Nothing is guaranteed. So there'd been times when I never had to worry about the cost of anything. If I saw something I just bought it. If I wanted to go somewhere – anywhere – I just went. But there'd also been years when I didn't know where the next penny was coming from. For now, though, the good times would start rolling again. No more scrimping and scraping. No more charity shop clothes. No more crying over Joe losing one of his £50 Startrite shoes while frantically searching on my hands and knees under all the shelves in a supermarket because I really couldn't buy him another pair.

The plan was that the breakfast show would start at 6.30am and ease the audience (and me) into it for half an hour with a lively blend of music and chat and then from seven until nine we'd crank it up a few gears.

(WHAT'S THE STORY) MORNING GLORY?

Me and Bruno Brookes had both worked on BBC local stations and used to do a spoof on Radio 1 called 'Yours Truly with Alan and Julie' in which a couple of really lovely characters were really lovely to each other and all their lovely listeners and only talked about really lovely things. For too long, BBC local radio had been Radio Cosy. Parochial, insular, in a vacuum.

A comedy sketch on TV summed it up for me. 'Today, World War 3 broke out. But we're going to ask: "Does sitting in a comfy chair really relax your legs?"'

Now we were going to get stuck into national and international stories as well as local issues, making it a one-stop shop for news. Channel 4 News and Newsnight were my nightly fodder so I reckoned I could cope. This was a seismic shift with Northamptonshire at the epicentre of everything. Nobody in the area would ever need to tune to national and local rivals ever again. To borrow from The League of Gentlemen, no more 'local radio for local people'.

I was excited. I was in. I wasn't giving a thought at that stage to the practicalities. From May 1st, I would be what Dame Edna Everage called a housewife superstar but I had less than two months to work out how.

Paul had to leave the house to commute to London at about the same time my show would start. So with both of us gone who was going to take care of our boys and get them to school?

A neighbour had helped look after Sam and Joe from time to time. She was lovely and kind and had all the experience that came with being the matriarch of a large extended family. She also had a housebound husband so didn't stray far from home except to do the odd bit of cleaning and babysitting around the village. If she took us on she would be free by nine o'clock when her husband got up and I would be home by 11 to do the housekeeping and still be able to pick Sam and Joe up from school every day. Perfect.

Childcare is one of the most important and responsible jobs you can do. It can literally be a matter of life and death and it's crucial that children spend time with someone who's not only competent but a good influence too. So I offered to pay her well over the going rate. After all, if I didn't have somebody I could completely trust and depend on, I couldn't work. But if I could take the job we should all share the wealth. She was up for it, wonderful and never once let us down.

I know Sam and Joe would rather have had their mum in the mornings. I was a big softy with them and they could get away with more. They did carp on about her strictness, her funny old country ways of speaking and her foibles but she genuinely cared and loved them and became like one of the family, always joining us for celebrations and parties. So now it was just the small matter of getting to grips with cutting it on a make-or-break (for me and John Ryan) radio show, day-in, day-out.

On my own.

I was petrified. I'd flown solo before, while operating the desk myself. But not since the Radio 1 Evening Show, 12 years ago. In the meantime I'd only had to talk, not work the controls, and since then my great mate Bruno had pronounced that women were actually biologically incapable of doing that.

Added to that, I'd also had the stuffing knocked out of me by being unceremoniously dumped by BBC radio twice, courtesy of Radio 1 and then Radio 5 Live. However, as soon as I clapped eyes on the clapped-out old desk I felt a bit better.

Radio Northampton had evidently seen no investment since

its launch in 1982 so its dowdy brown hessian-lined studios and archaic analogue gear were comfortingly familiar. However, as the big day loomed I got less and less confident that I could cope. On the eve of the first show I nearly rang John Ryan to bail out. Only the shame of letting him and my family down stopped me from committing career suicide.

And so, after a restless night of the stock-in-trade nightmares all DJs suffer from time to time, in which they have nothing to play or say and 'die' on air, I swung out of bed bleary-eyed at 5am and half an hour later shuffled out to the pristine new car glinting in the dawn's early light.

I'd treated myself to a dream machine; the kind of convertible I'd coveted every time I'd chugged past a nearby dealership in what my grandma called my 'bloody old jalopy'. I reasoned that if I was going to have to get to work like clockwork – whatever the weather – at an ungodly hour every weekday for two years, I was going to travel the 10 miles of twisty country lanes in reliable comfort and style, roused by rock music blaring from big fuck-off speakers. (Other more practical, cheaper and equally reliable cars were available).

And when I wasn't working hard I could play hard. I was going to enjoy the spoils at last.

Top of the pump-me-up playlist was Guns n' Roses' 'Appetite For Destruction'. The track 'Out To Get Me' was particularly motivational on dark dismal mornings and apart from scream-ing my lungs out with Axl Rose, those early morning drives were thinking time – quiet and uneventful.

Except on one dark morning when I turned a bend and was confronted by an upturned car in full flame, lighting up the winter skies, with a dirty, dark-skinned, dishevelled bloke crawling out of the wreckage. He wouldn't let me call 999 and desperately tried to communicate in broken English that he'd just finished a night shift (presumably for a poxy wage that no local would want) and was terrified of being caught, arrested and deported. To the extent that he'd shun medical help and see his only means of transport totally torched. His desperate face always haunted me when listeners rang the show about bloody foreigners coming here for a cushy life taking local jobs or benefits. I could now see both sides.

Immigration, car crime, road safety, town centre decline, recycling, pot holes, school standards, building on the greenbelt, all became cause celebres as did the rather ugly but symbolic Northampton Lift Tower which, er, 'thanks' to my show, still dominates the Northampton skyline. More to come on that campaign. The show was buzzing with listeners calling and writing in. They drove the agenda while I was their voice, taking officials to task and holding the authorities to account.

But it was hardly a walk in the park. What did BBC Radio Northampton make of me? Well, I was a woman – the only one the BBC let loose anchoring a breakfast show – and a disc jockey, not a proper journalist. A showbiz blonde airhead? Maybe. But not a lot anyway.

Please note. In the mid-'90s the Director General, John Birt, banned music between 7am and 9am on local radio. Breakfast shows were handed over to newsrooms to produce the speech only output. As was Drivetime except that was punctuated with Abba records. Newrooms now ruled the roost with the peak time shows that bookended each weekday.

Fine if it's any good. Back in 2000, in the leafy shires, it seemed to me that it didn't matter to some of my new colleagues if it were absolute shite. Some never seemed to venture out. Instead they scoured the local papers to find out what was going on and cherry picked items.

There were some really great people there. But a small clique of self-serving time-servers tyrannised the place. A clique that was not going to allow a flamboyant new manager to come in and upset the cosy status quo with his flagrant grasp of modern life and popular culture, with an obscene passion for public service, some tiresome Reithian aspirations to entertain as well as inform, and a naked ambition for the success of the station.

On the plus side, John Ryan was male. And white. But he wasn't middle aged (being the wrong side of 30) or middle class. He hadn't had the decency to go to university, had a white van man dad, and horror of horrors, had come from commercial radio.

And, good grief, he was gay. And very open about it.

In his enthusiasm for swift change, he made little attempt to disguise who he rated or hated and, to be honest, was a bit gung-ho in his approach to entrenched BBC HR procedures.

After a couple of journalists complained about him, he was quietly sent packing to a desk job in Broadcasting House.

On his leaving day we were assembled in the newsroom where David Holdsworth, then head of the BBC's Eastern region made a generic type speech about John.

Were those satisfied smirks on some faces behind him? I found it all so cowardly and said something along the lines of:

"When I first walked into BBC local radio I was struck that it was in the grip of white, male, middle-class, middle-aged, heterosexual Christians called Jeremy – all wearing chinos and driving VW Golfs. That was two decades ago in Leeds. Looking around here today nothing has changed. I'll only know it has when somebody like John Ryan gets to run a station again."

Eventually he did. Radio Leeds! But not before he'd served a two-year sentence in admin. That was his punishment. I'm still not clear what his crime was.

I do know that John Ryan was trying to do his best for BBC listeners. Alan Partridge on Radio Norwich wasn't just a figment of Steve Coogan's imagination – BBC local radio has always been plagued by pompous prats in sports casuals, peddling piffle.

The Controller of English Regions (all local radio and TV in England) Andy Griffee, cut a diminutive little figure in his chalk striped suits. Fast walking and smart talking, he had huge presence and was very sharp. Certainly not someone to mess with. I poured my heart out in a letter to him about everything from subtle hostility to downright verbal contempt, from sabotaging me on air with long-winded cues into what turned out to be blank tapes, to ignoring my requests for a drink.

I couldn't leave the studio and had been talking non-stop for two hours when I fainted live on air once because it was so hot. After that I always took in a flask. When I left they presented me with a coffee machine. I described the 'oh, that'll do' attitude and piss-poor productivity which resulted in a lack of decent content for the show.

Bernie Keith, our rather more petite Charles-Hawtrey-meets-Kenneth-Williams-style mid-morning turn, also put pen to paper about his own struggle to survive. I don't remember us getting a reply but soon we got a temporary editor who had been loaned from a nearby station.

Nikki Holliday looked disarmingly girly with a fulsome

figure, long curly hair and a big round open face but she made it very clear, very quickly, that she wasn't taking any prisoners or any shit. She brought with her a trusted producer for breakfast, Joanne Griffiths, who was also talented and determined, but... bloody hell, another turn up... she was black. We were on a roll. The old guard were left in no doubt that only total commitment and top-notch content would wash with this regime.

One morning, in September 2001, this was tested to the max. When John Ryan and I had talked by the canal about wanting the station to open up to the wider world, we could never have predicted that it would be shaken to its core on 9/11.

Under the old regime, coverage of the horror in the US would probably have stretched to getting some old biddy on the phone to reminisce about having been to Disneyland Florida once with the grandkiddies. On the morning of September 12th, 2001, Joanne and Nikki were phone bashing before dawn and got reaction from Whitehall to Washington. Nobody was putting their feet up in a comfy chair today.

One expert on terrorism and security spoke with all the authority of a real spook and obviously knew his stuff but it was weird when he asked if I ever worked in Broadcasting House. "Don't worry then," he intimated gravely. "You'll be OK there. It's one of the safest buildings in the UK." And with that he was gone. We tried to look him up later, could find no trace, and realised he'd called us. For years after, I always took trainers to work in case I had to leg it fast from a BBC building.

For the next few months we linked up with a talk radio station in Madison Square Gardens. Their presenter John Bachelor became quite a fixture on the Northamptonshire airwaves and in a reciprocal arrangement I became the accidental voice of the BBC in New York City. John Ryan's global radio for local people was now a reality. If only for all the wrong reasons. Fear and confusion meant we'd become one big trans-Atlantic support group trying to make sense of this new world order and wondering what we were all in for next. We were brothers in arms. Until the US actually took up theirs and unleashed them on Al-Qaeda.

News of the American assault on Afghanistan was greeted with whooping and hollering in the studio. A jingoistic let's-nuke-the-lot-of-'em 'Go Bush Go' mentality. I didn't know what to think about George Junior's tactics in what he seemed to call 'The War on Tourism'. I just thought that, as the local branch of 'the world's most internationally respected news organisation', it was important to dryly stick to the facts without inference, comment or emotion.

After the show I was put right by Nikki. It was the only time I doubted her judgement. She was angry that I hadn't conveyed any enthusiasm, approval or excitement on air. My whole tone was wrong. Omitting to big up the action amounted to professional failure on my part. I'd not only missed a trick in bringing in new listeners, I'd very possibly alienated our existing loyal audience.

Had I failed to capture the public mood? History will judge the Afghan war. The British public already has. All I know is that under very real pressure in a live and volatile situation, I didn't surrender to a media mob mentality. I refused to become a cheerleader for Uncle Sam and I'm not apologising for that.

Me and Bernie Keith were a winning combination in the morning and the number of listeners increased by nearly 50%. Job done, Nikki Holliday was on her way to troubleshoot at some other troublespot. There's a name to watch out for in BBC management.

Our next boss was a colourful character called David Clargo who came bursting onto the scene just in time to enjoy all the benefits of John Ryan's revamp of the station. Clargo's claim to fame was that he'd been the Milky Bar Kid in the TV ads. He was still blond and, though no longer bespectacled, he did look like he'd enjoyed more than his fair share of confectionery over the years.

Every three months, when the listening figures came out, he'd rush out of his office quite literally flapping. "I'm cock-a-hoop!" was what we came to expect every quarter. He had a great work-hard, play-hard attitude to radio. We had plenty of reasons to celebrate, so we had some great parties.

As the DJ, I knew that the first few notes of Bananarama's 'Venus' would have him throwing caution to the wind and twirling us round the dance floor. By now, any miserable bastards were in a minority, so there was no holding us back.

"I'm cock-a-hoop!" came the cry as he rushed in to tell us that we'd been nominated for the Sony Radio Academy Best Breakfast Show Award in Spring, 2002. We were going to the ball.

The annual bonanza at the Grosvenor House Hotel was now an evening affair so we were stuffed into gowns and tuxedos, tucking into mass-catered chicken and rubbing shoulders with the glitterati. Hundreds of them at around £150 a head.

After necking down copious amounts of 'free' booze we came away tired and emotional and, sadly, empty-handed. My mantelpiece remained bare. Beaten by John Humphrys and Nicky Campbell, we were disappointed but not really surprised. John Ryan had wanted us to take on the big boys at Breakfast.

THE BIRD AND THE BEEB

Tonight we had. We must be doing something right.

It was the first awards since 9/11. We could have entered our own Morning After The Devastation The Day Before Show. I've seen bosses rubbing their hands in glee when a natural disaster like flooding hits their patch and they can see a gong in their sites. Or the jealous gnashing of teeth when a human tragedy like a big murder case lands on a rival station's doorstep. Pain makes prizes. But I'd rather win a piece of perspex that's not splattered with some poor bugger's blood.

Unfortunately, there was no nice way to do the decent thing and to avoid feeling like a complete shit in early 2002.

During the early days in Northampton, I'd remained the Independent's radio reviewer and was asked to join a panel discussion on stage at the Radio Festival. (Nowadays the BBC bans presenters from being newspaper columnists, unless they're Jeremy Clarkson, but I was still getting away with it.) I had a big moan about disenfranchised listeners.

Why wasn't there a music station for the likes of me? I was past it for Radio 1 where the current policy was only to play brand new stuff. And I couldn't listen to all the whining women on Radio 2 (not presenters – there hadn't been any since 1995) like Whitney Bloody Houston and Mariah Bleeding Carey.

And 'bands' like Westlife.

Bands should have dirty guitar licks. Bands that filled festivals never got aired. Bands that had sold millions of records and were still rocking deserved a radio station that was too – as did us fans.

And finally, that station had arrived.

As I came off stage at the Radio Festival, a figure stepped out of the shadows. "Hi Liz. I think I might have something of interest to you. A new station. Working title Network Y. I think you might be right for us. Would you like to audition?"

It was too good to turn down.

I had to tell David Clargo I was deserting him for what was to become BBC Radio 6 Music. Although tearful, it was au revoir not goodbye. We were to get back together in Coventry just over three years later.

But for now, back to the lift tower.

Cobblers.

Because the town once produced most of the nation's shoes, that's the nickname for Northampton's football team. They were managed for years by Alan Carr's dad. As a young lad, Alan had travelled with him in the car to away matches on Saturday mornings chuckling at Bruno and Liz on the radio. And he decided then that he'd be on the radio one day. He told me that as he started his own show on Radio 2.

Northampton also produced the world's longest lifts. Long after that old factory was shut down, developers bought it, and in 2001 announced they were intending to cram dozens of new houses on the site. This meant demolishing the old lift testing tower.

Hang on.

It was the county's most prominent landmark and was listed. So they claimed it was unsafe because of 'concrete cancer'. The locals were soon revolting (stirred up by me), the council's own engineers investigated, and a preservation order was slapped on it. Result.

I fought with planning law and the law had won. I was now a bit of a local hero.

I'm so happy to see it still dominating the skyline. Not because it's lovely but because it means I'm nearly home. See for yourself by casting your eyes left next time you're heading south on the M1 around Junction 16.

All these years later I can say "see that useless concrete monstrosity? I did that." I don't know whether to burst with pride or hang my head in shame. It's an absolute eyesore.

And that, dear licence payers, is my public service broadcasting legacy to the people of Northamptonshire.

I'll get my coat.

Chapter Sixteen

WHAT'S THE FREQUENCY, KENNETH?

6 Music hit the ground running on March 11th, 2002.

This was the first new BBC music station in 35 years and its presenters were a mixed bag of first timers and old hands. But the line-up said it all. Phill Jupitus, Tom Robinson, Bruce Dickinson of Iron Maiden, Suggs from Madness, Brinsley from Aswad, Andrew Collins. And me. Comedians, musicians, writers. And the odd DJ. 'We play what we like' was the slogan.

This was music radio for real fans by real fans. On 6, pop wasn't used simply to punctuate the prattle. Here the music was fundamental, not incidental.

There'd been two camps at Radio 1. Music-loving Annie

Nightingale, Johnnie Walker, Janice Long, John Peel and the Kershaws were sectioned off on the third floor. Real 'crazy guys' like DLT, Bates, Gary Davies, Steve Wright and Bruno were a level above on the fourth.

6 Music was definitely 'Radio Third Floor'.

Bands from R.E.M. to Radiohead, Pink Floyd to Pulp, The Byrds, the Beatles and Buzzcocks could now be played during the day. Nirvana wasn't just for night time. New bands got prime time.

6 Music was 'Radio Evening Show' 24 hours a day.

I was getting to meet some amazing new artists – and several of my old heroes – both inside and outside the studio.

Like Mick Jones, from The Clash, who saved me, big time.

One sunny day I was walking from the station to the BBC when a bloke came running out of a pub, shouting "you're Liz Kershaw aren't you?" He was very thin but very stylish. I didn't recognise him at first until he told me who he was. Bloody hell. *Mick Jones* knows *me*! He wanted to give me a CD by a new band he was producing called The Libertines. Would I give it a play on my show?

He also came in as a guest and then later we went to a Tottenham Court Road drinking club. I'd had a few when I left to catch the last train. All of a sudden, a girl snatched my handbag and ran off. I was stuck in London with no money, no keys, no ID and no hope. I burst into tears but Mick took me to his house, let me sleep on his sofa and then gave me £20 to get home the following morning.

I thought I'd better make the gesture of sending him a cheque for the twenty quid. He only bloody cashed it!

Oh well. If you're going to get mugged in London you might

as well be saved by a member of one of the coolest bands in the world!

Bands like Franz Ferdinand and Black Rebel Motorcycle Club also brought in their debut albums as 6 Music quickly gained a reputation for playing interesting, new stuff. Radiohead helped choose the tunes one afternoon after Johnny Greenwood had insisted they talked to me, and legends like Jack Bruce of Cream were awesome. We had such a good time he sent me his entire back catalogue on CD. The Who's Roger Daltrey came to promote a gig. Bert Jansch brought his guitar. It was absolutely magical to see his fingers running all over the fret. Kevin Ayers had been a favourite on the Annie Nightingale show back in the '70s. For the first time ever I got to play 'Stranger In Blue Suede Shoes' myself on the radio. "Thank you ver-ree much."

Ian McClaggan from The Small (and big) Faces shared his hangover cure. A hot bath followed by steamy sex. Dave Davies was obviously the modest sibling in The Kinks. Sister Sledge were 'So Excited', The Temptations were so cool and, Edwin Starr, after some 'eye to eye contact', invited me to his Leicester home for some real southern hospitality – grits (ground-corn food of Native American origin).

Artist Peter Blake described how he'd created one of the most iconic album covers ever for Sergeant Pepper. It was good to see familiar faces from Suede, Echo & the Bunnymen, The Specials, The Bangles, Def Leppard and ABC again.

When Guy Garvey of Elbow, Huey Morgan of Fun Loving Criminals and Jarvis Cocker came on the show nobody knew that one day they'd become 6 Music DJs too.

Coldplay came by but we were chocka so I just smiled and waved through the glass. Lovely lads but their music's a bit lame for my liking. 'Hey Liz, why didn't you say hello?' they wrote in the visitors book. It soon filled up. But to be honest, 10 years on, I'm stumped. I can't decipher half the rock 'n' roll handwriting. And I still feel a bit of a shit about Coldplay.

The Director General didn't need an invitation. He'd just pop in to see who was around and hang out chatting about the stuff we were playing and what gigs were coming up. That was all cool.

Greg Dyke was cool. He was also a thoroughly bloody decent chap. When the Hutton Inquiry into the death of Dr David Kelly criticised the BBC in 2003 for false reporting and poor news management, he took the rap. At 6 Music we lost one of our biggest fans. The BBC lost its top DG. I never saw his successor on the shop floor. Not our bit anyway. Mark Thompson was a news man. Remember, he knew nothing about Jimmy Savile. Or any of those other DJ types, it seems.

An exec once told me that when Thompson was running BBC 2 he went to see him with an idea for a new music show.

"Who'd present it?"

"Jo Whiley."

"Never heard of the guy."

This was my dream job. And I'd never earned so much. When 6 Music dragged me away from Radio Northampton they doubled my money. Once again I was stashing it away for a rainy day. A few years earlier I'd been home alone all day and watching every penny. Now I hadn't time to spend anything. Between getting up in time to get Sam and Joe to school, to arriving back to pick them up from their after-school club was an 11-hour day. The evenings were family time. I went to gigs at the weekends and, as a family, really made the most of the festival season.

WHAT'S THE FREQUENCY, KENNETH?

Going to Glastonbury for 6 Music was a blast. I'd been before for the BBC when 5 Live sent me twice to capture the atmosphere as one of the crowd. The usual stuff. The toilets, the security, the police operation, births deaths and marriages. Everything you'd expect in a temporary town the size of Wigan. In 1997 I was camping and covered in liquid mud. It was knee high in places and when I saw Annie Nightingale with her walking stick (she'd just been mugged in Cuba) stuck and struggling I had to actually pull her out. It was filthy and made me so violently sick I was throwing up between reports.

Now, in 2002, I was back for 6 Music and it was all about the bands. Ian Brown had gone solo after The Stone Roses and was happy to talk about that over a smoke. Not for me, thanks. I got into enough trouble when I was out front watching his set. My producer spotted two little white tablets in my palm. I was just about to take a swig of bottled water when she knocked them out of my hand. "Liz Kershaw. How dare you take ecstasy in full view of the public!" I was proper miffed. They were my last two Smints.

As dusk fell, the sky turned pink with the setting sun and a thousand camp fires on the hill facing the Pyramid Stage. Just magical. Being right at the front watching Roger Waters doing a decent job of recreating the full Pink Floyd experience, I remembered a John Walters story. In 1975, Pink Floyd's two latest albums, 'The Dark Side of the Moon' and 'Wish You Were Here', had been massive. On a visit to Radio 1 they invited him and Peel to their huge upcoming gig. "Here. Take these. They'll help you though the set." Walters kept the two small pink things he'd been given carefully tucked away until he was safely by the stage at Knebworth. Popping them in his mouth he was in for a shock. They were only rubber earplugs weren't they?

Backstage at Glastonbury, away from all this performing, a constant stream of chauffeur-driven limos were arriving at a lavish marquee covered in BBC logos and with pastel coloured tented ceilings, a free bar and comfy sofas. Seemed like a good place to have a sit down.

"Can I come in and get a drink?" I showed him my 6 Music ID. No good.

"No. You need a special pass."

Looking past him I could see that you had to be a BBC director or at least Head of Drama to get one.

So I joined Donovan who was sitting alone outside on a bale of hay waiting to perform with Chorley lads Starsailor. Nobody else seemed to know that this unassuming long-haired older gentleman was once the Bob Dylan of Britain. He was delighted that I did and that I'd interviewed some of his old muckers like the folk singer Vashti Bunyan. So much so that his daughter Astrella Celeste asked me to help out at his surprise 60th party three years later.

I was all poised on stage in a London club as his A-list mates from the '60s waited for the birthday boy. He was led in to a rapturous welcome and I opened my red book.

"Donovan Philips Leitch," so far so good. "You were born on the 10th of May, 1945".

"No I wasn't Liz."

"What?"

"I was born in 1946."

"So you're not 60 today then?"

"No I'm 59. I wondered what all the fuss was about."

"Oh, hell. Oh well. Donovan Philips Leitch. This is your night!"

It was a great one too. Everybody was very laid back about it coming a year early. Hippies eh?

Back at Glastonbury 2002, there was one rock god I had to go find. I trekked to the other side of the site to find him in a tent in a long, white, flowing kaftan. I'd briefly (!) spoken to him on the phone. Now I had to grab my chance to say hello in person. His long blond hair hung down his back as he turned to see who was reaching up to tap him on the shoulder.

"Hiya Robert. I'm Liz Kershaw. Andy's..."

"Liz! Liz! How great to meet you!" Obviously no offence had been taken by me doubting he was the real deal when he'd called Our Andrew's flat 15 years earlier.

That Christmas he agreed to do a special for me. So we recorded it in a pub one afternoon with a pile of albums. While he chatted about his career I sat thinking 'this is what it's all about. When I cut that skint student's locks off back at Uni in 1975 and he paid me with a vinyl copy of Led Zep IV, I never dreamt I'd one day be getting it signed by the man himself. Mr. Robert 'Squeeze My Lemon' Plant.'

"Oh, yeah Robert. Why did you sing such a lot about your er... lemon?"

"Liz, I was 17 when I started. I didn't know about anything else."

The next time I saw him it was bad times, not good times. He was wearing a woolly hat and big coat, huddled in a doorway in the cold, waiting for us. We were all in Suffolk and in shock. It was November 12th, 2004, and John Peel's funeral.

Less than three months earlier, John had celebrated his 65th birthday with a big party in a marquee at Peel Acres. August 30th was my Joe's birthday too. He was 10. When I told Peel, he said Joe could bring his mates if it meant we could all come.

So I hired a stretch limo to take us all in er... style. Joe and his posse loved the disco lights but weren't so impressed by the paint job. It was bright pink. Oops. Still, getting there was a scream. Especially when the driver, who was more used to drunken hen parties, had to pull up on the side of the A14 so that his Coca-Cola-fuelled little passengers could have a pee.

I'm not sure Joe's mates enjoyed dancing to the indie sounds of Peel favourites Camera Obscura and The Wedding Present but they had a good feed and a good time was had by all.

My last memory of Peel is of him standing in disbelief, glass of red in hand, waiting patiently as our flashing cerise limo did a 25-point turn attempting to get out of his narrow country lane.

Our Elizabeth had surpassed herself this time. After much amusement he waved us off with a bemused shake of the head and a kindly chuckle. And we were gone. In October, so was he.

Yet another premature death. Walters had already died unexpectedly in his sleep in 2001. Walters had been like a father to Our Andrew and when I arrived at Radio 1 he'd taken me into the fold too.

"Our Andrew and Our Elizabeth, have come down to London frum't north," Walters would start. "They come for their tea and Helen makes them a nice salad. 'Eh oop! This 'as got apple in it!' This isn't salad. Where we come from a salad's a slice of ham, a bit of lettuce, maybe a tomato, a slice of boiled egg..." We just used to let him roll.

Such stories of our lack of sophistication were fondly trotted out at every social occasion. After one of his parties he dined out on the same story for years: "Good. They were going at last. Me and Helen saw them safely off the premises as they ran for the last London train. And then... and then... they watched it leave on the opposite track. That was it. The last train home. These two just stood there gawping on the wrong platform. They could have ended up in Eastbourne. They had to come crawling back, asking to stay the night." He loved it.

And now Peel hadn't survived his dream holiday in Peru. For Our Andrew it was like he was losing his close family.

Huge crowds had gathered under grey skies outside Bury St. Edmunds cathedral. The select few (there were still hundreds of us) who'd got through the barriers and satisfied security (it was like jostling to get into a really miserable gig) were now packed in the pews. People were chatting in hushed tones. The fella next to me took the time to explain why yer average rock star's preference for young chicks comes with problems. "She's gorgeous obviously. But it's so boring. I mean we have nothing in common. Nothing to talk about. But it's the sex you see Liz. If I don't have a shag in the morning I have to have at least one off the wrist to set me up for the day." I turned to see a sobbing fellow DJ throwing me a filthy look. Don't blame me! I'm only listening.

He shut up when the coffin came in to heartfelt applause. John's brother made a truly moving speech, most poignant when he spoke of Ravenscoft Junior's miserable formative years at boarding school. And Paul Gambaccini brought the house down. Then the organ struck up and the singers Peel had made famous leapt to their feet. It was a right din. A cacophony of Billy Bragg, Jack White, members of The Undertones, Robert Plant and more, each attempting 'Abide With Me' in their own distinctive yet incompatible styles.

A reception in a barn followed the service. Some famous faces seemed to need to prove how close they'd been to John by winning the wailing stakes. Pete Wylie, meanwhile, organised the 'best black coat at a funeral competition.' Was he any less upset and respectful? I don't think so. John's wife Sheila obviously wasn't offended. "Congratulations Our Elizabeth. Oh do you and Our Andrew have to go so soon? Oh please stay a bit longer."

"We're really sorry Sheila but we have a train to catch. The last one to London."

Now together forever with Peel and watching down from that great party in the sky ("glass of red, bit of cheese"), Walters was not going to have the last laugh on this occasion.

6 Music was run by Radio 2's Controller, Jim Moir, and his sidekick, Lesley Douglas. We also shared the same building as Radio 2 and we were allowed to attend their swanky Christmas do. When this was scrapped everyone there blamed a certain DJ for – in one of their 'unguarded' moments – letting slip to a newspaper how much it cost. Thousands. But as long as the bosses could write those kinds of cheques, they wined and dined The Talent in London's swankiest eateries. The Cafe de Paris, Reform Club and The Lyceum.

"Good evening Liz. And may I say what a splendid décolletage." Big Jim was receiving us all personally. But when it came to taking our seats I noticed that on the very top table with Jim and Lesley were several of Radio 2's biggest stars like Wogan (of course), some of their younger male signings as well as couple of the more favoured independent producers. I just got used to sitting over by the kitchens with the likes of Suzi Quatro, Sybil Ruscoe, Janey Lee Grace (from Steve Wright's posse) and the newsreaders like Fenella Fudge. I knew my place.

In early 2003, Jim announced he was retiring. Naturally, Lesley really wanted his job.

At the Sony Radio Awards in the May, I spotted Roger Lewis, who I used to work for at Radio 1, in a huddle with Lesley and a big wig from commercial radio. By now, all three of them were in the frame to run Radio 2 and 6 Music. I'd always liked and respected Roger. "Good luck with the Radio 2 Controller's job Roger," I called to him in passing.

The next thing, I realised that Lesley was at my side. And seemingly furious at what had been a throwaway greeting. Shit.

I fretted all night and the next morning I decided I'd better send her a grovelling email apologising because she obviously was 'not amused' by my 'tactless joke'. She replied that she just felt ill at the thought of Roger getting the job. She needn't have worried. Before long Lesley Douglas became our controller.

Later that summer, I went to see Director of Radio and Kershaw fan, Jenny Abramsky, about a number of issues. One of them being that Lesley Douglas had got Jim's job and I was afraid for my future.

Even though one of Lesley's right-hand men had assured me that "you're OK as a 6 Music DJ Liz because you're not like a normal woman. You're not feminine. You're more like a bloke." I don't think he was being nasty. He was just a bit thick.

THE BIRD AND THE BEEB

A BBC director's life is very busy. They have meetings to chair. Consultants to commission. Opinion formers to schmooze. Expenses to claim. With the best will in the world they can't waste too much time hearing from the operatives and you always knew Jenny's patience – and your time – had run out when she'd pull her cashmere pashmina even tighter round her ample form. End of conversation. She'd given Lesley the job. She was a fan. Live with it Liz.

Perhaps if Jenny had listened to my concerns then, Jonathan Ross and Russell Brand would never have been given enough rope to hang themselves and the BBC could have saved a fortune and the feelings of a national treasure.

When Lesley replaced Jim, it didn't take her long to 'refresh the schedules'. She shunted me from my weekday show to weekends but softened the blow by promising me stand-in work on Radio 2.

Soon I was free again most Mondays to Fridays. How was I to fill that gap?

Fortunately, David Clargo came calling.

In early 2005 he asked if I could join him from that September when he launched his new station, BBC Coventry and Warwickshire. Taking him up on his offer would mean I had to work seven days a week for a while – five on local radio in Coventry and two on 6 Music – while using any holidays to do Radio 2 work that Lesley had promised. But 'get it while you can,' is the freelancer's motto. So I did.

Especially when I was also asked to regularly provide holiday cover at Radio Leeds by its new boss, John Ryan.

One morning, I found myself hosting the weekly mid-morning gardening phone-in with resident expert Dave.

WHAT'S THE FREQUENCY, KENNETH?

"The lines are now open so if you've got any questions for Dave we'll take the first call after The Bellamy Brothers..."

"The Bellamy Brothers and 'Let Your Love Grow' on BBC Radio Leeds. And now to answer your questions here's Dave."

"Yes. Thanks Liz. I don't know about growing love but if it's anything else..."

"Yes thanks Dave and here's our first caller. It's Doris in Crossgates on line two. Morning Doris. How can we help?"

"Well it's me bush yer see Liz," a gravelly voice told us. "I trimmed it and now it's gone all brown down one side. And I'm just wondering should I lop it all off or just let it keep growing."

Bad news for Doris from Dave. "I'm afraid Doris, with that kind of bush, once it's gone brown there's nothing you can do about it."

"Thank you Dave. Now on line four it's Brad in Kirkstall. Brad?" Surely with a name like that the next caller had to be a bit of a lad. No.

"Actually it's Bradley dear. And it's me plums Dave. They've gone all shrivelled. I think it's all this hot weather we've been having." Dave agreed that Bradley's succulents were suffering from drought.

But I was nearly wetting myself by now. I wasn't cut out for this. Best head back to 6 Music and Radio 2.

All the Radio 2 work turned out to be in the twilight zone. I covered for Janice Long from midnight to 3am or Alex Lester from 3am to 6am. The production staff were fab and so were the listeners. The shows were great fun, as was staying in Birmingham in a flat near Radio 2's overnight studio in The Mailbox.

Doing midnight until 3am, you come off air still buzzing.

So I'd have a glass of wine or two, wave to the milkman, and crash out at dawn. Then get up around 1pm, meet a friend for lunch (or breakfast or brunch or whatever it was), potter round Birmingham for a bit and then go out for a booze-free dinner and be ready for work at 11pm.

Covering the Janice Long show was just like working really late nights and was rather sociable and very manageable. I loved it. For a couple of weeks at a time anyway. Janice has been in that slot for knocking on 15 years and counting. Give that woman a daylight show.

On the other hand, Alex Lester made me feel physically sick. His show that is. I'd go to bed at 8am after a couple of snifters – this was my evening – and sleep until about 2pm. Then potter around Birmingham like a zombie hoovering up stuff I didn't really need in TK Maxx, before having a ready meal on my own about 7pm in front of the telly, and then having another kip from 9pm until the alarm went off at 2am. Alex has been doing this for nearly 25 years. Tucked away from 3am to 6am, he's Radio 2's best loved secret and, in my book, the unsung hero of BBC radio.

These stints on Radio 2 during the week fitted in really well with my two weekend shows on 6 Music. But what about when I was asked to cover a Saturday and Sunday morning show on Radio 2 from its Birmingham studios? How could I be in a London studio raring to go on 6 Music at 10am if I'd only hung up my headphones, two hours earlier and 120 miles away in the Midlands?

Best ask the boss. Lesley didn't hesitate. "Just pre-record your 6 Music shows." Fair enough. Lots of shows were recorded but sounded live. Like Steve Wright's Love Songs. A clause was put into my contract confirming that my show could be pre-recorded – with prior permission from management.

So from then on, when I was on Radio 2 and 6 Music, or if I just needed the odd Saturday or Sunday off, me and my producer would put in for a pre-record by email and set about recreating my live show. I naturally assumed that, as a £250,000-a-year Controller, Lesley listened to the output and was aware of its content. Which in those days, on my show and others, included instant interaction with the audience by text and email in features and competitions.

With a 6 Music show in the can, I could now pop up on Radio 2 or occasionally spend at least part of a weekend with my family and friends.

Great. For example, one Saturday – having had permission to pre-record the next day's show – I was able to go off to the Isle of Man.

Our Andrew's partner had bought a holiday home there and he was putting on gigs for the Manx Government. For the grand finale of the TT Races he'd bagged a top turn for the bikers.

"Our Elizabeth. Great to see you. I've brought you a drink." Robert Plant was installing me in his dressing room at the Villa Marina on the sea front in Douglas with a whole bottle of Rioja. "See you after the show."

The next morning we had an early start. With Robert Plant at the wheel of a tatty Ford Sierra he'd been loaned by the tourist board, a chick from the BBC and Our Andrew's mate, the Honourable Member for Montgomeryshire Lembit Opik MP, we set off to explore the island's ancient history.

We found the remains of Stone Age settlements, ancient round houses and, on a windy cliff top, a Viking burial mound.

This had been formed by placing an upturned boat, pointing out to sea, over a warrior's remains.

Robert was blown away. He had to take a moment to lie quietly on the grass and 'commune with nature'.

"Agh! Help! Get it out!" He'd made a career out of screaming and writhing around but not like this. He was back on his feet, dancing on the grave and throwing back his hair. On close inspection I could see a little black head poking out of his ear.

Having dragged the wriggling earwig out, I now had Robert Plant's ear wax down my little finger nail.

"Ooh. You could put that on eBay," Lembit laughed. "Except you're not allowed to sell body fluids."

Now how would you know a thing like that?

"I'm hungry. Can we get some lunch please?" I had a nice pub in mind.

"Aha! I've got just the thing." Swinging the car into a lay-by, Robert threw open the boot. "Here you are. We can share this." He handed me a soggy white paper bag. The tuna mayonnaise sandwich was seeping through it.

"How long have you had this?"

"Oh it was fresh yesterday. One of the roadies got it for me."

Crikey. This was a bit of a contrast to the excesses of the '70s that he'd been sharing with us all morning!

The next day he pressed something else into my hand. "Here, Our Elizabeth. I've had a really great time. I want you to have this."

And with that he was gone. I unfurled my fingers. It was a token for a free ice cream, from the seafront tea cabin in Peel. Well at least when I got there I'd know, if the cafe's not closed, with a smile I could get what I came for. "A cone please. Best make it a big one." And she's buying an ice cream of lemon.

Happy days. Ones which I wouldn't change for anything.

Even if, before long, having the odd day off from working a seven-day week was to almost cost me my sanity, my reputation, and most of my livelihood.

Soon the summer had melted away and it was back to the grind with the new show in Coventry.

Chapter Seventeen

I GOT THE NEWS

It all started with the familiar fannying about and ended in the usual costly cock-up.

David Clargo had made quite a name for himself on the back of our success in Northampton. He'd now been tasked with setting up a new BBC station in Coventry and had lined me up to present the breakfast show.

We'd agreed a fee and everything. We'd both signed the contract. I was committed, once again, to turning up like clock-work at 6am five days a week, bright-eyed and bushy-tailed and ready to give it all I'd got on BBC local radio for the next two years. He was committed to £300 a day. Nice.

With only a couple of weeks to go, he rang to say that he was very embarrassed but there'd been a change of plan. A spanner had been thrown in the works by senior management. Jon Gaunt, the one with the listener in her tights (or was it stockings?), had been on the BBC's local station in London since winning all his Sony awards and those glory days had made him a bit of a catch.

Now the big wigs wanted to send this 'Cov Kid' home. He was on bigger bucks than me and they needed to get their money's worth by putting him on the biggest show. Breakfast.

That meant there were now two of us contracted and potentially being paid to do the same slot.

Now there are plenty of BBC managers who think presenters can just be shifted around like tins of beans on the shelf, to increase sales or cut costs. After all, as long as we're not BBC staff, we are utterly dispensable. And flexible.

And we have no rights. Or feelings.

So their solution was simply to move me to the other end of the day. Oh well. Looking on the bright side, on Drivetime I didn't have to get up at the crack of dawn, but I'd still get the same fee. I was oblivious to the massive ructions this had all caused. The trouble was that poor David Clargo, who is human and does have feelings, had already signed somebody else up for that show. Lorna Bailey. Not to worry, he was told. She could be shunted off somewhere else. David was trying to keep all his balls in the air, everybody on side and was apologising to everyone, but seeds of seething resentment had been planted and they'd grow into something much worse.

The station was launched on September 3rd, 2005, in a blaze of publicity around the returning local lad made-good. Jon Gaunt. A couple of weeks in, all the top brass turned up for our launch party in a bar across the road. Pat Loughrey, the

Director of Nations and Regions, made a rousing speech. We were a fantastic new station with a fantastic line-up of presenters looking ahead to a fantastic future together. Andy Griffee welcomed Jon back to Coventry and me back into the BBC local radio fold. Trebles all round.

But what was Gaunty on about? "I hope you like early mornings kid," he was whispering in my ear. What? I was on at four in the afternoons. He was the one getting up with the lark. Not for much longer he wasn't.

Just before starting at Coventry he'd told the management that he'd been offered a 'Voice of White Van Man' type column in The Sun. The BBC had been considering its response. For two months. Now they'd finally decided that it would be a clash of interests so he couldn't do both. Naturally he'd have to decline The Sun's lucrative offer. According to the rumour mill it was worth £250,000 a year.

He was furious because none of the suits could come up with a convincing explanation why other names could remain on the BBC while still mouthing off in the papers. It was a complete no-brainer for him. After just six weeks on air the BBC was left with a multi-million pound new station and no Breakfast Show to speak of anymore. Gaunty had walked.

"Liz you wouldn't mind doing breakfast again would you?" I felt sorry for David.

"Not really. This new contract you've given me specifically says Drivetime."

"I'll give you an extra ten grand."

"I can start Monday."

Jon Gaunt has since left The Sun, been sacked by Talksport for calling a councillor a Nazi on air, and has been assisting those serving police officers who donned 'PC Pleb' t-shirts at the height of the Andrew Mitchell affair with their public relations strategy. Andy Griffee went to project manage one of Mark Thompson's grand designs, the latest redevelopment (again?) of Broadcasting House which came in at just over a billion pounds. Pat Loughrey left the BBC, trousering a now infamous, but secret at the time, £866,000. Helen Boaden took over his responsibilities. She had to stand aside (or step down) and then move sideways (or along – I get mixed up) during or following the Newsnight-slash-Savile scandal-slash-fiasco and Pollard inquiry into what she knew. Or didn't. Oh forget it. She was in charge anyway. For a bit. I think.

I wrote to her saying 'Hiya Helen. If you want to see life on the shop floor, come and spend a day here'.

She never replied. Or took up my offer.

The BBC had thrown a lot of money at this. Its new premises in Coventry were stunning and because it was adjacent to Coventry Cathedral and had grown out of a World War Two bomb site, the council called it the Phoenix Initiative. Next door they served Nando's chicken. It could yet turn out to be a complete turkey.

Wall-to-wall, floor-to-ceiling glass looked over a piazza and 16-inch plasma TV screens adorned the place. There was a sunny balcony. Air conditioning. Designer furniture. Showers. "We're so lucky to work here aren't we Liz?" I agreed with Clargo.

Around 50 other people on good money enjoyed this space – or at least that was the idea. I've never heard so much moaning. Mostly from those who'd been around for years. The BBC had been in Coventry for decades, first as a station in its own right, CWR, and then, when that failed, as an opt out from its sister station in Birmingham, WM. Some of the dozen or so old timers obviously felt swamped by all the new kids on the block and threatened by change. A few were enjoying the new challenge in the new place with all the new faces.

Bob Brolly was a cheery Irish fella who'd been a fixture on radio round these parts forever. He was on before me in the afternoons and always greeted me with a big hug, leaving me stinking of aftershave. You could always smell Bob coming!

Taking a walk through the city centre with Bob was like doing a presidential walkabout. Everyone knew him and wanted to shake his hand when he took me out to local restaurants and cafés, into the directors' dining room at Coventry City's home games, and round the bars to meet the fans after the match. He showed me round the patch and introduced me to everybody and anybody. A big welcome from a big-hearted man.

His producer, Fran, was a Coventry girl through and through and a real family woman. We hit it off and became friends for life. My own producer hardly spoke to me away from the show. I wasn't Lorna Bailey and, like so many others from the newsroom, she was obviously having trouble getting over the recent musical chairs in which one of their team had been left without a seat. Sod 'em. All I had to do was to trot out a bit of Abba or Captain & Tennille between the fluff they gave me to fill three hours and they left me alone. I wasn't proud – doing Drivetime was a piece of piss. Breakfast was a rude awakening.

It's hard to step into someone else's shoes. Especially if they're a self-styled 'local hero' and shock jock. Jon Gaunt's style was belligerent and so was his producer's. I don't think it was really him. With Gaunty he'd thought he had to play a part and he didn't cope well with the pressure of a live show. It was chaotic. He'd rant at all the reporters and junior staff. And me. (More than once he had me in tears). Guests were kept waiting so long they'd get fed up and not be there when he eventually tried to get them on, leaving a big hole in the show and dropping me right in it. None of it was malicious, and any problems on the show were always accidental – I just don't think he was in control or knew how to keep things running smoothly.

I'd see him through the glass bursting a blood vessel on the phone and stabbing his finger at the young lad sitting beside him who was a very bright graduate but a bit dreamy and talked slowly. I think his parents were Chinese. Anyway he was treated as a joke.

After the show, a hilarious post-mortem would be carried out in a nearby café. As the new girl at this blokey bacon butty fest I just had to bite my tongue and go with the flow at first. Poor Peter (the young graduate guy) would collar me afterwards for a cry on my shoulder. This wasn't right for me. Or the licence payers. It had been set up to suit Gaunty. Something had to change. And I wasn't the only one who thought so.

Things weren't going too well on the home front either. I'd been doing up a house I'd bought a couple of years earlier. My cowboy builder was making a meal of it and progress was painfully and expensively slow. I'd been working seven days a week and going there every Sunday afternoon after my 6 Music show to check on things and hand him another wad of hard-earned cash.

Something had to give. So I told Lesley Douglas that, reluctantly, I would have to give up working Sundays at 6 Music.

No wonder she seemed surprised. Normally nobody gives up on national radio for a little, local station. But she swiftly replaced me with her latest protégé, Russell Brand.

Gaunty's old producer had now been replaced too. The BBC Coventry and Warwickshire management had agreed that, if they wanted a different kind of breakfast show, it needed a different kind of leadership.

Andrew Bowman was the brightest and youngest of the bosses there and offered to step into the breach himself. He was brilliant, has since got out, climbed up the local radio ladder and is practically running the show (all of them) at BBC Radio Manchester.

Before he took over, the breakfast show's agenda was usually set the day before. I'd get calls in the evening telling me what the news would be the next day. The newsroom staff weren't clairvoyants. Some of them were just making an easy life for themselves.

So I'd be driving up to Coventry at 5am listening to 5 Live and I'd hear a story we should be covering but knowing damn well we wouldn't because, the way things were set up, we couldn't.

Nearby Nuneaton may have been nuked overnight but where were our reporters? "Oh sorry. Karen is on an off-rota day to-day." Meaning she's taking time out to research possible future stories – i.e. she's spending the day reading the papers. "Oh no can do. Angela is working from home today. Her cat isn't very well." Or "oh 'fraid not. Roger's not on shift until 10 and his mobile's switched off."

It really got up my nose that some people could get away with not pulling their weight. I'm not in any way putting myself in the same bracket as the guys who currently still go out day-in, day-out in Helmand Province risking life and limb. But imagine if they're not given the right briefings or boots or bullets by the supply chain back on base. They die.

If I didn't get the right material to put out on air I died on my arse.

Andrew Bowman wasn't taking any more of this shit. He shook up the Coventry newsroom operation, encouraged and nurtured the good journalists who had a sense of public service and were keen to get on, and as a result the station's output went from strength to strength. We had real, genuine issues right on our doorstep and it was time to tackle them.

Soon we were breaking news and properly reflecting what was really going on in the area, tackling topics like the decline of major industries, including the sudden loss of thousands of jobs at Peugeot. It was heartbreaking to hear grown men cry.

We had dying town centres so why did councils allow more and more out of town shopping malls to be built when the likes of Coventry actually was a 'ghost town'? Why were there so many deaths from infection in local hospitals? Who was supposed to be caring for the elderly? Why did some of our councils have such poor track records on schools, housing, and child protection. And of course potholes. Always potholes.

We had our fair share of disasters to deal with. Major flooding swept away listeners' homes. We couldn't fix the weather but why weren't the water companies and Environment Agency doing more? A huge warehouse blaze killed four firemen. Why were these huge hangers still unregulated?

Questions, questions, questions.

I believed that I was being paid to ask them and to get honest answers whatever they might be. Because the BBC, as far as I'm concerned, is there to provide a platform on which the facts are set out for the consideration of listeners and viewers.

It's not there to tell them how or what to think. Unfortunately, in my experience, too many people forget that.

During my time on local radio in both Northampton and Coventry, the issue of immigration was a hot topic and the mantra was 'immigration benefits us all. Multiculturalism is good. If you don't like people from other countries coming to live here then you must be racist and not let on air.'

I didn't think we should be censoring debate by excluding anyone who didn't fit into an unspoken editorial policy of what was 'right' or 'wrong'. For example, if someone wanted to come on the radio and say they don't like what's happening to their neighbourhood or town because of the scale and speed of change that's resulted through thousands of Poles moving in, you can't just label them bigots and ban them.

I don't buy it that the BBC has an intrinsic political bias – left or right. But, just as in my childhood when Blue Peter seemed to assume that children everywhere had lovely homes and gardens, it still has a comfortable middle-class view of life.

That might be OK with BBC pros, like me, who are university-educated and living in Chiswick or Didsbury, or in a leafy village. But that's not everyone's experience.

Take life in my home town of Rochdale. It's changed almost beyond my recognition. Here's a simple example. Just driving up the road to my mum's looking for somewhere to pick up some fast food – pies or a butty – I see that the traditional bakers I grew up with have all gone and been replaced by exotic takeaways. That's just a fact. And that kind of cultural change must be quite devastating, never mind inconvenient, for some locals. And if they want to talk about that they should be allowed to say so without being labelled ignorant or intolerant.

Unless, of course, they are spouting hatred, inciting violence and are so offensive that they're breaking the law. So I kept insisting that we must talk about immigration and its effects and that we must listen to people with all kinds of views. I kept saying that more and more people will vote for the BNP and for UKIP in sheer desperation if their voices were not heard and their concerns not addressed.

Why couldn't we have any of the local BNP councillors on the show alongside their Labour or Conservative or Green colleagues. Hello? Hadn't they been democratically elected too?

And if they were never on the air then how could their views ever be challenged? If they hung themselves with their own rope then all well and good. But to banish them because they're the 'nasty' party is censorship. And that's wrong.

Another hot topic was climate change. Guests were lined up to tell us we were destroying the planet and had better turn our heating down and stop using our cars. I didn't know if that was true. I still don't. Yet when I was introducing an item on extreme weather or flooding, I'd be handed introductions that would begin with 'we all know that our habits are causing climate change and that we are seeing the effects of it today in...'

Sorry but we didn't.

A red pen was going right through that. By all means let's hear from an expert who wants to put that view to the listeners. And one with the counter argument. But let's not load the discussion up front. And let's deal in facts.

So why did it seem sacrilegious to insist on doing just that? That there was also the possibility that the world's climate has been continually changing, and if it is now, that could be a part of natural, cyclical phenomenon?

BBC local radio needs a big rethink and a shake-up. We are all citizens of the globe now. People aren't so rooted and parochial as they were. And its 40 stations in England aren't even in the right places anymore. So the licence payers of, for example, a thriving, rapidly growing modern 'city' like Milton Keynes aren't served at all because it was just fields when the BBC last looked at the map over 40 years ago.

And it's not as though these services come cheap. BBC local radio is comparatively heavily staffed and tied into long expensive leases in prime city centre sites. Although last time I asked (about four years ago) local radio management couldn't even claim to know what each individual station actually cost to run, never mind how much they cost per listener.

Plus they're not even trying to do what it says on the tin anymore. Local radio decided some years ago not to be Local. Not to attempt to serve the entire Local community.

They now target by age. So exclusively to the over-55s. This was to appease commercial rivals and to stave off political pressure to shut down. 'Let the independent local stations have the younger audience while we go for the oldies, and maybe they'll leave us alone,' is the thinking.

So 'Dave and Sue' were born. A fictitious cosy married couple aged around 55 with kids and grandchildren. Sue was a school receptionist and Dave was a plumber. We had to have them in mind whenever we opened the microphone. And apparently these over 50s can only handle a roster of around 50 songs from around 50 years ago.

One day I was greeted by an almost tearful manager. "I'm

afraid Dave has died Liz." It took me a few seconds to realise he was living out the latest corporately dreamt-up scenario. Thankfully, that bollocks was knocked on the head when its architect and supremo was pensioned off.

Somebody needs to listen to *real* listeners and to work out why, with around two thirds of the UK hooked on the BBC's national radio stations, over 80% of us never bother to tune in to its local radio. It needs to get its licence payers on side.

Even me.

Last winter for example, I tried to find out if my house on the Kent coast would be inundated by the biggest storm surge in 60 years. In 1953 hundreds of people died. Could I and my property now be swept away?

So I headed to the local BBC Kent website for the latest news.

There was no information about what was happening locally.

I thought that the BBC Director of News, who runs local radio, would want to know that. So I emailed him.

From: Liz Kershaw
5/12/2013
12.14

I hope you're enjoying life at the BBC. I have for the last 30 years, but once again I am embarrassed to be watching the BBC news channel. Yesterday you spoke to staff from New Broad-casting House and said "the BBC is the best news organisation in the world. The question is, is it good enough? Do we break stories? Do we tackle important issues with sufficient impact? Are we keeping up with, or setting the pace?" Clearly not. As you know, the BBC News Division employs 8,000 people, 5,500 of whom are journalists. Hundreds of these journalists are located in the BBC's 40 local centres in England. The East Coast of England faces the greatest storms and worst risk of flooding, damage and potential loss of life for 60 years and yet we have News Channel co-presenters Carrie and Simon interviewing a non-plussed fireman from the Isle of Skye on the phone. He told them the storm had passed and, no, he wasn't called out and didn't expect to be either.

Reading out unconfirmed information sent in via text by a reader: "We will have to check that..." (Yes – preferably before you go on air in the future). Interviewing a reporter on a beach in Redcar, staggering around, outlining the potential problems hundreds of miles away in Suffolk, Norfolk, Essex and Kent. Where are the BBC's reporters? No doubt sitting comfortably in nice, warm offices scanning their screens, local papers and maybe Sky News. I have worked in local radio off and on for 30 years, I know what I'm talking about. I have a house on the beach in Kent and it is in danger of being inundated. I would like to know what the conditions are like down there. I pay a separate licence fee for that address and where is the service for which I'm paying?

Best wishes, yours sincerely, Liz.

He came back with just 20 words suggesting that I contact the local manager directly. When will the BBC 'Officer Class' listen and learn from its troops on the ground?

Later that very day, Nelson Mandela died and the News Division sent 140 people (ITN sent nine) all the way to South Africa to cover the long expected demise of a very old man. A great man. Who they were now all suddenly and reverentially referring to by his Xhosa clan name, Madiba.

Any coverage of the storms disappeared altogether. What about the elderly here whose homes could be inundated and their families who might be drowning? What about those of us who had spent that day battening down the hatches and preparing for a dreadful, possibly life-changing weather event? Apparently we could just sod off.

At Coventry, we hit a rich seam with our MPs' expenses. One local likely lad had claimed for new guttering and electric gates, false oak beams, stone cladding, a new leather corner sofa and a 42" TV. I got him to admit that while technically this hadn't broken any rules, it was immoral. So then, to deflect criticism from himself, he tried badgering me on air about how much I was being paid. He made a formal complaint to my boss when I wouldn't say at the time. I couldn't. The BBC wouldn't let me. There were confidentiality clauses in contracts.

But since those gagging orders have been scrapped I can now reveal what I was on.

I can reveal a lot of other things too.

A daily rate of £300 meant I could be on more than the basic salary of a backbench MP but only if I never had a holiday (we don't get paid for taking a break). Or if I was never ill. (Although being self-employed is quite the cure-all). Presenters don't get publicly funded juicy pensions or golden goodbyes. Or an office. Or even a desk to call our own for that matter. Or expenses for travelling to work. Or renovating our homes and landscaping our grounds.

But like MPs we do have to be across all the big issues, be able to quickly assimilate masses of information, be accomplished at public speaking and act as an advocate for the public who pay our wages. We also have to know the law, operate six computers at once, keep time, and be good company. So the best current affairs radio presenters have to be an MP, a barrister and even a reliable, friendly techie all rolled into one.

So should MPs be paid more? Well... while some of them clearly deserve double, others seem so shockingly stupid I wouldn't (as we say up north) 'give 'em house room'.

And I'd like to hear any politician, who thinks presenting is a doddle, doing a job swap one day with, say, Nicky Campbell. I know who'd get my vote.

I did meet one politician whose stellar performances in the media suggested he'd cut it if he turned his hand full time to broadcasting. Tony Blair. The BBC runs an annual scheme called School Report in which kids get to interview public figures for radio and TV. When a Coventry school was chosen to go to Number 10 I was invited along too.

From the mouths of babes eh? The children were nervous at first but Tony was great with them and when they got going it was really touching to see their trusting young faces as they hung onto his every word, eagerly awaiting his pearls of wisdom in answer to all their earnest questions. They were given a guided tour of some of the grand salons and posed with the PM for photos in the Cabinet Room. Back in his parlour, with the microphones turned off, Tony sank into his sofa, dropped his guard and made my jaw drop.

The conversation had come round to those green issues. Fossil fuels, carbon emissions, saving the planet blah, blah, blah. He suddenly came over all weary and sighed. "Liz, we in the UK could shut everything down and turn everything off. Everything. And within two years all our efforts would have been wiped out by what's happening in China now."

Blimey. I'd had other people arguing that on my show and I'd secretly agreed with them. But this was straight from a world leader whose government had signed us all up to the Kyoto Agreement in December 1997. All his energy policies and taxation strategies, including raising fuel duty and selling that to us as a green tax that would help save the planet, seemed geared to getting us to cut down on our consumption and drive us back to wooden huts and horses and carts.

OK. Now he was admitting that turning down my thermostat and wearing a woolly jumper around the house, not filling the kettle and crawling along at 60 on the motorway was a complete waste of my time. And energy. Right. I've never switched my telly off since.

My only regret is that I didn't make more of the moment. I should have asked him what he knew about UFOs. Or, more seriously, the WMDs in his Iraq dossier and what he thought about the death of Dr David Kelly.

Chapter Eighteen

SOMEBODY'S WATCHING ME

As well as desperately trying to help kick our operation into shape, I was having other troubles as well – and these ones had consequences for those closest to me.

It's important that the audience knows you're on their side. That you're their ally. Some of them may fondly think of you as a friend. Others may seriously believe you really are. The dangerous ones want to take that a stage further. They're convinced they're having a personal, even sexual, relationship with you and expect you to spend time with them 'in real life'. Every presenter has a similar story to tell. Some funny. Others shocking. And some plain scary.

Before email you'd get letters, sometimes with disturbing handwriting, the worst in green or red ink, offering outrageous compliments. 'You are more beautiful than Olivia Newton John' was one of the daftest.

Some believed you were married to them and even that they'd somehow fathered your children. Even though they were locked away in prison or hospital.

Unless they were actually threatening, the BBC's advice was to ignore them. Mmm. That sometimes wasn't enough! I'd known colleagues who'd had deranged admirers turning up outside work or even at their homes and had to get the police involved and go to court.

In the early summer of 2006 I'd had emails from one guy, praising me. I'd politely replied to thank him. Then he started asking me out.

I tactfully explained that wasn't going to happen and why. But then one day, when I was on air, a different kind of email altogether from him popped up on one of the screens. He said he was in my village. Well he'd got the name right. He said he knew my children were in the primary school. One of them was. And he said he was going round there before I got home. And he'd be waiting for me too.

I ran out of the studio as soon as I could and David Clargo stayed uncharacteristically calm. He knew to call the BBC Investigation Unit. That's manned by ex-CID officers and one of them was immediately on the case.

I rang Joe's school and at the end of the show drove like the clappers to get home. The stalker was using a false name but through his email provider he was contacted, and given a quiet warning at a meeting on neutral ground at Warwick Services on the M40. The BBC detective assured me that he'd left him in no doubt what he was in for if he persisted.

While all this was going on I was very scared. When I was told how easily anyone could find out where I lived I was absolutely terrified.

But I was assured that this guy posed no physical threat and that he just really liked me.

After that, someone emailed me for a while with constant abuse and then started on me on Facebook.

For all I know he could have been the stalker. Or even someone I actually knew. It goes to show. You never know who's out there.

One morning, after a staff meeting in Coventry, one of the reporters beckoned me to one side and whispered that he agreed with me about the breakfast show. He said he too was really unhappy about the production and content. I didn't really know him but I knew of him because he'd been the butt of most of the jokes from the breakfast team and I was sympathetic. He asked me out to lunch. This was the first of many in the rather posh local restaurants he introduced me to over several months. Always at his invitation but I always paid for myself. And for the pleasure of listening to him.

He told me he hated working there. He hated his colleagues. He refused to join the union. He wouldn't socialise with them. He'd got nothing in common with these people. He was better than them. He wasn't getting the recognition he deserved. He was too good for the place. He was going to walk.

He was bitter about his pay saying that, at 45, the BBC was forcing him to live with his parents. He told me that he'd been at odds politically with his father, now a retired chief constable, for policing the miners strike on behalf of the Thatcher government in the early '80s. However, his father was delighted his son was now a BBC man. But he insisted he didn't belong at the BBC at all, he'd rather be a freelance hack running his own agency selling stories to the tabloids.

At first he seemed like my greatest supporter, saying how much he rated me. That we were both intelligent, creative, like-minded people. He was certainly very bright and articulate. And he wasn't your stereotypical BBC local radio man-in-slacks. He was unkempt. Bohemian. An eternal student. A rock 'n' roll rebel. 'Crikey,' I thought. 'I've got a fan and ally in the newsroom. Hallelujah!'

However, the management didn't seem as keen on him. I'd hear bosses bemoaning his attitude, his dishevelled appearance and his work. He'd been at the BBC in Coventry for eight years already but they still didn't know how to handle him. His line manager wanted me to help out. Or rather she wanted out, I came to realise. Her husband was seriously ill and she was taking a lot of time off. And even when she was in the building she wasn't on the ball. I'd been warned before I started at Coventry by an old colleague who now worked in Birmingham. "Watch her, Liz. she's only there because they had to move her out of here. Nobody trusted her."

"I'm at my wit's end with him Liz," I was told. "But he seems extremely fond of you. Can you have a chat and tell him how much we all value him."

After the station had been on air for a few months, it held a series of receptions at its new outposts in public libraries. The press came and so did local bigwigs, including the mayor and mayoress. Nobody else ever brought their mum and dad.

I was getting a few nudge-nudge, wink-wink comments from a couple of colleagues. "Oh are you going to lunch again? Do you think he likes you then?" They were so bitchy and parochial. So I couldn't be bothered to explain about platonic friendship. I just smiled. Let them think what they liked if that's what they got off on. They really should get a life. I wonder now if they were winding my lunch date up the same way.

Before long he got just as tedious. I'd given him plenty of support and advice but he didn't help himself. He was still a loner and wouldn't join in. He wouldn't come to works parties and he was torpedoing his own career. He knew how to work the system, spending afternoons in the pub, going missing, not pulling his weight. He'd even drop me in it on air so he was letting me down personally as well as professionally now. I could see why management was despairing of him. He was his own worst enemy. I didn't understand him. He saw success as an entitlement so he wouldn't put in the effort or take the chances he was given. That wasn't my way.

I was working seven days a week, two on 6 Music and Monday to Friday in Coventry, going to bed before my children and getting up at dawn. And as well as a family and home to look after, I had other serious pressing problems. My brother was living on the edge and I'd got builders ripping me off, not to mention a stalker threatening to abduct my kids while I was at work.

And... oh yes, by the by... I was fighting off cervical cancer. I'd had one operation 10 years earlier after a dodgy smear test. Now the scary cells were making a comeback and I'd have to go under the knife again. To fit it in with work, and because I didn't fancy another NHS special, I went private. The operation was arranged for a Saturday morning and I was told I'd need a few days to recover. So I got permission to pre-record that weekend's two 6 Music shows and took the Monday and Tuesday off at Coventry. I was too embarrassed to tell anybody why.

After being laid up for four days with Paul nursing me and waiting on me hand and foot, I knew it wouldn't go down well if, after only being there a few months, I had any more time off.

So I was back in the car at dawn on the Wednesday. It was too soon. During the show I could feel something was very wrong. I had to rush to the loo during the five minute news break, deal with it as best I could and then dash home.

I'll spare you the gruesome details but the specialist told me that if things didn't heal I'd have to face up to a full hysterectomy. I was absolutely dreading that. The idea of losing my womanhood was awful and so was the prospect of having to take weeks off work.

Would the BBC wait for me? Would they have me back? Would I be out on my ear and broke again? As well as not being a proper woman anymore?

All in all, I had so much else on my plate that I simply didn't have time, energy or inclination to deal with my troubled colleague and his, to me right then, non-problems. Never mind trying to shag him as he was to claim later.

I'd realised by now that he knew nothing about my woes. Because he'd never asked. It was all about him. He wasn't a true friend or ally. In fact he'd started having a go at me about anything and everything. How much was I earning? Why was I invited to that and not him? More and more petty jealousies came to the fore. I learned that he wanted to be a presenter. Preferably on a national radio station like me. He was jealous of me and at the same time happy to hang on my coat-tails to further his career.

I'd been getting more reluctant to spend time with him outside of work. And then he well and truly crossed the line. He took me on a short drive early one evening in April, 2006, because he insisted he had a great local story to share with me.

It was still sunny when we swung off the main road from Coventry to Kenilworth and into some woods. At the end of a rough track a group of men was standing round a parked VW camper van. As our car approached they slowly started to walk towards us looking menacing. "What the hell is this?" I asked.

He explained what 'dogging' is and I realised these guys weren't happy that we were spying on their illicit and illegal activity from a BBC branded vehicle. So now I was panicking and pleading with him to get us out of there. He was roaring laughing as he put his toe down and got us away just before they could get their hands on the door handles.

He drove to Kenilworth and parked up at a pub near where he lived. He was boasting that the landlord had barred him so it was obviously a badge of honour that we got served. I was recognised by a group of students who were surprised but pleased to see me there. He was irritated by this attention and went over to have a word. They were laughing as he walked back to me.

Could all this get any more odd? I told him I thought his behaviour was a bit weird and, anyway, people at work were talking about us which was starting to get difficult. I needed to know what he was thinking to make sure that spending time alone with him was not all going to end in tears. The dogging experience had been a new low and I had to sort things out. What was the real reason for him getting me on my own outside work? Was he maybe expecting more than friendship from me? I really didn't expect a yes but I had to ask.

Actually I was wondering by now if he might be gay and too scared to be honest about it. Everyone talks to their mates about their love lives. He never went near the subject. He just didn't behave like everybody else did. There was absolutely none of the physical contact that's normal between friends or colleagues, gay or straight, married or single, male or female. Nothing. No greetings with a kiss on the cheek. No arm round the shoulders. No hand on the arm. No hugs. Nothing. He was almost asexual and I'd started to notice that he didn't really laugh with his eyes. And, at 45, who still lives with their parents?

We could have talked it through sensibly, laughed it all off and moved on. But he just blew up. His reaction was totally disproportionate and anti-social.

I remember the horsey bits best.

"Yeah, right. I want kids. If I did get a girlfriend she'd be 25. Still fertile."

"I beg your pardon?!"

"Well you're hardly a fecund young filly are you? More like a menopausal old nag".

I was absolutely stunned. What a way to respond. It was particularly hurtful as I was facing 'having it all taken away'. Well. There was certainly no pretence at respect or friendship now. How dare he speak to me like that after how nice I'd been to him. This was totally over the top, vicious and unnecessary. What a nasty, hurtful, rude bastard. What a fucking cheek.

He got characteristically superior and said he was off. I told him if he left me there, that was it. He walked out. Fantastic. Miles from home and on my own. I tried to find a taxi but then went back inside the pub to wait for a mini-cab. The students called me over. What was I doing with him? He was well known round the local pubs. Barred even. I explained I worked with him and I'd thought he was my friend. Eventually the cab came and took me to my car in Coventry and I drove home.

Did I leave him some voice messages or text him? Probably. I was as furious as I was upset. And he'd frightened me. I didn't want anything more to do with him outside of work again. I could have gone snitching to management. But this was personal and I dealt with it in my usual way. Directly, myself and very clearly. And for me that was the end of it. For nearly seven years anyway.

Meanwhile, he spent time in a mental hospital. He'd been off work for months and had asked for redundancy before he ended his life in a psychiatric unit in October, 2012. It was devastating. I was heartbroken for his mother. I know what it's like to have someone you love imploding and running you ragged. I had every sympathy. And I understand why a grieving family looks for someone to blame. But their troubled son's problems were not caused by me.

What a waste. He had some great qualities including a sharp inquiring mind and a rich radio voice. I was very sad it had come to this because, at one time, I had been genuinely fond of him and wanted to help.

Mental illness is still a taboo. The signs are often dismissed by families and firms alike because it's somehow shameful and people don't know how to handle it. But a sufferer can be as dangerous for their co-workers as someone coughing over them with TB. Even now, with more awareness that mental health problems need to be taken seriously, only one single penny is spent on mental health for every hundred spent on the NHS. And 34 out of 51 local authorities have reduced their budgets for mental health since 2010. This can't be ignored.

If the symptoms in this case hadn't gone unrecognised and had been properly dealt with, this colleague might have got better and still been alive today.

Sadly I've loved and lost enough people to drink, drugs and mental illness to know that much.

Chapter Nineteen

PANIC (HANG THE DJ)

Who'd have thought that little old me would ever be caught up in a Royal scandal? That my name would, for a few months, be inextricably linked with the Queen's?

And that I'd be forced to mysteriously disappear for three months by the BBC.

In July, 2007, portraits of Her Majesty Queen Elizabeth II were suddenly slapped next to headshots of Liz Kershaw DJ across all the papers and TV news bulletins. Alongside photos of the Blue Peter cat and Pudsey Bear. At least the Daily Mail distinguished me with a banner splashed across my face. It had one word on it. 'CHEAT'.

So what had this gang of four got in common? Well, we'd all been shafted by the BBC. Or, as it was actually reported at the time, we were all at the heart of what came to be known as The Great BBC Competition Scandal of 2007.

A couple of weeks earlier the Queen had taken the rare step of formally and publicly complaining to the BBC. She'd had good cause. She'd been made to look like a rather nasty piece of work in a TV trailer. A film crew had been allowed access to a photo session at Buckingham Palace. The Queen was to pose for the renowned rock photographer Annie Lebowitz. Fully robed in full Knight of the Garter regalia, and being a stickler for punctuality, she'd been filmed hurriedly sweeping along the Palace corridors to honour her appointment time with Lebowitz but the footage was cut to suggest the Queen was leaving rather than arriving at the shoot and the trailer left viewers believing she'd taken umbrage with the photographer and had stormed out in a temper. The Queen, it seemed, was prone to behaving like a proper prima donna.

Having now worked my way through most of its departments since 1984, I was ashamed of the BBC but not all that surprised.

This was an incident waiting to happen.

I'd become resigned, by now, to the fact that getting rid of experienced in-house programme makers and replacing them with cheaper, younger production staff and desperately competitive independent production companies, would one day lead to a major embarrassment. Still, it was one thing not knowing the ropes and failing to properly contract a performer. Or to forget to arrange the necessary work permits for an American band, so that their session had to be cancelled and a radio show ruined. It was quite another to misrepresent the Monarch.

The BBC grovelled profusely and the Controller of BBC 1, Peter Fincham, was 'resigned'. We've since been told, at a House of Commons Public Accounts Select Committee hearing in September, 2013, by the erstwhile Director General Mark Thompson that he was advised by lawyers that, as this Controller hadn't been directly involved in the scam or even aware of it until the complaint from the Palace, there were no actual legal grounds on which to sack this senior manager. However, the Chairman of the BBC Trust, Sir Michael Lyons, was determined that somebody must pay so Fincham was publicly sent packing. With, as the public would only learn years later, half a million quid of licence payers' money. He went to an even more lucrative job running ITV.

That done, Thompson, a devout Catholic, who, after being educated by Jesuits, had seriously considered the monastic life himself before opting for the media, then decided to purge himself by opening a corporate confessional. An email was sent to all of us. Were there any other production practices that were a bit dodgy and that could potentially land the BBC in more hot water?

Er... not half.

At 6 Music we'd been duping the public almost since Day One. I'd tried telling Director of Radio Jenny Abramsky at our meeting in the summer of 2003 that a Today programme deception that had preceded the death of Dr. David Kelly was just the tip of the iceberg. That I'd observed a rather relaxed attitude to detail on the shop floor. And that potential whistle-blowers needed someone to turn to. So how about a presenters' guru to whom the likes of me could voice our concerns without queering our pitch with management?

PANIC (HANG THE DJ)

Now, four years later, we were suddenly being asked to collectively come clean. As good Catholics like Thompson and Kershaw-the-convent-girl knew, confession equals automatic forgiveness and absolution.

So what was my sin?

Well, I'd always thought it wasn't quite right to 'fake' competitions as part of a recorded show. While I took genuine professional pride in the fact that I could pull it off – sounding live when I wasn't – I'd feel really bad when I was next in live and saw all the emails that listeners had sent in at my behest and in good faith while I'd actually been off enjoying myself elsewhere.

It made me feel like a bit of a shit actually.

But recording a show to get a day off meant presenters still got paid, which was nice, and it suited the 'suits' who wanted on-air continuity and consistency while accommodating some work/life balance for us DJs.

It had been agreed by Lesley Douglas in my contract that permission for pre-records always had to be sought first from management. In the case of mine, my producer or I would email 6 Music's Head of Programmes, Ric Blaxill. Sometimes he would apparently refer the request upwards before he came back with the go-ahead. I can't remember such a request ever being refused. So everyone seemed very happy and in the loop.

Well maybe not Mark Thompson. Yet.

Since starting at 6 Music, over five years earlier, I'd had six producers. The best one I've ever known in all my time in music radio was the fifth, Leona McCambridge. We got on like a house on fire. It was a very sad day for me when she was moved off my show in 2006 and replaced by Jude Adam. But she was being promoted to weekdays and Leona deserved every success so I was delighted for her.

She was so bright, knowledgeable, thorough and conscientious and also blunt to the point of being hilarious. It was her no-nonsense honesty that prompted her to immediately respond to Thompson's trawl for misdemeanours with an email outlining the practice on 6 Music of pre-recording shows and the inevitable faking of competitions within those shows.

We had no idea, no concept whatsoever, about what would happen next.

On Wednesday, July 17th, 2007, into the following Thursday morning, I spent hours dressed in a pink satin gown with a white fur stole and tiara waving a white satin gloved hand at crowds on the streets of London from the back of a pink Rolls Royce. At the wheel of FAB 1 was a chauffeur in full grey uniform and a peaked cap.

I'd been in my element playing Lady Penelope, my childhood heroine, for a TV special. The press officer from the old days at Radio 1, Jeff Simpson, had gone on to produce Top of the Pops and was now making a film about the iconic TV series Thunderbirds for BBC4. This new BBC TV network had smaller budgets than he was used to and, feeling the pinch, he'd asked me to help. He knew I'd jump at the chance to do this just for fun. It was best to film in the early hours to make the most of the capital's relatively light traffic so we worked from midnight until around 5am.

I was knackered, so the next day I was still recovering and flopped out on the sofa when the phone rang. It was David Clargo from Coventry. He'd known I wouldn't be in work that morning. (Obviously you can't record a breakfast show with fast moving news so he'd agreed to give me that morning off and booked a dep). And he would be seeing me tomorrow.

So what could he possibly want at 2.15 on a Thursday afternoon?

"We just want you to know that we are so very, very sorry about what's happening at 6 Music. David Holdsworth and I want you to know that you have our 110% support."

Eh?

What?

"Oh sorry Liz. Didn't you know?" He was panicking now. "Oh you'd better speak to Lesley Douglas. Sorry. Sorry Liz. See you tomorrow. We're thinking of you. Good luck. Bye."

It took me another half an hour of frenzied phoning to get through to Lesley, the Controller of Radio 2 and 6 Music. She said that she was about to have a very strange conversation with me. In just 15 minutes time, at 3pm, I was to be named (and shamed) by the Director General in a major announcement to the media.

Mine was one of six programmes that had been chosen from the many 'admissions' he'd received in response to his call for a collective mea culpa.

And under no circumstances must I talk to the media.

Director of Radio, Jenny Abramsky (everybody's boss), then rang me and apologised for the fact that, unfortunately, because my show was eponymous, my name would be dragged through the mud and that would be hurtful but, she continued, she absolutely knew that none of this was of my doing. 'It was a production matter' and that's why she was definitely not taking me off air.

So what did she mean by 'a production matter'?

THE BIRD AND THE BEEB

Well, in a live radio situation the presenter has complete control of the microphone and output. With that power comes responsibility. So if you say or do something wrong you're to blame. And in 20 years on national radio I'd only got into hot water twice; once for smashing up a studio and once for describing working from home as 'cottaging'. Otherwise I'd managed not to swear or drop me or the BBC in it.

But in a pre-recorded show, the producer was directing operations and, should the situation require it, was duty bound to correct my cock-ups. And as a back up, all pre-recorded output had to be listened to and signed off by their boss. This practice would become pivotal in 2008 when Russell Brand's recorded phone calls to Andrew Sachs were broadcast with the approval of Lesley Douglas.

I was relieved I had Jenny's support and understanding. But there was one thing I just didn't get. And I don't think she did either. I was genuinely puzzled when I asked "but Jenny, why just my show?"

She explained that I'd pre-recorded competitions and that the audience had been deceived into thinking they were live.

Yes, yes, yes.

I already knew all that.

And not only was I not denying it, Leona had volunteered that information to Thompson in the first place. But I was fast realising that Jenny didn't yet know that this was common practice and common knowledge. It never occurred to me or Leona that we would be singled out and held up as an example.

It was quite obvious that Jenny was completely in the dark and she was having to rely on information from her sources. And, until now, those sources had not included me.

PANIC (HANG THE DJ)

A few minutes later I watched News 24 in disbelief as Mark Thompson stood in front of Broadcasting House to purge himself and the BBC.

Until 20 minutes before Thompson named my show, I'd no inkling that I was about to be publicly shamed. Nobody had bothered to discuss it with me. Thompson hadn't investigated this story. He hadn't checked his facts. He couldn't possibly be sure of the full picture. And yet he was the BBC's most senior journalist. Its Editor in Chief.

That afternoon, Jon Sopel, on News 24, smugly reported that I had made up calls to cover up the fact that nobody really phoned my show.

Bollocks. The BBC was just making things up now.

Channel 4 News reported that my deceit 'was systematic' and all the news outlets reported that 'a new producer took over at Christmas (2006) and stopped the practice immediately'.

Absolute crap.

Someone was really spinning a yarn.

The public was being told that Liz Kershaw, in cahoots with her producer, had decided, off their own backs, to pre-record shows and fake competitions. That we were somehow mavericks and that my show was a one-off aberration that had only just been brought to light.

Lesley Douglas was quick to assure me that the media must have got the wrong end of the stick.

Really?

I did a bit of digging and found out that the line about 'a new producer took over at Christmas and stopped the practice immediately' was actually written – word for word – in an official BBC press release.

The assertions that the 'faking' of competitions was confined to my show on 6 Music and only during the time in which Leona was producer, and that it was very obviously outlawed, covert, and came as a complete surprise to everybody else, was damaging and utter crap.

Nobody had stopped anything. Pre-recordings had happily continued under Leona's replacement.

The day after the news broke, I put all this in a letter to Jenny and Lesley.

Jenny was genuinely shocked and told me I must inform Lesley. That's a bit rum isn't it? Me, a freelance disc jockey, needing to tell a BBC Controller what was going out on her own networks?

Jenny also told me I must "rebuild trust with my audience" by apologising on air the following day. So, I drafted what I was going to say and she emailed "I'll be thinking of you. Love, Jenny." On Saturday, July 21st, Lesley Douglas rang me when I was on the train to work to advise me how to open that morning's show. Including which records I should avoid.

I did what I'd been told and began my show with:

"First of all... I am being my usual cheerful self today in 'the show must go on style' but please don't mistake bravado for arrogance. I can assure you I am anything but happy clappy after this week.

"So those of you who've seen the papers and telly I'm sure you've got lots of questions. I can't go into detail because there is a BBC investigation underway into the production of my recorded shows and I've been asked not to talk about it in detail.

"But you deserve some answers before today's show.

"In 2005, I presented 250 shows on 6 Music. 243 were live.

The Radio 1 gang in 1988

The kids are all right! My dad visits Radio 1 in 1988

I know my plates. Peel doing Walters' washing-up in 1987

Born To Run. 'Just wrap your legs round these velvet rims. And strap your hands across my engines.' In LA on my last holiday before I became a mum, 1989

And my nights out with Paul were numbered with Sam on his way!

Bouncing baby Sam, just days before being struck down by meningitis

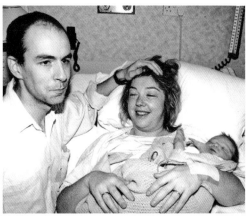

More drugs Liz?... asks new dad Paul

Proud mum Liz with Sam and Joe, 2003

Start 'em young! Two-year-old Joe works his passage across Lapland, reporting for Radio 5 Live

Radio Royalty! (And Bruno). With my heroine and mentor, Annie Nightingale, at The Savoy, 1989

Doreen Davies, who gave me my
big break at Radio 1 in 1987

Ooh Gary Davies. With Radio 1's
'bit in the middle' celebrating 30
years of fun, 1997

The boy next door. Me and Binksy
at the London Hilton in 2003.
Playing out together after 43
years (and still counting)

The jubillant BBC Radio Northampton Breakfast crew at the Sony Radio Academy Awards in 2002. Standing left to right: Antonia (our roving reporter) Clargo (the boss) Joanne (my ace producer) and sitting right, trouble-shooting supremo Nikki Holliday

Friends reunited. Leeds legend Martin Kelner with his old Radio Aire mate, Helen Boaden, (now BBC Director of Radio) at the same do

Bird spotting. DJs past and present at Radio 1's 40th birthday party, 2007

Pop meets politics. Drinks on the House of Commons terrace with my old friend and now LibDem MP Tessa Munt. Oh, and Jimmy Page of Led Zep

With Annie Nightingale, at the Sony Awards in 2003. And right, a guest of The Zep at the premiere of their 2012 film Led Zeppelin: Celebration Day

This charming man. Tony Blair at Downing Street, 2007, when I took a group of Coventry kids to grill the PM. Privately he explained the futility of the UK trying to cut down on its energy usage

The future starts here. At Radio 2, 2001, young Sam tells William Hague what he needs to do if the Tories are to win a General Election. He resigned as party leader not long after! A great bloke

Democracy in action. Speaking "as a licence payer" outside Broadcasting House during the brilliant Save 6 Music campaign, 2010. The listeners spoke in their tens of thousands, the BBC Trust had to listen, the suits were beaten, the people won. A much-loved, unique service was saved. Result!

PANIC (HANG THE DJ)

Seven were recorded earlier because either staff were on holiday or I couldn't be here because of a kid's birthday or because I was live on Radio 2 at the same time. Lots of radio shows are recorded.

"This one has been singled out because in order to make my show sound live, the Ruff Riff Competition went ahead and I was asked to get you to take part when in reality, on those seven occasions, nobody could really win. If you took part you probably feel quite cheated. Quite right. I never saw your texts but I read your emails and felt uncomfortable that you'd believe that I was really here when I wasn't. I even replied to some of you but I never spoke out to stop it.

"So I apologise unreservedly. For being a coward. I'm sorry.

Some of you will be listening for the first time because you have never heard of this show before but have seen this show flagged up and are curious. You're very welcome. We have a good time on a Saturday morning and I hope you stick with us.

"There will be those who have never liked me and are tuning in to hear me squirm. Enjoy your schadenfreude.

"There are those of you who feel betrayed and want to know what the hell I was thinking. Please wait for all the facts to come out and then make your mind up about me... Sorry again for being part of a charade that deceived you.

"And there are those of you who are thinking 'oh what the hell? I enjoy the show, just get on with it Liz'.

"OK."

After the show, Lesley texted me to say she admired me for my courage in getting through it all and that I should now go and enjoy my family holiday. A year later, the BBC suggested to OFCOM that apologising to the audience was my own idea.

That management hadn't been aware that I was going to until I did.

I had hundreds of supportive emails from the public. They were so lovely. And certainly helped me feel a lot better, so I've kept them ever since in the same folder with all the crappy stuff from the time.

Meanwhile, I'd got a holiday booked and was getting out of the country for a few days. I was off to Ireland to meet my late grandma's relatives for the first time ever. Sadly this wasn't the happy family reunion I'd been looking forward to. They were clearly wary of their now infamous cousin. My reputation as a scoundrel had preceded me. One relative even announced I was a gangster. That hardly made me feel any better. Now I'd gone from being a radio presenter hosting a show that occasionally pre-recorded its output – the same as loads of others – to being a criminal.

I landed back in the UK on the evening of July 31st to find a phone message from Lesley Douglas. "Nothing scary," she said. "I just wanted to update you." I rang her immediately but she texted to say she couldn't speak to me. It was another three days before she did. She told me not to come in the next day. I was being taken off 6 Music until September. And the two weeks I was booked in for on Radio 2 in August were also cancelled. I've never been on Radio 2 since.

I tried to get a reason out of Lesley and Jenny but I never did.

I later learned that the Deputy Director General Mark Byford, along with Chief Operating Officer Caroline Thomson, had been grilled by a Commons Select Committee on July 24th, 2007, and MPs had demanded to know why I was still being allowed to broadcast on the BBC.

PANIC (HANG THE DJ)

At that Committee hearing, Caroline Thomson told MPs that "the producer who was responsible for the period in which these problems occurred (Leona) is no longer producing the programme. When the new producer arrived, at Christmas, they saw the practice and immediately stopped it."

This was now the party line. If only Byford and Caroline Thomson had gone along to that committee having been made aware of all the facts, those MPs could have been told the truth. That recording competitions had been accepted production practice in BBC radio – that actually, it was possibly endemic.

And that if the BBC ditched me, it might have to lose some of its bigger stars such as Jo Whiley, Tony Blackburn and Dermot O'Leary – just three people whose shows were subsequently reported to Ofcom for also pre-recording competitions.

And, the tight knit Senior Management Club would have been forced to accept responsibility and take the rap themselves.

On Monday, August 6th, I got the biggest shock yet.

I was at the coast and got permission to go in to Radio Kent to access my BBC email. That's when I made the disturbing discovery that all the most recent emails arranging pre-record-ed shows, had disappeared from my inbox. Jenny Abramsky seemed as horrified as me when I told her that and immediately used her considerable clout to get IT to find them on the server and reinstate them to my account.

She also asked IT to find out who'd deleted them. But they found it had been done from a 'hot desk' so they couldn't tell her.

Jenny now accepted that the BBC had put out false informa-tion about the timing of my new producer's arrival and the BBC's awareness of pre-recording on my show.

Then I heard from poor, earnest Leona that she'd been sacked.

Lesley Douglas had taken the trouble to go down personally to her home in Hampshire and, with Leona's mum there for support, had delivered the devastating news that she was finished at the BBC.

The Radio 3 Controller, Roger Wright, was investigating all this for Abramsky. I'd been told that he didn't need to speak to me but I insisted that he did. I needed to tell him that it was unfair for the BBC to single out Leona and stop me speaking out about it.

I laid it on the line to Roger in no uncertain terms. Leona had done nothing that her predecessors had not done. Jude Adam had stopped nothing whatsoever.

Leona, as far as I could tell, was nothing but a sacrificial lamb. It was disgusting, a disgrace.

Roger Wright informed me that his inquiry was confined to certain dates set by Mark Thompson so most of the evidence I was giving him was inadmissible because of that.

Similarly, Jenny wished to impress upon me the importance of protecting the BBC brand. She was determined that as few people as possible would get hurt by all this.

Oh I see. So if this was an exercise in damage limitation, what about the collateral damage? Me.

I was really scared now.

All this was very wrong. The truth of the situation was being deliberately ignored. I decided it was time to take this up a level. I'd known Mark Byford, the Deputy Director General, socially for years and I thought at least he'd understand my concerns because he was a qualified lawyer. I rang his mobile and started to explain that I felt that clumsy attempts at a cover up were getting out of hand. That management wouldn't be able to justify singling out Leona in a court of law and that the BBC would end up with egg on its face. Suddenly he blurted "I can't have this conversation Liz," and terminated it abruptly.

Meanwhile I couldn't get anything out of Lesley Douglas. When would I go back on air? Next week? Ever? What was going on? By now I was relying on programme listings on the 6 Music website to find out if I was expected to turn up for work or not.

How can it be right for someone to find out if they are on the radio by having to surf the internet?

Then, out of the blue, in October, Jenny rang me to say she was putting me back on air. But first I had to go and speak to Lesley who said she understood what I'd been through and how sorry she was, as a mother, because she'd been at her wits end herself at times, waking up in the night and worrying if she was going to lose her job. But now it was all over.

Welcome back Liz. Kind of.

What she didn't say was that while I'd been suspended from 6 Music, she'd signed up a new duo, Adam and Joe, for my slot. Did she not expect me back? When I asked, she put me straight in a shirty text: 'That is not your slot!'

A minion then rang to say my show had been shortened by an hour and shunted to later in the afternoon.

When I tried to contact the Controller herself, all I got back was that I should get over it and move on. But the shockwaves just kept on coming.

I wasn't warned of the series of on-air apologies that Ofcom had insisted were broadcast at the start of my show. Or that I was to be held up as the bad girl of broadcasting to the tens of thousands of BBC staff and presenters at its Restoring Trust Workshops.

The last thing anyone wants to do is drop their colleagues in it. But I'd had enough.

Me and Leona had been honest and now she'd lost her career and I'd been publicly punished. Meanwhile, cowards who'd kept their heads down behind their desks and said nothing had so far got off scot-free.

I'd given Jenny Abramsky enough hints that other shows had been doing the same as us without ever naming names.

Now I decided to give her just one.

Since becoming Controller of 6 Music, Lesley Douglas had replaced most of its starting line-up with comedians – Stephen Merchant, John Richardson, Russell Howard, John Holmes, and later, Adam and Joe. She always had an eye for young male talent and in 2006 reeled in her biggest catch – Russell Brand.

She'd given him my Sunday show when I suddenly gave it up in March, 2006, because I needed one day a week off work. Leona carried on producing that slot. For one week and one week only. Russell Brand immediately took against Leona and being told how to behave on the BBC so he rang Lesley Douglas.

Leona was told to go back to the office and Head of Programmes, Ric Blaxill finished the recording of the show – complete with competitions that had staff posing as contestants.

In all the time that me and Leona were being hung out to dry, everybody kept quiet about Russell and Ric doing the same thing.

But now that Jenny Abramsky had been told, she got stuck in straight away and the matter was finally reported to Ofcom.

Evidently she wasn't the only one who was shocked.

"Liz there's a call for you." It was seconds after 10am. I'd just come off the air in Coventry.

Oh. OK. Somebody must be keen to speak to me.

"What the hell are you playing at?"

"Sorry?"

"What do you think you're doing dragging Russell into all this?"

"Well I just want a level playing field. A bit of fairness actually."

"You do realise you could be making things a lot worse for you and Leona don't you?"

I was shaking but I wasn't going to show it. "Really? I don't see how. But thanks for your 'concern'." Gulp.

Suddenly Leona won her appeal against dismissal for gross misconduct and was 'unsacked'. Quietly. The press office never announced that. It seemed to have finally dawned on BBC HR that with the evidence we had between us, they'd be taken to the cleaners if Leona took them to a tribunal. Now she was 'leaving by mutual consent'.

Rubbish. She loved her job. It was her life. Only a big wad of licence payers' money could've convinced her to go. But even though we still got together for a gossip and a giggle, I could tell that the subject of her departure from the BBC was strictly off limits.

The following summer, Ofcom announced its rulings. On July 30th. My 50th. Nobody had warned me that I'd be getting splashed across The Mail as I splashed in the Med.

Happy birthday Liz. This time it was quite a star-studded party as other BBC shows and stations had now been rumbled.

THE BIRD AND THE BEEB

Radio 1 got a bill for £75,000 for faking Jo Whiley competitions after they'd been brought to light by a journalist. The BBC tried to defend poor Jo. The press were told that obviously she hadn't realised that she'd been talking to Radio 1 staff, not real 'listeners'.

BBC London was billed £25,000 for similar deceptions on the Tony Blackburn show which had been flagged up by a listener.

Programmes controlled by Lesley Douglas cost the BBC £220,000.

6 Music was fined £115,000 for my show, £17,500 for the Russell Brand show and £17,500 for Clare McDonnell's programme.

For Dermot O'Leary's show, Radio 2 was fined £70,000.

As well as fining the BBC in 2008, Ofcom, in its adjudication, also slated Thompson and his board for being selective in what it had chosen to report 12 months earlier. It ruled that BBC senior management had no right to decide what was serious and what was none of Ofcom's business.

I'd been trying to tell them for over a year. If the papers had known back in July, 2007, about the Tony Blackburn, Jo Whiley, Dermot O'Leary or Russell Brand shows, would they have made headlines out of me?

I doubt it.

In September, 2013, The Times reminded its readers of the whole saga. Unsurprisingly now, with all these big names to spice up the story, I didn't even get a mention.

Chapter Twenty

IT'S THE END OF THE WORLD AS WE KNOW IT

So where did all this leave me then?

Well, in late 2007, I was getting to grips with my new compact 6 Music show. I was still in touch with Leona and I was happy to hear she had created her own niche in her boyfriend's conference business.

I was still scared of Lesley Douglas. But not for much longer.

By now, Russell Brand had moved to Radio 2 because in Lesley Douglas's eyes he could do no wrong. However, left in the hands of an independent company with only a young producer to keep control, his Saturday night show was soon in trouble. We all know the story now of how Jonathan Ross and Russell

Brand called Andrew Sachs and left unsavoury messages about his granddaughter and how that was heard on October 18th, 2008, by an investigative reporter. He immediately tipped off the papers, which, when the BBC failed to face up to the initial outcry, whipped up the nation into an angry mob.

If that show had been live and the obscenities had been instantaneously broadcast unchecked, there would have been demands for the presenters to go, an official BBC apology and maybe some regulatory sanctions. But that wasn't the case. It was recorded. And the producer was au fait enough with BBC rules and standards to check about leaving that content in this show with Radio 2's Head of Compliance, Dave Barber.

I knew Dave and he would have been understandably twitchy for several reasons. Firstly, he was lovely but a bit of an old woman. Secondly, he was very new to this job. In fact, the job itself was new. It only existed because of Competition-gate. Thirdly, he was understandably nervous. Everyone was now utterly paranoid about scrutiny. Nobody wanted his job and, most significantly, Russell Brand was the Controller's pet. He always got his own way and had already seen off around six producers in just over two years on her two stations. So poor Dave Barber emailed Douglas and asked if the 'funny' phone calls should be allowed to go out on air. He got a one-word reply. 'Yes.'

Jonathan Ross, understandably, got hammered by the press over this. But I just couldn't believe he'd ever deliberately set out to hurt anyone. I'd known him since 1986 when he did a voice-over for Livewire before he got his first TV show

He'd always been irreverent and gobby. But also big-hearted

and generous of spirit. And pocket it turned out.

In 2007, my Sam asked if he could come into work with me one Saturday. Not to watch my show (as Peel once said that's like watching someone in a typing pool), but to meet Jonathan, his telly hero, who was on Radio 2 on Saturday mornings when I went into 6 Music.

So I went to Jonathan's studio and asked him if it was OK to bring Sam along the next week. "Sure. What shoe size is he?"

A bit random but very Wossie.

"Er... size 13."

"Oh, Christ. OK. I'll think of something don't worry."

The following Saturday we stuck our heads round the Radio 2 studio door and were beckoned in. While the next record was on, Jonathan made a beeline for my little lad and made a big fuss over him.

He also handed him a suit carrier.

Sam looked puzzled.

"Go on. Open it then."

Inside was a purple and mauve shimmering two-tone suit with a bright green silk lining, a pink silk shirt and co-ordinating tie.

"It's yours young man. I'm too fat for it now."

Crikey! Sam was gobsmacked. Back home he checked it out online and found a shot of Jonathan on telly, looking much thinner, and wearing that get-up.

And so, having being welcomed soon after as a guest to the Jonathan Ross show, he swanned off to his school prom in an Ozwald Boateng suit which fitted perfectly. The trousers are sadly too short now. But he'll never part with it and I'll never forget that Jonathan Ross really didn't need to do all that for my Sammy.

For over a week, with Mark Thompson on holiday abroad and the Deputy Director General Mark Byford in charge, it appeared to the public that the BBC did nothing. I'm told Lesley Douglas could be found holed up in her office and burning the midnight oil. Yet nobody replied to emails from Andrew Sachs's agent nor apologised to him. Thompson eventually cut short his holiday, met with the BBC Trust, and on October 30th, 2008, after 12 days of stalling, the BBC announced that Lesley Douglas had resigned.

I was punching the air at the news. Now I could go and discuss with the Director General, how come this particular little corner of his empire, under Lesley Douglas's stewardship, had cost the licence payers another £150,000 – making a total of £370,000 in Ofcom fines in just over a year.

Lesley's departure gave me the confidence to write to Mark Thompson, the highest paid employee in the UK's public sector on £834,000 and, according to Forbes magazine that year, the 65th most powerful human being alive.

I'm not sure he ever read it himself. I've since come to wonder if he read anything during his time at the BBC. Apparently he had people to do that sort of thing for him, but I received an email from someone in his office and I was slotted into his diary.

I didn't want to just ramble on. He was the top journalist at the BBC after all. Best make sure he had all the facts at his fingertips at last.

I prepared a 12-page dossier, in four sections. I started by explaining who I was with a brief CV of my time at the BBC. Secondly, I related the whole saga as I have just now. Thirdly, I set out my complaints about the affair in bullet points and then I finished with the following questions:

– Why was my show singled out and, knowing what they did, why did 6 Music management allow it to be so?

– Did the DG know of the extent of the problem when he high-lighted my show in July, 2007?

– Why was I given no warning of his announcement until 20 minutes before it was broadcast?

– Why was false and misleading information given out in a BBC press release?

– Why were relevant emails from one individual deleted from my BBC inbox?

– Why was my current producer, who had continued with the offending competitions on my show, left in place when I had been removed?

– Why was I taken off 6 Music for three months?

– Why was I not allowed to present the shows I was contracted for on Radio 2 in summer 2007?

– Why have I not been on Radio 2 since? (I had been a regular since 2004)

– Why was I threatened with the termination of my local radio contract?

– Why was I strung along as to my return to 6 Music?

– Why was my existing 6 Music show scrapped?

– Why was the Russell Brand show on 6 Music, for example, not reported until I told Jenny Abramsky about it?

– Why did the BBC have a change of heart over the position of Leona McCambridge?

– How much has the BBC paid to make Leona McCambridge quietly disappear?

– Does the BBC now accept, after so many examples have come to light of pre-recording competitions, that the practice was endemic and fully accepted by staff and management?

– Can the BBC assure me I will suffer no financial loss at its hands because of the damage its actions have inflicted on my reputation?

Discuss.

In February, 2009, and armed with my dossier, I caught the train from Coventry after my show and arrived at Broadcasting House in good time for the meeting. At least the commission-aire was pleased to see me.

"Eh up, Liz. We haven't seen you in here for a while."

"Hiya Stella. I've come to see the DG."

"Bloo-dee hell!"

"I know. Get me."

I was led up to a part of Broadcasting House that I'd never seen before. The inner sanctum. The DG's office was in the 'bow of the ship' over the huge bronze front doors and under the nude statue of Ariel and to be honest it was all a bit manly and brown. Walls, floors, furniture. Yuck. I sat in an anteroom.

Beyond glass doors I could see a line of four or five secretaries all facing the other way through a glass window into the room beyond full of sofas and with views down Portland Place to Oxford Circus. I could see Thompson and a woman with a clip board. He was only here on certain days of the week. His main suite was in White City where he could be near to the things closest to his heart. News and Television.

As I sat there, I recalled what had happened in all the other attempts to get through to Thompson on my be-half since July, 2007. Lembit Opik MP had written to him twice to ask that I be treated fairly and the National Union of Journalists (of which I was a member) had also sent a let-ter about my situation. Both parties had been fobbed off with niceties and generalities about how the BBC didn't discuss individual cases etc, etc. Oh well. I was here myself now. He had to discuss my own case with me, didn't he?

I'd been waiting a little while when one of the secretaries came out wringing her hands and wincing a bit. It was the same one I'd just seen going in to speak to Thompson. He'd glanced my way and then swung round and some furious discussion had taken place. I was about to find out what that had all been about.

"I'm afraid I've got some rather bad news. There's been a diary error and the DG won't be able to meet you after all."

After all I'd been through and all I'd done to build myself up to this moment, part of me was crushed.

The other was fighting mad.

"Perhaps you could tell the Director General that this meeting has been arranged for some time," I said. "I came down here today, all the way from Coventry, in good faith, having got up at 5am and having already done a full shift for the BBC. Please tell the Director General that I am not leaving and will wait here until he sees me." Next thing you know...

"Liiiiz! Great to see you." Thompson was now thrusting his arm out as I was shown through.

"Come in. Take a seat. Coffee?"

Jacket-less, tie-less, sleeves rolled up, slight stubble. He was a study in casualness. Yet he seemed anything but relaxed.

"How are you?"

"Well I..."

"Great. Great. Can I just say that I'm glad we've all been able to put the last year or so behind us. I think it's so important that lessons have been learned and that we can all move forward."

"Yes but I haven't," I said. "I can't. I didn't want to waffle on today so I've written this."

I handed him my file.

"I didn't expect you to be able to answer all my questions today. So I'd like to leave this with you and when you've read it perhaps then we can have a discussion."

I can't remember how we filled the rest of the time it took to finish my coffee but his Chief Assistant, Jessica Cecil, was writing furiously on her pad throughout, only looking up to nod at her boss in agreement. So she'd be able to tell us I expect. And a lot more besides I'd wager.

She's always been at his side as a witness taking notes so it's amazing he doesn't remember more about his last years at the BBC isn't it?

Eight weeks later, I'd heard nothing. So I wrote to him again. Still nothing. So I wrote to him again. Finally, after nine weeks – and 12 pages of details and questions – I got a single side of A4.

Here are the highlights... 'I think important lessons have been learned from your experience. We have a responsibility to look after our people effectively through good times and bad... I hope it is of some comfort that your feedback will inform how things are managed in the future... Many, if not all, of the figures you name are no longer with the BBC... I'm not sure what an investigation would achieve or how it would help ensure that things were 'put right' as you suggest.'

Super.

He was right about one thing though. Everybody involved had gone. Or was about to.

The Director of Radio, Jenny Abramsky, (on a salary of

£316,000) had surprised us all by retiring in September, 2008. With an undisclosed lump sum commensurate with her £4million pension pot which pays out £190,000 a year. In January, 2009, she was made a Dame of the British Empire.

The Controller of Radio 2 and 6 Music Lesley Douglas had left the BBC in October, 2008, with an unconfirmed lump sum of around £250,000. And, after 22 years, because she'd been allowed to resign, with her BBC pension intact.

Head of Programmes 6 Music, Ric Blaxill, was forced to 'resign' in 2007, and went very quietly, so I'm guessing not empty-handed.

The Controller of Radio 1, Andy Parfitt, (responsible for the Jo Whiley show) vacated the post in July, 2011, with 31 years of accrued pension rights. And some kind of 'sweetener'?

By then Thompson had announced to the Trust that he was toppling the top of this pile.

The Deputy Director General, Mark Byford, left in 2011 with over a million in cash £1,022,000) and a pension pot of £3.4 million. He currently draws £164,000 a year or £13,000 a month.

In early 2012, Thompson announced he was off and he left in the September with over 30 years of pension rights based on his salary (£834,000 in 2010).

In January, 2014, the BBC announced that it would be funding a new partner called Lonesome Pine. Lonesome Pine is the production company owned by Lesley Douglas

I know I was involved in a scam that cost the licence payers over a hundred grand and I've always been really sorry about that. But compared to the millions trousered by those who were in charge, that's peanuts. And anyway, I'm still paying for it.

THE BIRD AND THE BEEB

In late 2008, I stood, with a tear in my eye, as Sam walked through the gates of Clare College, Cambridge for his entrance exam and interview in the cloisters.

I watched a porter greet him and guide him through into the quad that stretched down to the River Cam.

The rain was falling softly on the bicycles chained to the railings by chattering students with weighty books under their arms and colourful college scarves thrown round their necks. The lights of the Kings College chapel threw shadows across the wet cobbles and I couldn't have been any prouder.

A month later we heard the good news. Sam had been accepted and would study Computer Sciences. That's my boy.

I wanted Sam to be able to make the most of his time there and these things don't come cheap. So I thought I'd just check with David Clargo, who was still my boss at BBC Coventry and Warwickshire, that I could count on having a job and funds to see Sam through Cambridge.

His response floored me. It was devastating.

"I'm sorry Liz. But I won't be able to renew your contract next time," he said. By July, 2009, I would be finished on the Breakfast Show.

Blimey. That was over eight months from now. How clear cut. How matter of fact. What a huge blow. I felt absolutely let down by Clargo. I'd helped him get this job. To win awards. I'd just fronted another big community campaign and hosted a televised gala evening in Coventry city centre. All the bosses had come along and were full of congratulations. There'd been no hint of this.

He rambled on about the station not achieving the targets set by his bosses. They'd decided that 17% of the local population should be listening. That was the national average over its 40 local radio stations. However, long established ones in other cities like Birmingham and Manchester only ever got 10% or less. We'd recently reached 15% but was saying he had to try something new. I knew he was massively overspent. So he'd certainly benefit by replacing a freelancer with a member of staff. They didn't show up on his bottom line.

I felt utterly shafted. I'd been good for and loyal to Clargo for over seven years in both Northampton and Coventry. When exactly had he planned to tell me if I hadn't brought it up? His new boss, Cath Hearne, led me a right dance. Three times I went to meet her for a chat over coffee at a local hotel. First she was hoping to find me a new role, then she was talking to her finance people about it and in the end she was sorry but she couldn't help me any further. Her boss, David Holdsworth, by now in charge of all BBC local radio and TV, agreed to see me.

"You realise that you are one of the highest paid presenters on local radio don't you Liz," he said. I knew he'd got rid of a few more big names already around the country.

"I'm afraid we just don't pay those kinds of rates anymore. You've been a great team player. Who knows? I may decide we've made a big mistake. We may end up asking you back!"

"Thank you David. I appreciate that. Don't forget. I'm always just on the end of a phone," I smiled, while thinking 'Oh thanks. Big deal. Fuck that'.

Clargo kindly agreed to a pact. We'd not say a word to anyone. So for nearly eight months it was our secret. That way I kept face around the place and on air so I was able to do the job justice while I kept on smiling and got on with it. Of course, in hindsight, I can see that doubling my pay during that time would have also helped. As we now know, that perk was lavished on Mark Byford, the departing deputy Director General, to help him keep 'focused' while he worked his eight months 'notice'.

But, hey, I just made programmes.

And anyway, I had other things on my mind. My dad was dying.

For the last three weeks I worked at Coventry I had to do the show, finish at 10am, drive for three hours up to Blackpool, sit with my dad for six hours, drive home, go to bed at 11pm and get up again at 5am to do it all over again. Everybody but the listeners knew what I was going through. A member of BBC staff would have been given paid compassionate leave. But as I've explained, I had no rights to that. Or feelings.

In July, 2009, I told my work friends, gave a week's 'notice' to the listeners and ploughed through their hundreds of bewildered emails. In an email, David Clargo wrote: "I am very sad to let Liz go. She has made a huge contribution to this station with her forensic mind and wonderful warmth with people." He went on to reveal who my replacement was to be. A male member of the management team. So staff and 'free' then.

Cath Hearne marked my exit with a group email welcoming in 'a new era'. It was tactless and very hurtful. I replied by trying to warn her that she should watch her own back. I'd heard about a plot to oust her with a vote of no confidence. Someone sold the story of my email to The Daily Telegraph. I know who it is. They are not there either any more.

A dozen or so close workmates organised a farewell breakfast and presented me with a necklace and a couple of the newsroom staff came to tell me how much they'd learned working with us. Lots of listeners also dropped off leaving presents with heartfelt messages. I even got flowers, homemade cakes and chocolates from children.

And apparently, I wasn't the only one leaving that day. By the next set of data, a third of the audience had as well.

On the last day, I finished the show by thanking my listeners for having me for the last four years, I played 'Don't Look Back In Anger' by Oasis and I walked out into the rain.

I didn't think things could get any worse.

My dad died a week later.

Chapter Twenty One

DON'T LEAVE ME
THIS WAY

Jack Kershaw was a hard act to follow.

I'd watched him so many times in the school hall, holding assemblies or at numerous functions with the audience hanging on to his every word.

I was no stranger to public speaking myself now, but it's one thing talking to the Women's Institute in the village hall, or even addressing a party conference. It's quite another to try and summarise a loved one's entire life when they are lying in a box next to you.

Somehow I didn't actually cry until they played his chosen songs. (Typically he'd got everything organised in advance).

The ones he used to sing to me as he put me to bed when I was a little girl. 'Somewhere Over the Rainbow' and 'When We Grow Too Old To Dream Your Love Will Live In My Heart'. If he'd specified Our Gracie's 'Sally' I'd have collapsed.

One of the reasons I've never had a wedding is because I just couldn't face post-divorce argy-bargy between my parents. But you can't avoid a funeral. Thankfully, my mum, my dad's first wife of 17 years and the mother of his children, showed good grace and dignity and didn't insist on attending. So avoiding any conflict for all of us.

But there was still an awkward 'second family' moment when the mourners' cars arrived at the home my dad had shared with his current wife. There were two cars. Who was to get in the one closest to him directly behind the hearse? His blood relatives? His children? Or the spouse who he'd chosen to spend his last years with? And her supporting offspring? Tricky eh? In the end, after a lot of shuffling around and delay, me and Our Andrew took pole position. As we pulled off towards the funeral, I couldn't help thinking of my grandma's take on her son-in-law. "Eeh, Jack Kershaw were a proper nice fella," she once said. "If only he'd been able to keep his pants on, we wouldn't have had all this trouble."

My dad's demise in 2009 brought me face-to-face with the NHS. And having seen it up close and personal while it's treated my elderly relatives since 1995, I have to say that treatment has been a disgrace.

On my first visit I was relieved he was in a bright new ward. Until I noticed what he was doing. He was bent over his tray attempting to get at his lunch. I watched as he stabbed, puzzled, at the plate. I then saw that a taut sheet of hardly visible clingfilm had not been removed by the staff. Eventually I had to intervene. His pride was hurt and that hurt me. But he had to eat.

As the weeks wore on, things wore him down and he was less reluctant to ask for help with the most personal tasks. Could I accompany him to the bathroom? If he could be helped to walk he wouldn't use a bed pan. When I wasn't there he had to. I love my dad's memory too much to go into any more degrading details.

Could I ask a nurse to cut his toe nails? The nurse said no. Health and safety. The chiropodist had to do that. "There's only one for the whole hospital. It'll be about a week." So I did it.

Being there at meal times was forbidden but I insisted that as I'd travelled so far, I wasn't leaving. Sometimes, after the meals had been delivered, the staff would withdraw to their station and I'd be the only able-bodied soul on the ward. There were eight elderly men and nobody to assist them. I couldn't sit by and watch. One man with only one good arm had been handed a roll with some spread... in a foil wrap. I could only watch him struggle for so long before I tactfully offered to slice and butter his bread.

I was asked for all kinds of help and sometimes for information. Or just a chat. Sometimes I had to wade in. I couldn't just sit and watch the man opposite throwing his covers off again. He had no pyjama bottoms on. I went searching for a member of staff. She started ranting that it was none of my business. I explained that I thought an elderly gentleman's dignity should be hers. And by the way, my father is Mr. Kershaw. Not Jack to you.

DON'T LEAVE ME THIS WAY

My dad, now trapped in a failing body but still sharp enough to complete the daily crossword, was horrified by all this communal humiliation.

And why was he even on this ward? Because he was over 80? He had a heart complaint but only after my call to the hospital's medical director did he finally get into Coronary Care with access to treatment someone my age would have got without question. But it was too late. Again.

My first taster of what we can all currently 'look forward to' was in 1995.

"Tell you what. Why don't we just put a pillow over his face and finish him off here and now?" Our Andrew was beside himself with rage and, between sobs, I was beside him nodding in support. "There's no need to take that attitude," blustered the consultant. "All I'm saying is that the prognosis is not good and by forcing food on him you'll just be making it worse for him."

"So we just starve him to death then?"

"Well he's dying anyway. We could put a tube in him but that would just drag it out. As I say it's just a matter of time."

Two weeks' time as a matter of fact.

That's how long it took my kind, courageous and proud grandad Wallace to slowly and painfully waste away. Day after day I witnessed the deliberate deprivation of nutrition that resulted in his 'accelerated' yet agonising, undignified death. If the geriatric consultant was suggesting this was some form of euthanasia – it was not. Euthanasia is Greek for 'good death.' There was nothing good about this. This was systematic torture. Pure institutionalised horror.

And this was before the NHS had even come clean with its Liverpool Care Pathway policy.

On May 8th, 1945, VE Day, as a member of the British Army, he'd danced with the crowds in St. Peter's Square in Rome. Now on its 50th anniversary, Wallace Acton, having fought the Nazis, now looked as though he'd been liberated from Belsen.

We hardly left him, but caught up in that culture we couldn't help him. Cause of death then? Being 87, apparently.

No wonder alarm bells rang when, four years later, my 89-year-old grandma was taken to the same hospital.

She became so bloated with an overdose of fluids, that the wedding ring she'd never removed in 60 years was unceremoniously snapped off with bolt cutters. Once smart and stylish, her hair was matted and she had faeces under her nails. I cleaned her up. I fed her the meals that were dumped on her trolley to go cold and then, untouched, taken away. Mostly I just talked to her. The nights were long but I realised if she was on her own she would have no voice and be left to suffer. Sometimes I kept awake by fixing my eyes on an old Band-Aid under the bed. It never moved in three weeks because nobody cleaned that bit of the floor. As well as washing my grandma, I wiped windowsills, the locker and sink.

When she cried out in agony I went and asked for painkillers. The night nurses chatting round their station were obviously irritated. More than once I waited and waited until I couldn't stand her suffering any more and stalked the dark gloomy corridors until I found a doctor only to be told "she's very old you know."

I was treated as a bloody nuisance but I didn't care as long as she was cared for.

DON'T LEAVE ME THIS WAY

It was the way she was spoken to that really made me mad. "How–are–we–then–today–Norah?" the ward staff would slowly mouth up-close, shouting at the same time. Their manner improved once I'd put her photo on the locker. She was pictured all glammed up in her Queen Mother pose, draped in turquoise chiffon and surrounded by family on her 85th birthday. "Ooooh. Is that yer grandma then?"

"Yes it is. She hasn't always been pathetic and bedridden. And she's not daft so please call her Mrs. Acton unless she tells you otherwise. She's not a child."

She'd have been better off if she had been. Staff on a children's ward would be locked up for treating their patients in the same way. Other ladies would call to me. Sometimes they'd need a bedpan or simply to move. Mostly they just wanted a chat. Imagine children being left for hours on end without even a kind word, without pants, wandering pitifully around corridors looking for toilets. Or going hungry, or simply crying out for a drink.

Whenever I thought she was improving I'd nip home to see my children. Every time I came back she'd have suffered a setback. What was going on? So me and Our Andrew then spent almost three full weeks on that ward, taking turns to sleep in my car outside.

One morning, I was woken by laughter. Some nurses coming on duty had spotted me. One of them threw me a filthy stare.

A few minutes later she called me. "You'd better come quick. She's going." I was in time to see my grandma draw a very last soft breath. No more pain. She'd gone.

I soon learned that she'd just been dosed with morphine by the nurse with the stare. And died almost immediately. I'll never know if those events were in any way connected. But from the brusque, smug, businesslike manner with which I was issued the paperwork and encouraged to leave, I will always suspect so. And then I discovered the bedsores.

Black, yellow, oozing and undressed. A big hole had been eating away at the base of my grandma's spine and into her buttocks. I was told that the notes recorded that it had been treated and dressed. So why was it so rotten and where were those dressings? Where were those notes? Where was the clinical care? The consideration? The kindness?

In August last year, I was on holiday when I heard that my 78-year-old mum had been taken ill and was in hospital in Yorkshire. Fourth time unlucky?

Sam drove up first. He was very shocked at the state of his grandma. Not least because of the strong smell of poo in her room. Oh, here we go again.

So I rang the ward and was told to hang on by the ward clerk. She came back giggling and told me "the nurse says you'll have to ring back, she's just tucking into her toast" over background laughter.

Eventually a nurse came to the phone but was impatient and rude and when I asked about my mum's medication she blurted "I can't remember all that. I've given out all sorts of medication to loads of patients this morning."

She said a doctor would call me back but nobody did. So I phoned again.

The one who was brought to the phone turned out to have qualified just two weeks earlier.

Consulting my mum's notes he listed a cocktail of seven

drugs including a sedative. "Are you doping her like they do old people in homes to keep them quiet?" He denied that any of the drugs would change her mood or personality and that she was only being given a 'short acting relaxant – as if she'd broken her arm' just to prepare her for a brain scan which she had been getting worked up about. A brain scan? I thought she'd had sickness and diahorrea.

When I arrived the next morning the doctor said that for various reasons, after a full week, he still hadn't been able to get the brain scan done and he wouldn't discharge my mum until he had. And it was unlikely he'd get a slot today. Well could you please try? Fifteen minutes later we went down together.

Just as we left the ward, lunch was being served but I was told she'd just have to do without. The scan showed nothing was wrong with her brain so she could go home. So I left my mum alone while I went to the office to retrieve her valuables. A nurse was just starting the drugs round.

When I got back 20 minutes later my mum was unrecognisable, suddenly in a state of mania, cackling like a mad woman and ending each sentence with "because it's Tuesday." There was a small plastic beaker with traces of thick liquid beside her.

I was so shocked that I went to get the nurse. "Well wouldn't you rather have her like that than when she's being awkward?" She gave me a wink and a 'knowing' smile.

Hang on, she'd been admitted for vomiting and dehydration. Now she was completely gaga. That was it. Not again. I got her out of there. She was lucky.

All my elderly relatives' death certificates have stated that the cause of death was heart failure. Rubbish. We all ultimately die of that. It's what brings that about that is the real scandal here.

THE BIRD AND THE BEEB

I dread ending up on an NHS ward, old, trapped, vulnerable, powerless and neglected. Since I first spoke out about all this in 1999 on Channel 4 News, dozens of distressed relatives have contacted me. And now, with official investigations into the treatment of the elderly in NHS hospitals, many more families have gone public with graphic stories. The truth is out there. At long last.

Perhaps now, as a supposedly civilised society, we will face up to the most sickening aspect of all this. The hypocrisy. We currently outlaw elective deaths. People are prosecuted for bringing a loved one's suffering to an end. Medics, politicians and lawyers get up in arms about suicide trips to Swiss clinics. But how can openly planned, painless deaths be so abhorrent while cynically and covertly killing by deprivation and without dignity, is par for the course in our hospitals? When every day, all over this country, the very people who, since 1948, have believed in care from the cradle, and paid for it, are being routinely propelled to those graves by our 'marvellous' NHS.

That's why I readily agreed to do my bit for cherridee. Age UK had been on my show, knew what I'd seen and so asked me to be a patron and ambassador for its campaigns.

It's hardly rock 'n' roll is it? Fighting for frail old fogies isn't glamorous. But it needs doing. Because, until things are put right, unless you die suddenly or peacefully in your sleep at home, one day it could be you.

No wonder Our Andrew announced "I'm not giving up smoking. Sod my arteries. I'd rather go out with a bang than end up like that."

And from 2006 to 2009 it seemed he was heading that way.

Chapter Twenty Two

HE AIN'T HEAVY, HE'S MY BROTHER

How I wished my grandma was still around when Our Andrew's life was unravelling a few years ago. She'd have sorted him out. When we were at nursery school, he took a water pistol in one day. He hadn't been told he couldn't so he was indignant when the headmistress snatched it off him. "You don't snatch, you say please," she was told adamantly by this chubby blonde three-year-old. Her white powdered face turned puce as she locked him in her office. Twenty minutes later she was confronted by the formidable figure of my grandma. "Where the hell's Our Andrew?" He'd rung her from the phone on the head's desk and was swiftly released.

THE BIRD AND THE BEEB

Nope. It was down to me now, hundreds of miles away across the sea, to support him and to fly over whenever I could.

There's just over a year between me and Our Andrew but an old nursery teacher once told me "you two were like twins. Always inseparable. Joined at the hip." Being close doesn't mean you're not very different though. I was always cast as the smiley, sensible one. As for Andrew, "oh he's a little bugger with his tantrums." Or as Radio One producer John Walters described Andrew when he arrived in the office he shared with John Peel, "it was like someone had let a bluebottle out of a jar."

Now I had to force myself to keep calm and outwardly cheerful as I drove to the BBC to present a live radio show knowing he was in big trouble. And not for the first time.

"Don't you dare step foot in Rwanda," I warned him as he set off on one of his African trips. He recalls that as he narrowly escaped death at the hands of a brutal bunch of militia by picking his way through land mines for hours on end one terrifying black night, his biggest fear was "Our Elizabeth is going to kill me when I get home."

I should have been just as worried when he moved his family, in search of a dream life, to the Isle of Man in 2006. The Manx people are subjects of Her Majesty the Queen. But they don't enjoy the protection of her government. It's not part of the UK or the EU. No Human Rights Convention is recognised there. True, they've stopped flogging homosexuals. But would they really lock somebody up for 'losing it' after losing his family and his job?

Yes. In 2007, Our Andrew was banged up three times.

Now life was unbearable. My phone would ring night and day. I already had a load on my plate without this.

HE AIN'T HEAVY, HE'S MY BROTHER

It was so hard to cope that sometimes I just wanted to slam down the phone and cut him out of my life.

But I couldn't. I understood why he was like he was. I knew what he'd been through. And I'd already lost one of my dearest friends, in 1997, to depression and drink and I damn well wasn't going to lose my brother. So no matter what he did, however he behaved or what he said, I'd never abandon him. He was ill. He'd suffered a major breakdown. He needed help not condemnation.

So how did it come to this?

Ever since he was a child he'd been enthusiastic to the point of obsession. With his fierce curiousity and capacity for minutiae, if he latched onto a subject he made it his own. First it was wildlife. Then it was fishing. Next was motorbikes. At the age of 14 he took himself off to the Isle of Man on his own to watch his heroes in the TT. Then it was Bob Dylan. When he decided that the jingly jangly guitars of West Africa were for him he set off to Timbuktu with just a passport, a spare pair of undies and a tape recorder. The pants got pinched and he inherited the gift of a whole dead sheep. The tape recorder brought Radio 4 listeners an armchair adventure.

It's that passion that's made him professionally. But it brought him heartache and disappointment in his personal life. And a criminal record.

A born romantic, he's been like a bounding puppy with women. They've been like flies around a honey pot. Swarms of them. He still scoffs at my sisterly advice when we shared a flat together and I'd just seen another nubile girl nipping along the corridor to the bathroom. "Oh Andrew. Be careful. You'll get germs."

But when sometimes hastily-placed affections were shunned he'd be like a wounded hound.

In 1992 he was persuaded to settle down. Kind of. Babies followed but he never lost the travel bug. Michael Palin once said of Andrew "he made me travel a little further than I normally do." Hear, hear. I'm grateful for him leading me on hairy adventures across continents, into scrapes, opening my eyes and mind and filling my life with enormous fun and wonderful memories.

But it was horror that he brought home from Rwanda. Cosy evenings on the sofa watching the kids while supper cooked were out after seeing bodies butchered by machetes by the roadside and corpses spilling out of wells. He couldn't settle for small talk when he'd known the total terror of encountering demented, marauding militia on a moonlit road or missing a land mine by millimetres. He was bored and he started to booze.

Then came a series of body blows. In 1999, after nearly 15 years, he was 'let go' by Radio 1. At the time he'd won more awards than any other British DJ. But that didn't count with the now youth-obsessed-yet-ironically-middle-aged-themselves-must-get-down-with-the-kids Radio 1 suits.

Someone once gave me a sanity saving piece of advice: 'Your job is what you do. It's not who you are'. That's kept me going from crisis to crisis but it's not something Our Andrew has been able to grasp.

Then his beloved producer and father figure, John Walters, died suddenly in 2000, followed all too soon by the childhood hero who'd become his mentor and friend, John Peel, in 2004.

He said he wanted to rethink his life now.

They'd always had really happy holidays on the Isle of Man.

Now with typical gusto he decided that the family should move there. They bought a house by the beach in Peel and a boat and set off to live the dream.

But it turned into a nightmare when his partner found a text from another woman. He said it was innocent. She'd heard it all before and moved out taking his kids. This time the boy who's always been a bugger but used his considerable charm to get his own way couldn't get her back. He was left rattling around in that rambling house, alone.

By January, 2008, and already having done three short stints inside, he was now bound to the house while he awaited sentencing again. He'd been told he was going to prison for longer now. He'd pleaded guilty. He had no choice. He'd been advised that to defend himself would cost a further £20,000. He hadn't been working and his funds had been cleaned out by Manx lawyers, so was doing as he was told. "Taking it on the chin."

The website of the Isle of Man Law Society boasts that since the 1960s the number of lawyers on the island has multiplied tenfold. Maybe it's because, outside of bike racing events, there's not a lot else to do except take each other to court, obliged to use the breathtakingly expensive services of this local cartel.

I've never seen my brother through rose-coloured spectacles. He'd been a bloody mess and hurt the people who love him most. But this made my blood boil. What kind of justice was this? What kind of place has he chosen as his home?

The next month, while Andrew was inside, I went to Binksy's birthday party in Liverpool. Binksy's brother and sister-in-law are lawyers and Binksy was dating one too. So it was wall to wall with Liverpool solicitors and barristers and even a judge from Leeds who were all adamant that Andrew would never have been locked up in the UK.

My grandma would have been marching up to the prison now with her big handbag poised for action. But we weren't kids anymore. And I doubted the governor was a timid spinster in a crisp cotton frock.

And so it was then that I found myself, in early 2008, on the set of Porridge visiting 'Disgraced DJ Andy' as the tabloids liked to label him. And waiting with a bunch of trackie-bottom-wearing pram-pushing, chain-smoking lovelies in the lashing rain outside the island's dank, dark, Victorian prison.

Sniffed by dogs and stripped of all my personal possessions and identity I was led through huge creaking fortified gates into a yard straight off the set of a Jack The Ripper TV special. In contrast, the glaring ghastly yellow gloss paint of the visiting room walls was intended, I guess, to instill a sense of cheeriness in the visitor and inmate.

There, sitting at a crummy Formica-topped table screwed to the floor, in a high visibility jacket (of a yellow that incidentally clashed with the walls) was my little brother. He tried to put on a brave face but he looked dreadful. He'd been trying to sleep with his coat on, plagued by mice. When I'd rung to find out what I could send him, the warder was very jolly ("no files in cakes Liz!") and promised to look out for him. But I'd written to him every day and sent him supplies which he knew nothing of. The stamps and biros having been confiscated in case the glue and ink had been laced with drugs. He was allowed one visit a week and one phone call a day. No computer. He could have books, but only after they'd been checked for drugs in the spine. He said the boredom was crushing.

When I went to collect him seven weeks later he was badly undernourished, and covered in sores, his skin having had little sunlight. His hair was coming out in clumps, he was covered in flea bites and his legs were swollen from poor circulation due to cramped conditions.

As soon as I picked him up and we'd escaped the waiting paparazzi he was instructing me to pull into a shop. But he bought booze and three days later, as my plane took off for home, he was being re-arrested and locked up again. This time it was suggested that he came over here to recover on a suspended sentence as an alternative to another stretch. So I had a terrible dilemma. Could I take him in and expose my children to his current madness? I didn't have a choice. He turned up in just shorts and a t-shirt. In March.

For a week he carried on drowning his sorrows.

Then suddenly and typically he announced he'd been through enough and was going to quit drinking. And would I take him to a doctor please? We were told that it would be at least six weeks before he could get any sort of psychological support.

So we were sent away with a haul of pills and potions and we set about creating our own affordable version of The Priory clinic while he went cold turkey which meant days of shivering and shaking wrapped in blankets on the sofa. I'd hand out the tablets, logging on a clipboard what he'd had and when. I was terrified he'd die. One morning I couldn't see him moving at all so I had to check for breathing. He woke up startled to find me bent over him with my finger shoved almost up his nose.

Then his self-devised therapy was to make himself handy around the house. So he'd fix and tidy things. And build fires. He felt permanently frozen. He'd even be stomping around all night piling up logs and watching TV. Because he couldn't sleep. And neither could I. It was torture lying awake knowing I had to get up at 4.30 am to drive to Coventry for my Breakfast show. But, in four years there, I only let the listeners and BBC bosses down once when I rang in to say I just wasn't able to make it that morning. And why.

Every day when I got back home from work I'd listen. All day long, over pots of coffee in the kitchen he'd pour his heart out. I'd never heard some of these stories before. Like the one about a child of about 10 floating under a bridge in Rwanda. The kid's Man Utd kit caught his eye. As he emerged from under the other side of the bridge Our Andrew saw that this little kid's head had been hacked off. He sobbed as he told that story for the first time.

The most heartbreaking thing was to see him waiting for the post lady every day. Has she been yet? Any emails for me? Any phone calls? He wrote to his kids every day and to make sure the letters contained nothing which a mother could take exception to, I vetted them all first. After eight weeks of getting nothing back I couldn't bear to see him suffer any more. I picked up the phone. When I told him that their mother still didn't want him to communicate with his children he called her and told her exactly what he thought. These calls were illegal under the restraining order. When the Isle of Man police phoned and asked if he was with me, he ran off across the fields. I told them I didn't know where he was so they listed him as a missing person.

"Has your brother turned up yet?" my local police asked me on the phone. "It's just that we know he likes bikes and we've found a body in a ditch dressed in leathers." Lovely. Thankfully, by then, I knew Andrew was safe. But, so I couldn't be pressed for an address, I didn't want to know where.

I kept being pestered by the police. When they told me they'd leave me alone if I could prove Andrew was alive, I persuaded him to present himself at his local nick. A kindly copper was seemingly sympathetic. But as soon as we'd given him Andrew's address and left, the creep phoned his Manx mates. Andrew was carted off back to police HQ. But an officer there said the Isle of Man's paperwork wasn't in order and suggested Andrew made himself scarce. So he was on the move again.

After nearly a year of lying low on other people's sofas, he'd had enough. He decided that the only way to get his life back was to face the Manx courts again, sober this time, and flew back to the island. He was arrested as he put his key in his front door because he'd been spotted by 'someone' who'd immediately rung the police and he was locked up again.

This time he was sent home after one night. Only to find his house had been ransacked in his absence. He gave the Manx police names and evidence. But you know what? They did nothing. Then they tried to pin something else on him. An incident while he was off the island, in a shop he's never been in. Why? Because the culprit was kind enough to leave a name. Andy Kershaw. And that, apparently, is what passes for a fair cop over there. He put his house up for sale.

"When will your brother be back on the radio Liz?" I was asked all the time. "I used to love his shows. He's a brilliant broadcaster."

You know what. They were right. So in 2009, I decided to find out what, if any, future Kershaw minor had at the BBC. If only so I could give those loyal listeners a proper answer. So I made an appointment with the new Director of Audio and Music (Radio to you and me) Tim Davie. Best get it from the horse's mouth eh?

Tim Davie couldn't have been more of a contrast with his predecessor Jenny Abramsky. She was old school BBC through and through. And I'll admit that my first impression of Tim Davie was that he was a bit of a twerp. But he did get things done then and he did a fantastic job as Acting DG after George Entwistle was forced to resign in 2012.

But right then, this guy who'd come from Pepsi, apparently wanted to show he was still 'fizzin''. "I tell you what Liz. I shoot from the hip. I tell it like it is. What you see is what you get." Mmm. Right now I wasn't sure I liked what I was getting all that much.

"OK. We've got 15 minutes. What can I do yer for?" His eyes were on the clock behind me.

"Well, I was just wondering if, now that my brother's recovered..."

"Yeah, yeah. I know all about that. I know all the DJs."

"Er... you didn't know who I was until..."

"Yeah, yeah. Steve Wright, Chris Moyles... I've had lunch with all of them."

"OK. Well my brother had a breakdown but he's fine now and I was just wondering if he would be welcome back to..."

"Yeah, yeah. Great. No probs. Tell him to come and see me."

I had to explain that he couldn't. He hardly had a bean to eat never mind to spend on airfares and hotels. I'd come to petition the BBC to fly him over for a summit. If it didn't buy him a ticket I'd have to.

"And to be honest, Tim, because I also like to say what I think, I'm saying that I've got a lot less money than you."

So he stumped up a couple of hundred quid for Our Andrew's trip to Broadcasting House where, along with the Radio 3 Controller, Roger Wright, they worked out a comeback strategy for a broadcaster who, before he fell ill, had been one of the BBC's biggest assets. Andrew went on to make a series for Radio 3 which took him round the world again winning him more plaudits and many many column inches of rave reviews. For that he was paid an absolutely insulting daily rate. A pittance. Less than a plumber charges for a call out to a knackered dishwasher. But at least he wasn't washed up any more. He was back in the fold. Back on his feet.

Until he got floored by Radio 4's 'On The Ropes'. He'd refused to go on the programme. Why would he want to wash his dirty laundry in public with John Humphrys? But a producer had got hold of me and pleaded with me to convince Our Andrew to agree to it. After considering the implications carefully I told him I thought it would be good for him. It would announce to the world that he had indeed been on the ropes but now he was fighting fit and bouncing back. So he went for the grilling and came away confident that he'd told his story well and been careful to consider what his kids would think if they heard it. (Always a good litmus test).

Then the night before it was due to go out, and after days of heavy trailing by Radio 4 (including a John Humphrys interview with Simon Mayo on 5 Live about it) it was pulled. 'Someone' had heard the pre-publicity and complained. About what? That it apparently infringed upon the privacy of Andrew's children. Really? How could they claim that? They hadn't heard the damn thing. They didn't yet know what he'd even said. Who was in charge of Radio 4 scheduling these days? Its Controller? Or someone who had a very personal vested interest in keeping Our Andrew down and out?

When that Radio 4 Controller, Mark Damazer, left the BBC in 2010, (straight to a top job at Oxford University and with a nice little 'sweetener' of a few hundred thousand pounds) he said that cancelling 'Andy Kershaw On The Ropes' was one of the worst decisions he'd made at Radio 4 and that he regretted it deeply. No apology though. And a bit bloody late mate. I'd rung him on the day. His secretary was very sympathetic. "Yes Liz. I think you should speak to him," she said knowingly and put me through. In all my time at the BBC, I've never been spoken to so rudely by a more supercilious suit.

"What's it got to do with me? I'll tell you exactly what it's got to do with me Mr. Damazer. For a start it was me who was used by one of your producers to secure this interview in the first place. So I think I deserve more than anybody to know why it's not now going out. And also, I've spent the last three years keeping my brother alive. And now you've single handedly put all that at risk by publicly humiliating and misrepresenting him. That's why it's my business Mr. Damazer."

Our Andrew and I have resigned ourselves to the fact that while the BBC will, quite rightly, fall over itself to help staff struck down by, for example, cancer or heart disease, they are still unable to understand mental health problems. Anyway, he decided that he should now cut his losses and just get on with writing his book.

When it came out it was the same old crap from some quarters. He did an endless stream of interviews with hapless radio presenters who had clearly read The Sun. But not his book. So instead of any interest in his career or how he'd gone about rebuilding his life, it was another sensation-fest about boozing and brawling, raking up old allegations for which he'd served time.

Since then, despite being an expert on places like Haiti and North Korea, he's been systematically ignored by BBC News. And a recent Radio 4 documentary on Ivor Cutler, an artist who owed much to being a bit of a fixture on Andrew's shows, carefully avoided any mention of that. And how could BBC radio make a series about African music in 2014 without the voice of its DJ who, Stephen Fry notes, has played 'an unrivalled role in bringing world music to the ears of the west.'

In 2013, an interview with Our Andrew was featured in a TV trailer promoting the BBC's music output. Apparently Brand Kershaw is perfect for enhancing the cred of the BBC's music programmes. But not to present one. Even though Stephen Fry also cites him as 'the finest British broadcaster bar none'.

With his book published and a one-man tour ongoing and selling out, Andrew finally moved off the Isle of Man and in November, 2012, moved into the big new 'barn' I'd found for him on the Pennines. He shares it with his beloved dog Buster. And his children, Sonny and Dolly, visit every school holiday.

It's handy for the BBC in Salford and with the support of a couple of movers and shakers there he's been occasionally presenting Radio 4's Pick of The Week and regularly making films for The One Show on BBC TV.

The title for his own book came from a remark made by a friend. "No Off Switch." She was right. He hasn't got one. With him it's full on all the time. The journalist Francis Wheen has said that Andrew's life 'zooms along with the high-velocity recklessness of a TT racer. It's impossible not to cheer him on as he accelerates round the hairpin bends of his life, yelling hilarious defiance at anyone who tries to stop him.'

Life with Our Andrew has been a rollercoaster ride. The highs have been thrilling. The lows have been terrifying. And I'll admit there have been times when I've felt so desperate that I've wished I could just pull the plug on the whole bloody thing.

But now I'm relieved and delighted that he's still alive and kicking again. Hopefully we're in for an easier ride. And more adventures.

And one day, I hope I'll be able to say "Yes. Our Andrew's new show starts next week on radio..."

Chapter Twenty Three

(YOU GOTTA) FIGHT FOR YOUR RIGHT (TO PARTY)

Apart from the massive struggle to drag a 16-year-old boy out of bed and on to the bus every morning, life was, following my demise at BBC Coventry, fairly uneventful again in our peaceful country home. With Joe at school, Paul at work and Sam away at university, I filled my days in early 2010 just pottering around. If I didn't go out I couldn't be spending money. Money that I simply didn't earn any more.

And after all, although I was now virtually unemployed Monday to Friday (apart from writing the odd article for the Sunday papers) I still had a very important job to do. Home-making. We'd never eaten so many hearty stews and bloody big pies from such an immaculate kitchen. During the day, the empty house was quiet apart from the music I'd listen to for my 6 Music Saturday show and the telly. I will admit that, along with the rest of the nation's 'economically inactive', pensioners and shift workers, I did get sucked into daytime TV.

At 10am everything stopped for tea and Homes Under The Hammer, the property-porn show that fulfils the armchair voyeur's lust for schadenfreude whenever a 'greedy' investor gets their comeuppance. At least I could say my guilty pleasure was semi-professional.

With the money my grandma left me, I'd bought a house and a flat. I'd done them up with what I was earning and once they were rented out, I bought a couple more houses. The idea was that one day I'd be able to give Sam and Joe a home each. I could see, even back then, that the way things were going, they'd never get a mortgage when they started work. I also wanted to make sure that all my eggs weren't in the BBC's basket. And that one day I'd have some kind of pension. Bruno Brookes had told me to invest my little nest egg in the Dot.Com boom. I ignored him and I'm glad. Instead I listened to my dad.

"See that wonderful Accrington brick Elizabeth?" he'd ask, always pointing out the same house on the sea front near Blackpool. "That was sold for £8000 in the early '60s. It was a fortune then. It's just gone for £800,000. You can't do better than to put your money in bricks and mortar." Oh well. So far so good in that department anyway.

As far as broadcasting went, I was just glad to still have one show and that was on the coolest station on the planet so there were compensations to be had for not having more regular work.

(YOU GOTTA) FIGHT FOR YOUR RIGHT (TO PARTY)

To sit there every weekend, playing songs and having fun with like-minded people was a joy and it was keeping me afloat.

So imagine my surprise when, in early March, the BBC announced it was shutting down 6 Music. Apparently the station did not bring in enough 'unique listeners' to the BBC. Screw what we were trying to achieve on 6, screw that we had built up a loyal fanbase of listeners – apparently we had to go.

NO! I wasn't bloody having that! No way. I'd campaigned too long and too hard for a station like 6. There was nothing like it and, as a listener or DJ, nothing else for the likes of me.

If you need to understand what 6 Music is all about, watch the film 'School of Rock' starring the musician cum actor Jack Black for an insight into the rock 'n' roll ethos.

Not surprisingly I was just one of tens of thousands to be outraged. A protest group, 'Save 6 Music', was quickly set up and actively started to, as Jack Black's character says in that film, 'stick it to the man'. 'The man' being Director General, Mark Thompson.

I'd had a bellyful already. He wasn't getting away with this.

So, one morning, later in March, I joined the revolution with 6 Music's 'unimportant little' listeners outside Broadcasting House. If ever proof were needed that the BBC had no concept of popular culture, this was it.

And if, for all its costly audience research and focus groups, its senior managers were lacking evidence that this station's listeners were intelligent, passionate and vocal, here it was. Right on their doorstep.

The group invited me to speak and the people who organised the campaign were lovely. Articulate, intelligent, friendly, educated and informed. There were rocket scientists among this group! I remember thinking that the BBC had not realised what they had taken on. 'Save 6' organised a brilliant campaign and I was very happy to be involved.

My high visibility don't-mess-with-me-I-mean-business military style red coat came out. I got a band down there. We were denied a licence by the police so they had to play acoustically like a bunch of buskers, but they helped make the party swing. I took my turn with the megaphone, careful to start my little polemic with a disclaimer.

"I am speaking today as a licence payer not as a BBC presenter," I began, hoping that would keep the BBC off my back. But I soon got past being worried. What could they do to me now after the competitions thing? Fuck them.

My thrust was that although 6 Music had a comparatively small audience, it was no less valuable to listeners than any other BBC music service. Suggesting they were served by Radio 1 or 2 was like saying there was no room for Newsnight alongside the 10 O'Clock News. I recalled that the scrapping of Whistle Test in 1987 had been justified in a similar way. "Oh well. They've got Top of the Pops," went the argument. It was bullshit then and it was bullshit now.

And anyway. In terms of bums on seats, what about Radio 3? Why should the BBC spend 58 million pounds a year pumping out unamplified music by dead Germans and not a tenth of that on supporting contemporary British culture?

Because 'the man' didn't see pop and rock as culture at all? Was it still the 1960s in the BBC boardroom?

This was just before the 2010 General Election and a reception had recently been held in the Houses of Parliament for musicians, film makers, authors and the media.

(YOU GOTTA) FIGHT FOR YOUR RIGHT (TO PARTY)

Various politicians had wooed us with pledges of support for the creative industries, outlining their immeasurable but huge value in maintaining our influence abroad and reeling off figures on how much sales of books and records were worth globally to UK plc.

We were told that Harry Potter and Coldplay were better ambassadors for Britain in China than any embassy officials.

So why scrap a showcase for British bands (old and new) like 6 Music?

Outside Broadcasting House, through my microphone, I was speaking to the converted here. But thanks to the assembled press, the message started to reach a wider audience and the campaign just grew and grew. Boy, had Thompson and Co. underestimated this lot. 'Save 6 Music' petitioned him, the BBC Trust, and MPs. These licence payers were eloquent and organised. I did my bit of lobbying too. I didn't care anymore. I had nothing to lose. What was the BBC going to do? Sack me? They were shutting us down anyway.

Who to turn to then? Well, I did have some fairly power-ful friends. Ever since 'Pop Quiz' on Radio 1 in 1989 when I was a team captain and on one show I was teamed up with Bill Wyman's young girlfriend Mandy Smith as well as an ambitious, media-savvy young Scottish MP.

We hit it off and he invited me and a guest to the Commons for Prime Minister's Questions. So there we were, me and Our Andrew, just above the PM in the public gallery.

As Thatcher was wading in to the opposition, one of them was beaming up at me.

"Who's that daft ginger bugger waving at you all the time Our Elizabeth?"

"Oh that's the MP for Inverness and Skye, Charles Kennedy," I replied.

We both got matey with Charlie Boy and spent many an evening at parties round his flat with the likes of George Melly, Nicholas Parsons, Clare Rayner, and Honor Blackman plus some of his more 'fun' MPs like Lembit Opik and Mark Oaten. And Lord Rennard.

When he got married, Charles and his bride Sarah asked me to DJ at the do and I was once invited to speak about the lack of women in Parliament at his annual conference.

In the end, the party's powerful big donors ganged up on Charles. I was sitting next to one of them at a dinner. She had married her boss, a major industrialist, and lived in Regent's Park in one of those white houses that you pass wondering who can possibly afford to live there. She could. Her rubies, emeralds and diamonds would have put Liz Taylor to shame.

"If he doesn't get his act together he's had it," she hissed through gritted teeth whilst looking daggers at Charlie Boy knocking back another drink. Later, at another sitdown do he already seemed to have had quite a few when he was called by the MC. I couldn't imagine this going well at all but he rose from his seat, stubbing his fag out in the middle of my hot dinner, and gave a blinding speech. Then slumped down again.

Adrenaline is a wonderful thing. By the time of the crisis at 6 Music he had been ousted from the party's top job but was still a Right Honourable MP. And, with an election coming up, I reckoned he'd completely 'get' that the Lib Dems could have a natural constituency in Radioland among our lovely, free-thinking pro-democracy liberal with a small 'L', audience.

"You need to talk to our Media minister Liz." I was passed

onto a member of the upper house who was on some sort of committee that took a keen interest in the affairs of the BBC.

After I'd briefed him over a pot of Earl Grey in the House of Lords tea rooms he took the baton. Lord Clement Jones not only came to speak at our next protest in May, he also made sure questions were asked in The House. Did it really serve the licence payers well to close down a unique service? Thanks 'Tim'. You're a hero.

Meanwhile on the BBC, questions were now being asked of the Director General about his plans to scrap selected services.

Jeremy Paxman grilled Thompson on March 3rd, 2010, and his answers underlined just how little he knew, or seemed to care, about 6 Music's aims, ambitions, ethos or listeners.

Paxman: "How much money was wasted on these services you're now going to shut down?

Thompson: "All of these services have worked for audiences, er, for television audiences, radio audiences, audiences on the web..."

Paxman: "So in the case of a music station like 6, it's numbers really isn't it?"

Thompson: "Well I think it's also something else... with 6 Music, it's a relatively small audience, it's quite an expensive service to run, we could... we could..."

Paxman: "Well, so, of course, is 1 Xtra, and as we know their own DJs say there's no-one listening."

Thompson: "We could of course try to build its audience, but with Radio 1 and Radio 2 we have two 'popular music' stations and we believe, particularly by making Radio 2 rather a bit more distinct in what it's done, then we can use those two platforms to give a really rich and broad expression to popular music in this country."

Paxman: "So when a Radio 1 Xtra jockey, Tim Westwood, said on the 9th February 'I've been broadcasting to absolutely nobody for the last three hours,' was that an argument for a convincing audience?"

Thompson: "It might have been a joke, Jeremy."

Paxman: "I don't think so."

Thompson: "I–I – 1 Xtra... I believe 1 Xtra, in its niche, with its audience, is doing a good job. Point is Jeremy, we look at each of these services, one by one, we talk to the people who are listening…"

Paxman: "Sure. You justify BBC 3 for example on the grounds that it's a 'testing ground' that costs £115m a year."

Thompson: "I believe that BBC 3 and the quality of the programmes that..."

Paxman: "A very expensive testing ground."

Thompson: "I believe that what we're seeing there is new British comedy, drama, documentaries, which you would not see anywhere else on British Television... BBC4... The Proms..."

Paxman: "Do you know what they're broadcasting tonight?"

Thompson: "I don't. I can..."

Paxman: "I'll tell you. It starts with the news; then there's a repeat of a documentary; then there is Skippy: Australia's First Superstar – a repeat, no less; then there's Paws, Claws and Videotape, a clip show about famous animals..."

Thompson: "Er... er.

Paxman: "Then a bought-in film. Then there's Skippy: Australia's First Superstar again. Paws, Claws and Videotape repeated. Storyville, a repeated documentary. And then Paws,

(YOU GOTTA) FIGHT FOR YOUR RIGHT (TO PARTY)

Claws and Videotape again, but this time with subtitles! That's an entire evening's output!"

Paxman's disbelief mirrored mine and that of a hell of a lot of other people. The BBC suits had thought they could sneak this through without a fuss. They were badly wrong.

We lurched onwards for a few months not really knowing what direction we were going in.

Until, that summer. I was in the Arctic on a cruise ship, sitting in its crow's nest bar one lunchtime hoping we wouldn't be sunk by the huge icebergs we could see all around us. All of a sudden, the broadcaster Henry Kelly, who was onboard as part of the entertainment, ran in to find me.

"Kershaw, Kershaw, you've been saved!" he shrieked.

It took a bit of time for it to sink in that the BBC had seen sense.

A toast was proposed.

"Here's to the good ship BBC 6 Music and all who sail in her!"

"Hear, hear. To 6 Music listeners!"

"And Captain Thompson!" quaffed some wag.

I was delighted for the brilliant protesters who had done so much to fight their corner with charm, intelligence, courage and good humour.

Of course, it meant I still had a job and that was obviously good news too.

But I've never been the kind to worry about long-term security or I would have stayed in a proper job at BT. At the BBC I've always worked from contract to contract, month to month, mouth to mouth, year to year.

But it was great to know I could now carry on doing what I loved, on a station that I loved.

And since then, 6 Music's audience has grown to almost two million and counting.

Er... am I allowed to tell you that?

Chapter Twenty Four

OUR LIPS ARE SEALED

The reason I had always started any protest speech with "I am speaking today as a taxpayer" was because there was good reason for me to be wary of speaking out about the closure of 6 Music.

Over anything to do with the BBC actually.

My contract.

A standard clause insisted that presenters "must not discuss the BBC, its programmes or its affairs in public." I'm heavily editing that. It runs for several paragraphs.

This clause had been evoked (oh get me) and brought to my attention more than once over recent years.

With advice such as 'say anything to the press and you'll never work here again' or 'you can't mention that in an interview' or 'we have to vet anything you write and have copy approval on everything' or even 'I don't think it would do you any good to put that in a book Liz...'

The BBC needs to safeguard information that's commercially sensitive so it's only right to be secretive about new programme formats or corporate strategies that ensure the BBC's competitiveness in the broadcast industry. I fully understand and support that. But this is public service broadcasting. It belongs to the public. Our wages are paid by a poll tax. Call me old fashioned but I've always thought we are answerable to the licence payers.

So apart from certain stuff, surely the listeners and viewers have a right to know what's going on in their name with their money?

Surely we have a duty to inform them of certain matters?

And anyway, don't we all, in or out of the BBC, still enjoy freedom of speech in this country?

Er... no and no. And apparently not.

During the fight to save 6 Music, I was sent a new contract by BBC lawyers.

So even if they scrapped my station, a new signed and sealed deal meant they'd have to pay me a guaranteed sum.

It does make you wonder if there's any joined-up thinking. Why was the legal department, or even more importantly, radio management, promising to pay me for two years? Weren't they aware that the BBC might be about to close 6 Music down?

Well, let's see. I signed the contract, reluctantly agreeing to be gagged again and, to make matters worse, I also now caved in to a service company. What's that all about then?

Well, basically, the BBC doesn't like to make presenters staff because then they can't freely rearrange the goods in the shop window.

Staff have pensions and holiday pay and everything else that goes with being employees. And – as we all now know – they have to be generously paid off by the BBC if they're sacked. Or 'resigned'. Or made redundant. Even if they're crap or replaced immediately.

As a result, the BBC had always preferred to employ us presenters on an ad hoc basis with no employment rights at all. I've survived like that since 1987. But apparently, after donkeys' years, I'd now built up rights as an employee. And the BBC had got wise to that.

In 2010, I was under pressure to set up a company so the BBC could hire me through that. I didn't see why I should.

But it was compulsory I was told. Sign up or ship out. I've got an email trail from BBC lawyers writing to make it clear that 'it is now BBC policy that all presenters' services are engaged in this way'.

For the next two years, I stood the extra cost of extra accounting for a company I didn't need or want. And each year I paid tax. Twice. As a company engaged by the BBC and then on the 'wages' that I then paid out to myself.

Meanwhile, us BBC presenters were being vilified in the press for tax dodging. The suggestion being that because the rate of company tax is lower than personal income tax, we were willfully diddling the taxman. BBC executives were claiming in the press that presenters had a choice. Service companies were not compulsory. They were optional. It was up to individual presenters if they wanted to arrange their affairs in this way.

We were unable to defend ourselves because of those gagging orders. But one man decided enough was enough. Jeremy Paxman. So he went public with a letter to The Times on March 26, 2012.

'Sir,' he began. 'You use my photograph (Mar 24) to illustrate a story about the HMRC and service companies. But what you fail to state is that the BBC required me to form a company if I wanted to continue to present Newsnight.' Paxo was stuffing it to the press and the BBC.

Now, with 6 Music out of danger and emboldened by Paxman's lead, I just refused to continue with the charade.

In March, 2012, I told a BBC lawyer that I was dumping my service company and that its only director, me, would not be signing another contract. Liz Kershaw would though.

And I just carried on going into 6 Music and doing my show. For six months. Without being paid. Nobody seemed to notice that I had absolutely no legal status around the place.

Or bother to do anything about it anyway.

Obviously my returned, rejected and unsigned contract was gathering dust in an in-tray. Eventually somebody twigged. I was glad because my savings were running out.

An urgent three-party summit was arranged but the main man who'd called it failed to turn up, so that left me and the same lawyer making small talk across his office.

Eventually I got a call from their boss. A more senior BBC brief. Blimey. She seemed dynamic. She had a plan, some news. Maybe she'd 'learned lessons' because she was 'moving forward'. Deloitte, she told me, had been asked to examine the whole issue of how the BBC hired presenters and would be reporting back. In November. So until then I would get paid monthly and I'd get all my back pay. Result.

I never heard another word. Until the following March. By which time, after a full year, I still hadn't signed anything.

And then the whole fiasco started again.

But now the haggling wasn't over service companies. That battle had been won! Now I could really get to grips with those confidentiality clauses.

And other sillier bits:

"Why does this clause state that I have to agree to give blood?"

"In case the BBC wants to test you for drugs."

"OK. A little intrusive. But I have no problem with that." I could think of a few that would though.

"How about being on call 24 hours a day, seven days a week?"

"Sorry?"

"Oh, that's standard."

"Not for me it's not. The BBC is only guaranteeing me one show a week. The rest of my time is my own."

"OK. Scrub that."

"What about this 'extreme' activities bit?"

"Oh that's to make sure you don't render yourself unavailable by having an accident."

"It says here I have to ask permission."

"Yes."

"So I'm standing on a beach in the Med and I see a huge inflatable going by. People are having fun. I have to ring the Controller and ask 'Hey Bob. This big banana being pulled by a speed boat looks fun. Can I have a go?'"

"Er... I'll take that out."

"Now, these confidentiality clauses?"

"Yes?"

"They've actually been outlawed by the new DG."

"Have they?"

"Yes. On May 2nd, Tony Hall said he wants a culture where people feel they are able to speak freely about their experiences of working at the BBC so that we can learn from them. I quote: 'The measures we are taking today, including the removal of so called 'gagging clauses', show our commitment to change. This agenda will be a priority for the senior management team going forward.' He's even had The Trust take them out of his own contract."

"Really? Oh well. I'll delete a couple of bits out, but basically they have to stay."

"I really don't think so. You'd better check. But for now I'll sign the contract with a covering letter to say that I won't be gagged any more."

And that's how the BBC was brought to book.

And how I'm writing this one at last.

We've been made to keep quiet for too long. With dreadful consequences.

Chapter Twenty Five

THE MAN WITH THE CHILD IN HIS EYES

Now then, now then.

Have you heard the one about the wrinkly old DJ, a young girl, a campervan and a jar of jam? Actually it's not much of a joke. More of an anecdote. But one that always guaranteed roars of laughter among the old timers at Radio 1 when they trotted it out down the pub.

The story went that when he was on the road for Radio 1 with his Savile's Travels shows, Sir Jimmy Savile would routinely retire to his handy mobile home with an excited teenager selected from the crowd. What made one particular occasion legendary was that, as the caravan started rocking around ("as it 'appens" it always did), an old lady approached clutching a gift and, climbing the steps, started knocking on the door.

"Hello Jimmy are you in there?" Radio 1 colleagues look on laughing.

"Yeah. Go away!"

The old lady is now hammering on the door.

"But Jimmy, I've got something for you."

"Yeah, right. Piss off."

The banging continues.

"But Jimmy, I've made you some jam."

"Yeah? So what? Just sod off."

The caravan's still rocking. Radio 1 crew are now whooping it up.

"But Jimmy. I've brought you a present. I just wanted to thank you. Because I know how much you're doing for young people."

Assembled BBC staff are now rolling around uncontrollably.

Anyone fancy another round?

Stories like this soon convinced me that all the rumours I'd heard about local lad 'made-good' Savile, while living in Leeds, were true. He was a perv.

And not a man to mess with.

The word around town was that crossing Savile meant you'd get more than a calling card from his gangster buddies. Even before my arrival at Radio 1, Our Andrew had been warned to avoid this particular turn.

John Walters also intimated to us that Savile's 'selfless' good works were not all they seemed.

"Look at what he's wearing. Everything's branded. All his clothing is sponsored. He might be making millions for charity.

But he's not in it for nothing. He makes sure he's raking it in himself."

However, apart from when Walters was sharing his wisdom, Jimmy Savile wasn't really on my radar. Of course he had a huge TV presence with Top of the Pops and Jim'll Fix It but he no longer troubled the corridors of 'The Nation's Favourite'. He'd left just as I, as part of a new breed of presenters (like Nicky Campbell and Simon Mayo) arrived.

Like Our Andrew, we were in our 20s, university-educated, and had come up through local radio. We weren't a hangover from the Swinging '60s pirate ships or seedy discos. The times-they-were-a-changin' weren't they? Radio 1 was about to celebrate 21 years on air. It was coming of age. Unlike Jimmy's... erm... fans.

I didn't actually meet Savile until I went to interview him in 1997 for a BBC TV series about the history of UK pop. I had to talk to him because he'd invented discos. Or so he claimed. Actually, further research revealed that he had no qualms about stealing other people's thunder. His biggest creation was his own publicity machine.

Anyway, I was reluctantly paying him a visit in his famous penthouse flat overlooking Roundhay Park in Leeds and steeling myself because... well... he was a well-known, dangerous perv. Of course, at 38, I was well past my 'best before' date. Far too old to be in any peril myself. But I still found him menacing and revolting, sprawled on his leather sofa, cigar in mouth, legs akimbo and with chest hair and medallions on full display.

For the sake of the interview, I tried to bond. I thought he might be interested that I'd been a Radio 1 DJ myself.

THE BIRD AND THE BEEB

Not at all. I was just another bird to him. He couldn't have been less bothered. This audience in his inner sanctum was all about him and Sir Jimmy's relentless self-promotion.

After a tour of 'The Duchess's' bedroom – a rather gloomy shrine to his mother, which had been left exactly as it was on the day she died – and the rest of the miserable flat with its kitchen and bathrooms still showcasing '70s saffron and avocado fittings and tiles, he pointed out his trophies displayed on the teak, very-of-its-time, glass fronted wall unit with integral lighting. (I'd thought he was minted. Was Walters wrong? Could he actually be penniless? Or just intent on living in the past?) The whole place smelled stale and I was glad to get out.

But I was glad I'd been. It gave me something non-committal to talk about when he died during my programme 14 years later.

There are generally only two reasons why a radio boss bursts into a studio during a show. Either they're worried that something that's just gone out might drop them in it or somebody's just snuffed it.

On October 29th, 2011, I was live on air when the BBC heard about the death of Sir Jimmy Savile.

"Quick. Quick. You must have worked with him. Pay tribute somehow," was the message from upstairs.

Oh shit. Must I? There wasn't time during a three minute record to explain all my reservations about canonising this national treasure to someone who'd only worked at the BBC for 10 minutes. But the pressure was on. I quickly drew on my visit to his pad, recalling the miner's lamp and lump of polished coal on display. "He never forgot his roots. That he'd been born dirt poor and dragged himself up."

That done I added, "but I worked at Radio 1 and some very queer things happened during his time there. Now is not the time to tell those stories but one day they will come out. Meanwhile, here's how I'd like to remember him today. As the first presenter of Top of the Pops. Here's the theme tune. CCS and 'Whole Lotta Love.'"

Da dah da da dah...

Others were more sycophantic in their tributes.

DJ Dave Lee Travis said: "He was a powerful presence. We'll all be a bit worse off now he's not around."

Tony Blackburn: "He was just a big, over the top, personality. He did all these marathons the whole time, he was just great fun."

Even Royalty chimed in.

"The Prince of Wales and the Duchess of Cornwall are saddened to hear of Jimmy Savile's death and their thoughts are with his family at this time."

The BBC's Director General, Mark Thompson spoke for "all of us," apparently. "I am very sad to hear of Sir Jimmy Savile's death," he said. "From Top of the Pops to Jim'll Fix It, Jimmy's unique style entertained generations of BBC audiences. Like millions of viewers and listeners we shall miss him greatly."

Despite my on-air utterings, nobody at the BBC has ever asked me what I'd been on about. Why didn't anybody bother to find out what he was really like? They'd heard the rumours hadn't they? Didn't anybody think of checking anything?

Newsnight had.

They spent several weeks and thousands of pounds that autumn, looking into his extracurricular activities at a girls' school. Producer Meirion Jones, who'd had a long-standing interest in Savile, launched a formal investigation with reporter Liz MacKean into the star's association with Duncroft Approved School in Surrey.

Jones' aunt had been headmistress there throughout the 1970s and he'd grown up hearing stuff and had been dying to get stuck in to uncovering the truth. Now that Savile was safely out of the way, his editor, Peter Rippon, gave him the go ahead.

By this time it was an open secret that Mark Thompson was expected to leave before long for pastures new and the Director of News, Helen Boaden, and the Director of Vision, George Entwistle, were setting up their stalls for the top job.

On December 2nd, they both attended an awards lunch in London. Boaden claims she mentioned Newsnight's Savile investigation to Entwistle. He's said he didn't remember. But by this stage, his division, telly, had already announced that several Savile tributes would be sprinkled throughout its glittering Christmas schedules.

Less than a week later, around December 7th, the Newsnight investigation was quietly axed. Later that month the BBC press office confirmed to the freelance journalist Miles Goslett (he of the Brand/Ross/Sachs Radio 2 expose in 2008) that Newsnight's investigation into Jimmy Savile was well underway until it was dropped for 'editorial reasons'.

As Christmas approaches, the media executive's life is just one long social whirl and on December 20th, Mark Thompson was at a BBC drinks party when, over festive nibbles and mingling, foreign correspondent, Caroline Hawley, brought up the problem of Newsnight and Savile.

Thompson has said since that he can't recall any details of that chat but something must have stuck in his mind because the next day, he took the time, while up north visiting his new swanky outpost in Salford, to ring his head honcho in News, Helen Boaden to find out more about Newsnight's Savile investigation.

According to Boaden, (a year later, in a letter sent to the Pollard Review which investigated the situation), it was during this call that she informed Thompson that the investigation related to the sexual abuse of children.

The public still don't know anything about it. Miles Goslett had tried to get the story out there but had been rebuffed by seven national newspapers so at Christmas we were fed all those nauseating peak-time programmes celebrating Savile, stuffed with celebrities eulogising about his life and times at the BBC.

I was gobsmacked.

How could they be so gushing about Savile. How come we were still expected to swallow this crap?

It wasn't to last. The Sunday Mirror saw in the new year with a bang and it went public with some information on how Newsnight had been investigating stories concerning Savile's activities with 'schoolgirls' of indeterminate age.

This prompted Miles Goslett to go back to the BBC to ask when its Director General first knew about Newsnight's investigation but the press office refused to give him an answer.

On February 8th, The Oldie magazine went with Goslett's full story about the BBC, Newsnight and Savile. Goslett didn't pull any punches. He said that Thompson knew before Christmas about the nature of the investigation, the piece stated that Savile sexually abused underage girls, that some of the abuse took place on BBC premises and he pointed out that Surrey Police had investigated Savile in 2007 and that two other celebrities – both alive and involved in paedophilia – were also investigated by the Newsnight team.

The Oldie article lit the fuse.

That day, The Daily Telegraph emailed the office of the Director General to ask if The Oldie article was accurate. Thompson was also asked personally via his 'private' email address at the BBC. They received no reply. The Daily Telegraph repeated the claims from The Oldie article two days later on February 10th and in April, Goslett submitted a Freedom of Information Request to the BBC about Thompson's knowledge of the Newsnight investigation and whether he had informed the police and lawyers.

Goslett continued to get nowhere so eventually, after moving to The Sunday Times, he sent the BBC 14 detailed questions about what Thompson and Helen Boaden knew and when.

On September 6th, the law firm Mills & Reeve were paid by the BBC to write to The Sunday Times threatening to sue if it published any suggestions that Thompson and Boaden had a hand in cancelling Newsnight's sex abuse investigation involving Savile. This acknowledged that an investigation of this nature had taken place. Thompson has since said he wasn't really sure what was in that letter.

The next day another letter arrived at the BBC. Now it was ITV seeking responses to its investigation into Savile abusing children on BBC premises. ITV had been quietly delving into Savile's past for its documentary series Exposure and in September it started 'trailing' the programme it was about to broadcast about him.

THE MAN WITH THE CHILD IN HIS EYES

Finally, someone was going to nail him. I and many others at the BBC felt massive relief that the goings-on by Savile would be proven, even if it did mean the BBC was about to become embroiled in an almighty controversy.

Thompson left the Director General's office on September 16th, just a couple of weeks before that programme went out, but he would still be on the BBC payroll for another couple of months and 'on call' to assist his successor, George Entwistle, until he got to grips with the job.

That went well, didn't it?

On October 3rd, the truth was out there.

Exposure was the sensation sweeping the nation. And also quite an education. I genuinely hadn't realised until then just what the repulsive Jimmy Savile had actually inflicted on the young people 'he did so much for' nor what being specially picked out of the Radio 1 crowd by him actually involved. Of course I'd heard rumours and, as I say, was pleased that his behaviour was getting a proper airing.

But I had no idea he had been this bad.

I felt really sorry for his victims and I admired their guts for reliving the horrors.

And really angry about all those old twats laughing about it back at Radio 1.

Our old Radio 1 boss, Controller Johnny Beerling, who'd been at Radio 1 for 26 years including the 19 that Savile was there, seemed suddenly keen to make clear that he'd never had any inkling about his top jock's criminal activities.

On the day that Exposure was due to air he popped up with Nicky Campbell on 5 Live.

"After all Nicky, he never really mixed with any of you guys (his DJs) or the girls in the office."

Unwittingly he'd just summed up the institutionalised sexism on his watch.

"And anyway. He always had his producer with him."

Erm, yes, Johnny... and yer point is?

I was pleased to see my old mentor, Radio 1's mother hen, Doreen Davies, do her bit. She rang Beerling's predecessor, Derek Chinnery, to remind him that he'd had to formally interview Savile about child sex abuse rumours in his time as Controller (1978–1985). Chinnery now told Radio 4 "I asked, 'What's all this, these rumours we hear about you Jimmy?' And he said, 'that's all nonsense'. There was no reason to disbelieve."

Tony Blackburn was now saying "he was not a nice man, despite how the public viewed him at the peak of his success. There were always rumours circulating about him. All of us who worked at the BBC during the time of these heinous crimes owe it to the victims to speak to the police and the BBC Investigations Unit and help them in any way we can."

The new Director General, George Entwistle, then issued his dictat. Anybody who knew anything should speak out.

I didn't know anything about Savile so I just watched and waited to see what came out next.

The accusations and sickening stories just kept flooding in. Up until now, all Savile's accusers were women who'd been hit on in their teens but a grown man came out with his story of visiting TV Centre. Pictures of him as an eight-year-old boy scout on the set of Jim'll Fix It were splashed across our TV screens.

This man broke down as he relived the nightmare of Savile

inviting this innocent little lad into his dressing room on the promise of his very own medal.

We were spared the details but told that he was made to perform a sex act on his host. We were also told that he remembered another man popping his head round the dressing room door and doing nothing to intervene.

He later told Dame Janet Smith that, even worse than that, this man had actually stayed and joined in. I thought of all the times I'd taken my boys into the BBC. I'd want to kill anybody who did that to them.

There was little I could do now until one evening I got a call from the Radio 4 Today programme. I told them I had no evidence about Savile but they wanted to invite me onto the station to talk about the Radio 1 culture during Savile's time.

I was happy to help, so on Saturday, October 6th, a van pulled up outside our house. It was very early because the editor had decided I should be pre-recorded before the show. He was worried that I'd defame somebody.

Oh, please. I'd done enough live radio to know better than that and anyway I had no intention of naming names. This was about a culture, not individuals.

But I was worried about being recorded. I knew that way I'd lose control of what I'd said because I could be chopped and cut. This was a sensitive topic and the temptation for Today would be to sensationalise it.

Inside the van, the poshest BBC engineer I'd ever met was keen to chat about Savile but I was more interested in where this van had been before.

I reckoned this very nice man had been specially assigned to meet and greet the great and the good who usually appeared on this particular show and who must have sat in this very seat. I bet he had some tales to tell but there was no time for all that as James Naughtie was keen to get going.

I'm sure I told him a lot more about the BBC's archaic attitudes towards women than what went out later on air and I'm sure I touched on those confidentiality clauses in BBC contracts that meant we'd all been scared to speak out about anything before. But that was all dumped before I got into all that. The interview was cut and ended on a cliffhanger.

Naughtie had pressed me for a specific example of the sexist culture I was alluding to at Radio 1. So I told him about being routinely groped by a colleague who'd come into the studio while I was talking on air and stick his hands up my jumper to put me off my stride by fondling my breasts.

Had I complained at the time? Oh yes. And I'd been laughed at and asked "what's the matter Liz? Don't you like it? Are you a lesbian?" Tee hee.

Job done I got ready for work and made my way into 6 Music to do my show. I didn't realise that the shit had hit the fan. Just as the train was pulling into Euston station my phone started to ring.

The first call was from our Head of Programmes. He wanted to know if I was OK. Erm, yes. He told me that our Controller Bob Shennan and Director Tim Davie had heard about my appearance on the Today show and would I like to speak to them about it?

He also brought the news that the press had gone crazy and would probably be waiting for me outside the BBC.

Crikey. Why were they so interested in me all of a sudden?

I really didn't yet understand what an impact my story was having. After all, I'd been telling it for years and nobody had shown the slightest bit of interest. There were paparazzi on the doorstep and reporters trying to get some names out of me but I was keeping quiet.

However, the BBC suits were keener than I was to keep going over it. I took one call where I was asked "exactly what was I hoping to achieve?"

OK. First of all I never asked to go on the BBC's flagship news programme. They asked me. I told a story that I've been sharing since 1989 and nobody had batted an eyelid until now.

And nobody asked me about what I said on air the day Savile died about queer things going on.

I'll told them exactly what I'd hoped to achieve. Apart from helping Savile's victims get taken seriously, I'd like to think that, if anything good was to come out of the situation it would be that no women coming into the BBC would have to put up with the kind of crap I've had to – ever again.

I'd told our Head of Programmes that I really didn't want to speak to all and sundry up the management chain. I knew that constantly repeating myself would be a waste of time and I was worried, from past experience, that it could be dangerous too.

Stuff had got buried. Ignored. Changed.

I'd been passed from pillar to post on shifting sand until I could hopefully be brushed under the carpet.

No.

Now I was realising how big this was for the BBC. And if they were serious about wanting to get to the bottom of it, there was only one place for me to go. The top.

THE BIRD AND THE BEEB

"I'll speak to the Director General if he's interested," was all I said. He was interested. I was led into George Entwistle's office three days later.

Chapter Twenty Six

VIDEO KILLED THE RADIO STAR

The Exposure show on ITV had given dozens of people the courage to come forward and plenty of friends in the media were now happy to share their supporting stories too.

Carol Vorderman said it was about time all this came out and told me about one of her experiences at the BBC. In the mid -'80s, when she had a few years on Channel 4's Countdown under her belt, she thought she'd like to branch out a bit into other types of telly so she approached a big shot in the BBC's Light Entertainment department.

Along she went for an early afternoon appointment only to be kept waiting while he got back from what had obviously been a long liquid lunch. Then, sitting back in his ample chair, feet up on his massive desk, he eyed her up and down. "Sorry love. You're no good for us. Yer tits aren't big enough."

And a veteran DJ that I bumped into in the street near Broadcasting House said she was glad I'd spoken out. "It wasn't the touching that was the worst. It was the words. Awful," she said.

"OK. So please don't leave it all to me. Why don't you go public then?" I pleaded, but she wouldn't. No wonder. It's hard to put your head above the parapet when people are queueing up to shoot you down.

Since speaking out on Radio 4, it had felt like it was me on trial. On 5 Live's Richard Bacon show, (I wasn't invited to take part) the ex-Radio 1 DJ Mike Smith accused me of 'a heinous crime' – smearing people at the BBC. And it seemed he doubted my story anyway because, when pressed on whether what I'd described was illegal, he said it was absolutely appalling "if that happened."

I was doorstepped by reporters and photographers at home. We had to bolt the gates while the phone rang off the hook.

Nobody would be satisfied until they knew who'd felt me up. Get over it. It wasn't about one silly old fool who was no longer stalking the BBC corridors. It was about why he knew he could get away with it at the time.

The only other time I'd ever been granted an audience with a Director General, he'd been intimidating and I was dead nervous. Now it seemed the other way round.

George Entwistle was a different kettle of fish to Mark Thompson. Not slippery or cold. Or as lofty. Clean-shaven and with glasses, he wasn't such an imposing figure but, all in all, he seemed a thoroughly decent chap. And he was alone.

No Jessica Cecil covering his back taking notes this time.

He asked who'd groped me. He was a very nice man but obviously not a player like his predecessor. I could already sense that he wasn't very worldly, a bit out of his depth and vulnerable. So I told him it was best if he didn't know. That way he couldn't be pressed to reveal a name and I wouldn't end up in a libel court.

There had been witnesses and they'd had plenty of time to come forward to support me but hadn't. So, as things stood, I knew I couldn't prove anything. He understood that.

He asked why I thought Mike Smith had attacked me on 5 Live for what I'd said on the Today programme. Good question George. He seemed satisfied with my answer.

I told him that since the Radio 4 broadcast, two women my age had told me that, as teenagers, they'd each written to another Radio 1 DJ, only for him to turn up on their doorsteps at boarding school and at home. He'd taken them to gigs and football matches. They'd both been 13. I warned George Entwistle that he should brace himself for other BBC stars to be implicated and he said he'd already had other big names brought to his attention. By now he was ashen-faced and didn't seem that surprised at anything any more.

He asked me more about my time at Radio 1 so I described the set up and some of the Savile stories I'd heard and his grey face started to look a bit sweaty. He told me that he was despairing because the BBC didn't even have records of who worked there in Savile's time. Could I possibly recall and write out a list? I produced one I'd made earlier. "Erm... this name here," he was pointing at my pad. "Tell me about him. The police tell me his name keeps coming up."

"Of course he's retired now," I began.

"Well I don't care if he still works here or not. If he's drawing a BBC pension he's still accountable to me."

Crikey. The beast had stirred.

Entwistle was fair and decent with me and he didn't pretend he knew everything – which was a huge change from his predecessor.

"Look, Liz. I'll be honest with you. I've never worked in Radio and I know nothing about it," he said. "I have absolutely no idea about the culture back then."

"Well actually some of that culture still..." I started to explain.

"Do you think you could come back again and help us further?"

We shook hands on it and I left him staring out of the window, no doubt wondering what the hell to do next.

What he did was ring a QC. She's told me since that it was on that evening that she got a call from Entwistle asking her to lead an inquiry. The Dame Janet Smith Review into the culture at the BBC that had allowed Savile to operate as he did.

Result.

Meanwhile, Nicky Campbell had been dying to speak to me in order to get all the gossip. We'd gravitated towards each other at Radio 1. He's ferociously bright and doesn't suffer fools gladly so I take it as a great compliment that he doesn't think I'm one.

Over the years we've had plenty of laughs, revisiting our fab days at the fun factory, swapping stories about the ridiculous antics of some of our not-so-Great Mates.

I think Nicky was feeling a bit vulnerable now because, a year earlier, he'd been roped into one of the BBC's Savile tribute films. He recalls how, when he arrived at Radio 1, Savile told him that becoming a DJ there was like a bloke "getting the keys to Pandoras's box." He'd been paid a couple of hundred quid for his Savile memories and now wisely announced that he was giving that to charity.

He'd been leaving me texts, about our fondling friend. He knew exactly who it was because, as he said on his show that week, I'd told him all about it at the time.

But he understood why I was keeping schtum. And, after hearing Mike Smith slagging me off on the Richard Bacon show, he thought it would be only fair, and probably a damn good listen, to get me on his. I texted him back. 'Yes fine. Just get 5 Live to ring my home number. I'll be here.'

On the Thursday morning I could hear him flagging up the fact that I was coming on but nobody had rung me yet. Then just before show-time I got a frantic call on my mobile. A 5 Live producer was desperate for my home number. "Oh. Don't you have it there?"

"No Liz. It's nowhere to be found on the system and neither is your mobile number. We had to get that off Nicky just now."

Weird. I gave her my landline and a few minutes later I got on Nicky's phone-in.

Why was this weird? Because I'd complained to the 5 Live Controller, Adrian Van Klaveren, about not being given a right of reply to Mike Smith.

I'd told him I'd not been contacted and that was in breach of BBC editorial guidelines. He'd come back to tell me that he'd been assured that I'd been phoned on my mobile and my home number but hadn't replied to either. I told him my phone logs disputed that and 5 Live has since confirmed to me that they hadn't had either of my contact numbers.

Van Klaveren went to replace the editor of Newsnight after Peter Rippon dropped the Savile film and had to 'step aside' but Van Klaveren never returned to 5 Live after letting another unsubstantiated and libellous piece go out on the BBC. The Lord MacAlpine film. He's been re-assigned to working on archive-based BBC shows to mark the Centenary of World War 1.

The offers began to pour in as everybody wanted to speak to me. The most astounding call came on the following Monday in a conversation with an agent I vaguely knew.

"Fancy the jungle, Liz?"

"What? You mean in Australia sitting round the camp fire waiting to be humiliated on telly? No thanks. Not for me."

"But you could get a fortune now!"

"Really?"

"Yeah! Since you've said about being groped yer really hot!"

"Mmmm... posing in a bikini whilst popping a couple of testicles in my mouth? No thanks. I'd like to think we've moved on."

A few weeks later, the BBC's Investigation Unit rang to ask if they could give my number to Operation Yewtree – the police investigation in historical sex abuse cases at the BBC. I said "no, but I'll ring them." The detective I reached on the number I'd been given was in a car and sounded a bit spivvy to be honest.

"Hi Liz. We've been trying to get in touch with you but we've realised we've been talking to the wrong Liz Kershaw," he laughed. Good start. Kershaw is not a common name. Even oop north.

"Anyway. Good to talk to you. Now can you tell us all about DJ X?" he asked.

"What about DJ X?"

"Well, it's just that you've said he groped you at Radio 1."

"No I didn't. I've never said who it was."

"Well everybody knows it was DJ X."

"Do they? Well good luck with that. It's nothing to do with me."

"Now then Liz. If you don't make a statement about him people might think it never actually happened. That you made it all up."

"OK. I'm cool with that."

"But Liz. We need you to say what happened, the more women who come forward the stronger the case."

"Well call me old fashioned but I've got no evidence."

"Well have a little think about it and call us back."

I thought long and hard. And asked another detective.

"Are you're saying that just my word against some bloke after over 20 years is good enough for you? I'm sorry but as a mother of two boys I'm finding this all very disturbing. So you're saying my son could go to a party and years later be accused of rape and you wouldn't need any DNA or eye witnesses or CCTV pictures to charge him?"

"Well. If it was just one girl obviously the Crown Prosecution Service would probably throw it out. But if more than one girl came forward well..."

A week later I got another call from the BBC investigation unit. "Are you ready to make a statement to Operation Yewtree now Liz?" they asked.

No I wasn't and I wouldn't be. Ever. This wasn't justice. I was shocked, disgusted and even a little bit scared. I'd had previous experience of ancient incidents ending up in court on somebody's say so. At the start of 2010, I had found myself on the witness stand, taking the oath in Court No.1 at the Old Bailey after being called as a witness by a solicitor from Southport.

"I wonder if you can remember sharing a minicab from Birmingham to London with a blind man after a TV discussion programme with some glamour models about breast enhancement surgery in 1990?" he had asked.

Now there's something you'd hardly forget in a hurry is it?

I replied that I absolutely did. It was a show called Central Weekend Live presented by fellow Radio 1 DJ Nicky Campbell. I'd been on it a several times arguing various topics like "Is chart music shite?" or something along those lines anyway. I couldn't recall most episodes except for the one involving the solicitor's client, the blind man. And so, without being asked any more questions, or being told what the case was about, I got roped in as a witness for the defence.

I still didn't know what the charges were when I was asked why I would remember a journey from 20 years earlier. I explained that I'd been miffed that ITV had been so cheap on this one occasion that they expected me to share a ride with a stranger and that me and my fellow passenger had a memorable discussion about vision.

I'd asked him how, if he'd been blind from birth he dreamed because I did it in pictures, almost like a film. We chatted and chatted and laughed about the breast implant I was carrying that had been given to me by one of the glamour models on the show. Again, not something you're likely to forget eh?

Anyhow, a full 20 years following that journey, a young guy had come forward and accused the blind guy of sexual molestation after travelling together back to London from that very show. But there was no young guy in our cab. Just me, him, the breast implant and the driver and it was a good job I'd been tracked down to say so.

So I'd seen firsthand what *false* claims coming out of the blue, could do to an *innocent* man. I'd since spoken out truthfully about historical events that had been only too real. And I'd done that, not to single out any one person after all this time, but as an example of workplace culture many years before.

I'd never had any intention of naming an individual without proof. Or of now going after them. So, when Operation Yewtree came onto me, about a guy I'd never actually accused, I didn't want any part in it.

Meanwhile, back on Planet Thompson.

In October, 2012, ahead of our erstwhile DG's arrival at The New York Times as its CEO, it seemed he was rather busy clearing up any lingering misconceptions about his past life. He gave an interview to his new paper and took the time to write to Rob Wilson MP saying he'd 'never heard any allegations' about Savile during his time at the BBC.

But on the 24th of that month he told Ben Webster of The Times in London that he was aware, back in December, 2011, that Newsnight's investigation was about sex abuse.

Less than an hour later his aide contacted Webster claiming that Thompson had 'misspoke'.

The Times ran the interview anyway. It was all recorded and I've listened to it. It really has to be heard to be believed.

The BBC had, by now, been forced to respond to all the flak over the shelving of its own TV investigation into Savile by setting up an inquiry into the whole saga, the Pollard Review.

Nick Pollard had run Sky News and his brief was to get to the bottom of how the Newsnight investigation came to be quashed.

Who'd been involved and why? Was it simply a judgement call by its hapless editor Peter Rippon? Was it down to pressure from rival senior managers concerned about a clash of interests between News and Entertainment? Was it shelved because 'someone' had realised that revelations about Savile's sex crimes on their premises wouldn't sit well in the schedules with its uncritical yuletide beatification of the perpetrator?

In late 2012, Nick Pollard, assisted by a QC, interviewed all the players and he had to wade through some very conflicting evidence, to say the least.

It published its findings on December 19th, 2012, and the upshot was that Pollard concluded there'd been no conspiracy to save the BBC's face and that the Savile film had been dropped by Newsnight Editor Peter Rippon simply because he got the jitters. It was all of his doing.

Thompson was in the clear. Even though Pollard didn't mention a letter from Boaden, via her lawyers, that contradicted Thompson's version of events. How had that happened?

I decided to contact John Whittingdale, chairman of the House of Commons Media Select Committee to ask him why a woman's evidence to Pollard hadn't been given as much credence as that of her male boss.

Ooh, feminism eh? That touched a nerve.

We met in Portcullis House over coffee and, while sharing this righteous Parliamentarian's seemingly unlikely penchant for hell-raising rockers AC/DC, I convinced him that the licence-paying public, and us BBC operatives, needed this clearing up once and for all.

He wrote to Boaden asking her to confirm to Parliament that she had informed Pollard that Thompson had been told about the nature of the Savile investigation by Newsnight before Christmas, 2011. She did just that but her evidence, and further investigations into exactly what happened, have been shunted to one side.

For now.

Nick Pollard, speaking publicly for the first time since his report was published, told Radio 4 in August last year that he was not convinced he got to the bottom of the story "partly because of conflicting recollections by people, or no recollections offered to us."

He also told the journalist Miles Goslett (again, I've heard the tapes) that it was an error in judgement when he didn't consider Boaden's evidence about what she told Thompson in his report. In response, a BBC spokesman said the report's findings had been accepted and there was nothing further to add. Another £3 million of licence payers' money well spent then.

Back in October, 2012, I'd been trying to get a taxi behind John Lewis in Oxford Street, London. All of a sudden a cab pulled up and getting out of it was none other than Lord Patten, the Chairman of the BBC Trust. This was a pure fluke. Wow. Should I humbly slope away? Or should I grab my chance?

I bit the bullet.

"Excuse me Lord Patten. You won't know me but I've worked on national BBC radio now for 25 years now. I just want to say..."

He was glazing over already.

"I just want to say that I've lived through many BBC crises before and I hope that you won't allow the usual to happen." He wasn't responding.

"What I mean is that you mustn't just let the DG resign and sack some bloke on the shop floor this time. If the management in between are really to blame, it must be made to stick this time. They must be made to take responsibility. OK. I can see you're busy. Thank you for your time. "

Seems I was wasting my breath. After only a month or so in the job, George Entwistle was forced to take all the blame for past mistakes under Mark Thompson. He was so earnest and full of good intentions and he was genuinely trying to get to the truth about Savile and his cronies. But he wasn't a politically savvy player, he was too nice and he paid the price for that.

So the top guy had to go and he wasn't the only one.

Peter Rippon was packed off to a basement in Broadcasting House as Editor of the BBC's Online Archive, with a brief to create 'the definitive online collection of the BBC's television and radio journalism'. That'll be the doomed Digital Media Initiative then, which, after wasting £100million of licence payer's money in less than six months, was scrapped in May, 2013.

The BBC announced with a flourish that Helen Boaden's deputy, Stephen Mitchell, who was castigated in the Pollard Review for being 'exceptionally vague', had agreed to leave, even though Paxman got it out of the BBC on 'Newsnight' that Mitchell was retiring anyway.

So what was his punishment then, if he was already leaving? "Nothing" would be the answer to that.

Boaden herself also lost her job. Well, in News anyway. The

BBC had been brought to its knees by her division which according to the Pollard Review "had gone into meltdown" on her watch. So somehow it was decided she'd be best out of the way running a lesser department. She was made Director of little old Radio, collecting around £350,000 a year from the licence fee.

In her evidence to Pollard she'd mentioned attending a Radio Academy lunch where she hadn't taken any notice of the conversation because her table companions had just been 'some old DJs'. Mmm. That didn't bode well did it?

Without that kind of dismissal of those of us who work in the BBC's most loyally consumed and senior service, maybe the likes of Helen Boaden could have found out what we had to say about Savile. And maybe BBC News wouldn't have got us all into this mess.

Mark Thompson is now an uptown kinda guy, running another of the world's biggest media brands, strolling to work from his home on Manhattan's East Side to his high-rise New York Times office on 40th Street, open necked shirt, Starbucks in hand. On September 6th, 2013, Channel 4 News caught up with him on his way to work and he admitted that he and Helen Boaden had discussed Newsnight's investigation into Savile and sex abuse but he still maintained that he'd never misled anyone about what he'd known while he was at the BBC.

Maybe I've lost the plot.

But I think Thompson is best staying in New York. At least there he can still dine out on the kudos of the BBC.

Last time I was in the States, I decided to do some in-depth research into current US perception of the BBC brand. By asking a guy in a bar.

THE BIRD AND THE BEEB

"Hell yeah! Jeez, I lurve the BBC. Let's see now. Poirot! I lurve Poirot. And Downton Abbey. I lurve Downton Abbey."

Mmm. They are actually ITV so far then. Not to worry.

"And what about Jimmy Savile? What do you think of him now?" I asked.

"Jimmy Savile?" he was looking puzzled. "Is he in Downton? No? OK. Never heard of the guy."

Chapter Twenty Seven

SISTERS ARE DOIN' IT
FOR THEMSELVES

Does being a woman make a difference in the BBC?

Well judging by the not so politically correct title of this book you can probably guess what I'm going to say. All the clues are there.

Of course I accept that men and women are built differently. That's why they don't play football or cricket for the same team or why someone like Jessica Ennis-Hill will never take on Usain Bolt.

But if the skillset for a job basically requires you to be able to sit for hours on end in a comfy chair, think straight and talk sense, should it matter whether you have tits or testicles? I know that's crude but it really is the nuts and bolts of the matter.

I know full well that I've had some breaks simply because I was female and in the right place at the right time but I've also known for 30 years that some jobs have been just for the boys. I've been told that I'm an oddity at the BBC. And, statistically at least, I agree.

Recently I realised something about the seven 'line-managers' for my 6 Music show. From my producer and his assistant, all the way up to Director General, six of them are men. And with guys presenting the shows either side of mine, both with blokes in charge of those, it sometimes feels like I'm the only woman in the building. It doesn't bother me. I can be one of the lads. I just think it's an odd state of affairs in the 21st century.

When I was presenting breakfast shows on BBC local radio from 2000 to 2009, I was the only lone female doing that across the BBC's entire output. And last time I checked there was still only one woman let loose on her own at peak times in the mornings on the BBC's 50-odd stations. How come?

In 2008, when I asked BBC local radio management why this was the case, I was quickly told to shut up for my own good and warned that I must not do a planned interview with a magazine if I was intending to mention that.

So they knew. But did nothing.

As there is no other reasonable explanation for all this, it seems to me it can only be down to deliberate discrimination. And that's illegal. And, if it's happening at the nation's tax-funded broadcaster, it's also a national disgrace.

In 2009, I attempted to flag this up in an email to Harriet Harman MP who was the Minister for Women and Equality. Surely she would be interested?

Nope. No reply.

Nothing.

If only I could find somebody who agreed with me that a change had to come.

In December, 2011, at a champagne-fuelled festive party I finally found an ally. Nadine Dorries, MP.

"Don't I know you? Yes. You're on the radio aren't you? Not Janice Long... Oh I'll think of it in a minute," she said.

"Er... Liz Kershaw," I chuckled.

"That's it. You used to be on Radio 1."

"Yes. Twenty odd years ago!"

"Are you still on the radio then?"

"Yes. BBC 6 Music."

"Crikey. That's a long time then. There can't be many who can say that."

"No. Apart from Anne Nightingale and Janice I'm now the third longest serving female DJ in the country. But that's mainly because there've been so few of us. There were only three of us really back then. In fact, to be honest there aren't many more of us now!"

I thought that was it but I hadn't realised how much of this Nadine was taking in over a snifter at the bar. She's a tough cookie and hard to read.

A month later she invited me to the House of Commons where she was on her feet, supported by my long-time friend and now MP Tessa Munt, armed with a dossier of statistics I'd put together by simply collating information already in the public domain and readily available on the BBC's own websites.

Over to Hansard where the case is now set out in black and white, forever.

THE BIRD AND THE BEEB

January 23rd, 2011. 10.16 pm
Nadine Dorries (Mid Bedfordshire) (Con):
I was inspired to apply for this debate when, at a Christmas party, I met a very successful and very well-known BBC broadcaster who shall remain anonymous. What I was told shocked me, not least because that very famous individual told me that should he (that's me!) raise the issue within the BBC, life would be made so difficult for him that the end of his career would be just around the corner. I was given a quick resumé of how the BBC behaves with regard to female broadcasters. It was a shocking story.

What is even more shocking is that in the case of the BBC, the general public, 52% of whom are women, pay a licence fee to endorse the behaviour in question.

I think it is about time the Minister set up a Parliamentary Committee to scrutinise the decision-making process within the BBC. Whatever it is doing at the moment, it is simply wrong.

I am not advocating degrading quotas; I am talking about basic commercial common sense.

Let us begin with Radio 2. The most listened-to music radio station in the world has not a single female daytime broadcaster. Is that not shameful? Radio 1 has one daytime female presenter. However, Radio 2 has 'Sally Traffic', whose job seems to be moving in and out of one studio after another to massage the egos of the male presenters who are there throughout the day.

Although she outstrips most of the presenters in wit and rapport, I imagine that she earns a fraction of what the male egos do. Sally appears far more intellectual and witty than every male broadcaster whom she has to humour. However, the BBC bosses, whoever they may be, appear not to have noticed that.

SISTERS ARE DOIN' IT FOR THEMSELVES

Even though the BBC is wholly funded, one way or another, by taxpayers, half of whom, as I said, are women, the BBC bosses seem to feel that the person who pays the piper does not need representing on daytime radio.

Mr. Speaker, I am sure that you remember the amazing Annie Nightingale, and that you grew up, as I did, listening to her on Radio 1. She has more music knowledge in her little finger than the majority of radio presenters today on Radio 1. Do you know what Annie Nightingale does now, Mr. Speaker? She presents one programme, one night a week, from 2 till 4 am. That is where the BBC has consigned Annie Nightingale. Jo Whiley is on Radio 2 three nights a week from 8 till 9.30pm. That is as good as it gets. It is a double travesty. Vanessa Feltz is on Radio 2 weekday mornings from 5 till 6.30. Another music legend – I am sure you remember her name, too, Mr. Speaker – Liz Kershaw, is on Radio 6 on Saturday afternoon from 1 till 4. That is where the BBC has placed those fantastic women.

If the BBC placed a banner on top of Broadcasting House and wrote on it, 'The BBC does not believe that women deserve to be represented on BBC radio', that banner would be 100% accurate. It is frankly amazing that Annie, Liz, Vanessa and Jo have kept hold of their jobs at all, because we all know what the BBC attitude is to women of a certain age.

Let us move to news and current affairs. The Today programme on Radio 4 has seven million listeners a day. Many of them are influential and decision makers. Yet only 16% of the voices heard on Today can go two whole hours in the morning when listening to the Today programme without a single female voice, and have male voices speaking at you throughout all that time.

When questioned about the fact that there were no female voices on Radio 2 for two hours on one particular day, BBC editors said that that was okay because they did not receive any letters of complaint.

In conclusion, the left may have ignored the behaviour of the BBC while it was in government, but if the Minister continues that pattern of behaviour, I and others will view it as a dereliction of the duties of his office. What is he going to do to end the culture of sexism and poor-quality, male-dominated programming that we women are paying for, and are subjected to?

Tessa Munt (Wells) (LD): As far as I could see when preparing for this evening, there is not one woman with children in Radio 2's management above assistant producer level. That includes the producers, the executive producers, the head of programmes and the controller of Radio 2. That situation may not come as a surprise. When we look at the structure of the radio system and the controllers of Radio 1, Radio 2, Radio 3, Radio 4 and Radio 5, we see that only Radio 4 has a female controller. The Director of Radio and the Director General are both male. I am sure that the hon. Lady agrees that in local radio, it is horrific that only one woman presents a breakfast show, out of 43 such flagship programmes.

The Parliamentary Under-Secretary of State for Culture, Olympics, Media and Sport (Mr. Edward Vaizey): The representation of women across the media, but particularly at the BBC, is an important issue that is worth addressing.

Some 84% of reporters and guests on Radio 4's Today programme are men.

SISTERS ARE DOIN' IT FOR THEMSELVES

Indeed, on July 5th, 2011, one would have had to wait from 6.15 am until 8.20 am to hear one female contributor, alongside the 27 male contributors to that programme.

If (the BBC) is to maintain its pre-eminence and prominence, it must address the issue of gender imbalance.

The BBC agreement does place a duty on the BBC executive board to make arrangements for promoting the equality of opportunity between men and women. The BBC executive board is accountable to the BBC Trust, and it is the duty of the trust to ensure that the duty on equality of opportunity is met. The BBC, Channel 4 and S4C are all subject to the Equality Act 2010, which seeks to eliminate discrimination and harassment and to advance equality of opportunity. Under the terms of the Act, all those broadcasters must publish equality objectives every four years, and publish information to demonstrate compliance with the general equality duty.

I take my hon. Friend's point which is to draw attention to the public face of the BBC and to ask how female-friendly it is.

My offer to the hon. Member for Wells and to my hon. Friend the Member for Mid-Bedfordshire is to broker a meeting with both of them with the Director General of the BBC, Mark Thompson, and we will sit down and discuss this issue. It is an issue that we must keep pressing at.

Some people might regard it as frivolous or something that makes good copy for a parliamentary sketch, but my hon. Friend made a valid and fundamental point: we want to hear a balance of voices on the radio.

We do not want to set quotas or diktats, but we do want to maintain a dialogue and pressure.

House adjourned.

THE BIRD AND THE BEEB

In February, 2012, Nadine and Tessa got their meeting with Mark Thompson and handed him a report I'd put together setting out the facts.

On Radio 2 there hadn't been a female presenter during daylight hours on weekdays for 17 years since Gloria Hunniford was replaced by Steve Wright in 1995.

Indeed, across the entire week there was just one female presenter between 8am and 8pm – Elaine Paige on Sundays for a couple of hours. Across seven days' output of 168 hours only 33 were presented by women.

Radio 1 was no better with just 16% – 27 hours – of its airtime presented by women.

And what about my home, 6 Music? Surely the newest and coolest BBC radio station would be a shining example of equality?

Well here's the maths again. There were just four female presenters on 6 Music, on air for just 26 out of 168 hours a week. Or the equivalent of just over one day in every seven.

In case Thompson defended all this with tired old clichés, I also armed Tessa and Nadine with a full set of arguments.

Myth: Women don't like listening to women. Only male presenters can cut it with the daytime audience because it's predominately female and the housewives' choice for company is naturally a man.

Reality: There's no evidence for that. When we were growing up we loved Annie Nightingale just as much as John Peel. How insulting to female licence payers.

Myth: Girls don't aspire to be radio presenters.

Reality: Just as many girls as boys ask "how do I get into radio?" Indeed, more girls take Media Studies than boys do.

SISTERS ARE DOIN' IT FOR THEMSELVES

Myth: Women don't apply for presenters jobs.

Reality: And neither do men. Management hire and fire presenters as they pick and choose to do. There are no ads. There are no applicants.

Myth: There aren't enough girls who are passionate or knowledgeable about music to be DJs.

Reality: Have you been to a festival recently? Have you looked at the crowd? Try telling Emily Eavis who runs Glastonbury that.

Myth: Women just aren't well informed or authoritative enough to anchor the likes of the Today programme or other radio breakfast shows.

Reality: Mmm... Just like women listeners have to have their own little show later in the day. (That's Woman's Hour by the way girls.) How come women present TV programmes like Newsnight for example then? Try telling Kirsty Wark or Emily Maitlis that they're ill- informed pushovers. Or Jo Coburn who presents The Politics Show on BBC TV.

Myth: The gruelling early starts and hours of Breakfast shows don't suit women.

Reality: True, it takes enormous self-discipline and dedication. (It is tough going to bed at 9pm and getting up at 5 hitting the ground running). But do try out a few women. I think you'll find that even the weaker sex can manage that these days.

Myth: Presenting a daily radio show is not compatible with being a mum.

Reality: But yet it's suitable for a dad?

Myth: It's simply not a suitable job for women.

Reality: The required attributes/qualifications are a good voice. A sharp mind. Focus. Dedication. Discipline. Knowledge. Women have those.

Tessa and Nadine just wanted facts not flannel. And for the

BBC to come clean. And assure them that women would not be deliberately excluded simply because of their gender.

Neither me nor these MPs had any wish – then or now – to oust perfectly capable men from their jobs. I have two sons remember – we don't want them penalised for their gender any more than we want girls to be.

We just wanted to be told why, if over 50% of the UK population is female and paying for BBC radio, they've been kept off it?

I guessed that Thompson would be in denial because I had once raised the matter with him myself.

"Do you realise that on all of the BBC's 54 radio stations only one daily breakfast show is presented by a woman? Me," I'd asked him.

"No, no no. That can't be right," he protested.

"Yes. I know it's not *right*. But it's *true*."

As predicted, when he met Nadine and Tessa, he again avidly disputed the facts and figures.

But when they shoved my pie charts (I'd really done my homework) in his face he had to change his tune. These graphics represented the 24 hour clock on Radio 1, 2 and 6 and I'd filled them in with the traditional colours for boys and girls.

They were solid blue. Except for slivers of pink.

Unable to argue with those, he delegated the ladies away by passing them down the management chain. So Tessa then had meetings with the Director of Radio, Tim Davie, and the Controller of Radio 2 and 6 Music, Bob Shennan. Nobody seemed to know exactly where this was going.

In the Spring of 2012, and with Thompson on his way out, it was time for the BBC Trust to appoint a new Director General.

SISTERS ARE DOIN' IT FOR THEMSELVES

Tessa wanted each member of the Trust to know the score before they interviewed the candidates for the BBC's top job.

So she sent a copy of my report to each of the Trust members ahead of these interviews.

Its title 'Just 17' referred to a number that kept coming up. Only 17% of BBC DJs were female and that it had been 17 years since there'd been a woman on daytime Radio 2.

Her covering letter asked them to take this seriously and to make sure they appointed a successor to Mark Thompson who was actually willing to accept the statistics, accept there was a problem, and who could outline how they would deal with it.

Tessa had been very encouraged by Tim Davie during their meeting and, now that he was in the frame for the DG's job, she thought he might like to have all the facts at his fingertips when he got grilled by the Trust.

So I told Tessa that I'd drop off a copy of the report and her letter to him at Broadcasting House (incognito of course!) next time I went in to do my show.

I was terrified that, if my involvement in all this got out, it would drop me right in it.

What a crap secret agent I'd make! What a farce.

"Morning. I'd like to leave this for Tim Davie please so he can have it first thing on Monday. Thanks." I'd just popped into the BBC's main reception and was walking out again. (We're in an annexe next door).

"Er... hello! Sorry. Excuse me. You can't leave this here." The receptionist was waving the envelope back at me. "We can't accept it."

"Sorry? Why not?"

"Security. We're not allowed to take anything."

"But it's just a letter. I could post it now in that box right outside and then it would go miles round London and be brought back here on Monday."

"I know but that's the rules. Security."

"So I can't leave it then?"

"No. We can't accept it."

By the time I'd walked round the corner there'd been a change of heart.

"Morning Liz," one of our own commisionaires greeted me. "I've just had a call from BH reception. They will take your envelope. Just give it to me and I'll run it round."

"Blimey. Thanks."

Tim Davie didn't get the Director General job but a few months later, in May, 2012, while still Director of Radio, he hosted an evening at Broadcasting House for Sound Women. A new organisation for women working in radio. And those who want to.

"Hi Liz. Thanks for that stuff you sent me." He greeted me with a knowing grin.

"Me? Stuff!"

"Yes," he continued mischievously "You know. Your 'Just 17' document and Tessa Munt's letter. Broadcasting House reception rang me at home that Saturday morning to say you had a package for me and it seemed to be very important and urgent."

Bugger!

"Ha-ha-ha! You've got me there alright Tim. It's a fair cop!"

"Well anyway thanks. It's a real issue and we've got to do something about it."

Hurrah! Result. Someone on the BBC board, on side, and on

the case at last. Tim Davie should have been made Director General and did stand in for six months from late 2012 when George Entwistle left suddenly.

On Saturday, January 10th, 2013, I emailed him wondering if he realised what a big day it was for the BBC.

Something very significant was about to happen.

6 Music's latest signing, Mary Anne Hobbs, was starting her new show at 7am that day. With Edith Bowman on at 10am and me as usual at 1pm, for the first time ever, three consecutive music shows were about to be presented by female DJs.

Three girls in a row? Absolutely unheard of before!

And something I would never have put money on just a year earlier. This really was important and an exciting landmark in the history of BBC radio.

Tim emailed straight back with "yes, it's great isn't it Liz? We have a lot of work to do. But it's a start. Best. Tim."

What a shame that Tim Davie never came back to running radio. He went off to be head of BBC Worldwide.

Throughout Tessa and Nadine's campaign it's been snidely and widely suggested that my MP mates are being disingenuous because the gender balance is no better in their workplace. That only 16% of MPs are women. And that maybe they should try putting their own House in order first.

I've had that discussion with them. As I did at a party about 15 years ago when someone tapped me on the shoulder and asked me if I fancied running for Parliament.

My view hasn't changed.

Life in the House of Commons couldn't be more different to life in Broadcasting House. All the bogus obstacles that have been put in the way of women in the BBC are actually real and to be reckoned with in politics.

So I'm convinced that being an MP is no job for a mother. Or rather, should I say, for a woman with children under 18. To be an MP you have no choice but to spend most of the week in Westminster. And to qualify for a seat you must have a constituency. The House and your home can be hundreds of miles apart. You may not be able to see your children for days on end.

That must be very hard on all involved. I know that I really missed my mum being around when I was young when she was absent from home, attending endless council meetings in the evenings. Our relationship suffered and still does. Once your kids are away for weeks at a time at university or have left the nest altogether it's a different matter. All we need to do now is get rid of the ageism that writes off older women and puts them off standing as MPs and we'll have cracked it.

The best female candidates for Parliament must be those who are young, free and single or those who've already brought up a family and acquired the many skills along the way. Tessa and Nadine are perfect examples. Both over 50 and with their kids grown up.

Oh, hang on, that's me now, too! Watch this space...

At the BBC, I'm pleased to say things should now change, thanks to the latest Director General, Tony Hall.

In August, 2013, he announced: "I understand that it's not my BBC. It is yours. Everyone pays, so everyone should have the same chance of working for us. Talent will be the only requirement for success. If you have the ability, the BBC will give you the opportunity and we need more women in key broadcasting roles at the BBC. By the end of 2014 I have set the challenge of at least half of all local BBC radio stations having a woman presenting their high-profile breakfast shows – either solo or as part of a team".

Hallelujah.

About time. And straight from the horse's mouth too.

For nearly 50 years this situation has been at best ignored, or at worst, covered up. But from now on, nobody should be afraid to speak up or held back simply because they're female. Or male.

We're not asking for men to be sacked. We don't want tokenism. We don't want quotas. We'd just like a bit more fairness.

Tessa and Nadine succeeded in highlighting archaic and scandalous attitudes and have finally embarrassed the BBC's top brass into talking the talk.

Now let's see some action boys.

Chapter Twenty Eight

WHOLE LOTTA LOVE

You always worry when a band brings out its greatest hits. Is it all over? Well, I might be writing my memoir but I'm not ready to hang up my headphones just yet.

Even though I've been there, done that and got the gongs to prove it, I still have a few ambitions. Twenty five years after making a pilot at Radio 1, I still hanker for a late-night show (say between 10pm and midnight) reviewing the day's events by chewing them over with interesting guests and playing great music.

And I still dream of being able to present the Today programme or Newsnight with a Rochdale accent.

But will there still be a BBC to work at in the future? Has the BBC got one?

Yes, if it continues to do what it does best. Because when it does, it's the best in the world. As emails from Brazil to Brisbane tell me week in, week out.

Let's start with television.

Because of ever more rapidly developing technology, the media is changing faster than ever before and so is how we consume it. And this presents particular challenges.

We no longer have to wait a full week for Auntie to let us see the next episode of our favourite show. Or months for a new format to be created, commissioned, made and shown.

We're all Marxists now. As Carl said "the workers must have the means of production" and now we can 'film' our own stuff on our iPads and 'broadcast' it on YouTube. And we can get entire new series on-line in box-sets from Netflix and LOVEFiLM. We can record, pause and rewind output from thousands of sources from around the globe via satellite and the World Wide Web, on our computers, set-top boxes, smart TVs and mobile devices. Wherever and whenever it suits us.

It's all getting a bit blurred. Who'd have thought that my old employer, British Telecom, would be broadcasting TV and that the British Broadcasting Corporation would be accessed on a telephone?

And yet, every evening, 20 million British viewers still sit down in front of a tellybox in our homes for a traditional, shared experience. And talk about it afterwards, at school or work. Through these 'water cooler' moments the BBC has been the glue that binds this nation together. And it can still have such a place. As long as it concentrates on creating excellent 'Event TV' that's time critical and possibly interactive. Whether it's in entertainment and drama (Strictly Come Dancing, Eurovision, Sherlock, Doctor Who), sport (The Olympics), factual (Crimewatch, Watchdog) current affairs (Newsnight) or the big occasions (Royal weddings, state funerals and national celebrations).

BBC Radio is safer I'd say.

Video hasn't killed the radio star yet. Nor will it. Easy access and mass ownership of recorded music, whether on wax cylinders, 78s, vinyl, CDs or digital downloading, didn't snuff out radio listening. Because we don't listen to radio just to hear what we already love. We can do that on the likes of Spotify and YouTube and with any number of devices.

We listen to radio with a sense of community and to be part of something. That's why millions still gather round the wireless every morning for Pop Master with Ken Bruce or have a rant every lunchtime during the Jeremy Vine Show. Or start the day by tuning in to the Today programme or Your Call with Nicky Campbell, or spend Sundays with The Archers or Steve Wright's Love Songs.

Through most of its national (and now international through the internet) radio services, the BBC still reigns supreme with more than two thirds of the country, tens of millions of us, listening. Stations like Radio 4, 5 Live, Radio 2 and 6 Music are unique and the best in the world. Not least because they are uncluttered by ads.

Which brings me onto the licence fee.

I know it provides my bread and butter but I don't take that for granted. I pay it too. So I never abuse it. Every time I've faced incurring a cost at work I've asked myself 'how many people have had to cough up to fund me doing that?'

So I feel able to say with a clear conscience that less than £150 a year per household is peanuts. Especially when the Sky+ box my sons insist we need costs me nearly four times that annually and while subscribers are still expected to buy into car insurance and payday loans to line Sky's shareholders' pockets.

In any case, if the BBC had to rely on advertising revenue it would be stuffed. And so would its competitors. The cake is only so big. And now everyone – from our traditional terrestrial broadcasters to the emerging social media – are chasing increasingly thinner slices. For the BBC to try and grab a wedge would just starve out others. And the advertisers are cottoning on to the fact that we all skip through the ads now anyway. It's just not a viable or enduring business model.

Of course, the BBC must spend its income more responsibly and be more accountable. Some senior managers have claimed and wasted millions. For example, when I suggested making a show about the band The Smiths from their home patch in Salford, I was told I could but only if I were prepared to pay my own £60 train fare to get up there. Meanwhile, we learned that Mark Thompson, at one time on over £800,000 a year, had claimed back the cost of his £2.40 tram ticket from the train station in Manchester city centre to Salford Quays. And that one six-figure salaried exec had replaced her £500 designer handbag on expenses.

No wonder the public gets disgusted and fed up. I know I have.

But the licence fee needs to be protected and to be allowed to at least keep pace with inflation, especially as the BBC is being expected to provide more and more with less and less.

In 2010, the NUJ attacked the "shabby, behind-closed-doors deal with the government" forged by Thompson by saying "his decision to agree to freeze the licence fee until 2017 and take on an extra £340m in new financial responsibilities, such as the World Service and the provision of fast broadband, has proved a disaster for the corporation."

The World Service is indeed a huge financial imposition on the licence payers. It used to be funded directly by the Foreign Office from other taxation because its value to the nation was recognised by successive governments of all political persuasions. It still should be.

OK, cue Land of Hope And Glory!

The World Service and the BBC's other radio and TV networks are the best ambassadors for Britain that we have. You could shut down all our embassies and we'd still have influence around the world via the BBC.

Before 9/11 I was told by an Afghan journalist visiting Bush House about the avid way Afghans consumed the World Service. How it was a lifeline. How respected it was. Especially among women and girls who were banned from education and, under fear of death, were otherwise deprived of information from the outside world. He made me cry. And feel very humbled.

As I did in the African bush in Zimbabwe when, huddled round a campfire in the dead of night, I heard the World Service echoing across the vast open plains. As I do anywhere on earth when I see the locals huddled round a TV in a bar tuned to the BBC. As I do when I hear from friends in New York that a little station has started up there and is forging ahead by proudly modelling itself on 6 Music.

We may not appreciate the BBC because it's just there. And

we feel entitled to criticise it because we – not some twin tycoons or an aristocratic dynasty or a global media mogul – own it. It's ours. It's the tie that binds us in Britain. And the brand that defines us abroad.

It gives us status and influence on the increasingly turbulent world stage. It helps our small island nation punch above its weight in the international arena. This is so called soft diplomacy. But it's under attack. And its loss would hit us hard. The demise of the BBC would cost us all dearly, culturally, socially, financially and politically at home and abroad.

I love the BBC, completely believe in it, wholeheartedly support its continued existence and will always fight tooth and nail for that.

Acknowledgements

SIGNING OFF

So that's my story. A story of a little girl from Rochdale who grew up imbibing the BBC through programmes like Children's Favourites, Blue Peter, Doctor Who, Radio 1 and Top of the Pops, and who one day, through some happy accidents and hard work, found herself, along with her brother, rubbing shoulders with heroes from John Peel to Jeremy Paxman.

My journey has taken me through all of the BBC's national radio stations, BBC local radio and BBC TV. From pop to politics. Along the way I've been able to meet my music heroes, rub shoulders with royalty and politicians, and the great and the good of stage, screen and sports. And thousands of so-called ordinary people with extraordinary lives with whom I'd never have come into contact otherwise.

THE BIRD AND THE BEEB

The BBC has sent me around the world and the BBC brand has got me across borders and opened doors into exclusive events and amazing situations.

It's been a joy and a privilege. A complete blast. Or to say it in song...

I've been so lucky, I am the girl with golden hair
I wanna sing it out to everybody
What a joy, what a life, what a chance!

And I've often wondered, how did it all start?
Who found out that nothing can capture a heart
Like a melody can?
Well, whoever it was, I'm a fan

Altogether now...

So I say
Thank you for the music, the songs I'm singing
Thanks for all the joy they're bringing
Who can live without it, I ask in all honesty
What would life be?
Without a song or a dance what are we?
So I say thank you for the music
For giving it to me...

Thanks for having me. Thanks for listening.
Oh... before I go can I just do a few mentions please?

OK, I'd like to thank...

SIGNING OFF

My grandad, Nat Kershaw, for – at just 14 years old – facing the horrors of war in 1914 and then coming home to a life working in the mill to put my dad through college and bettering us all.

My grandma, Emma Kershaw, for fighting for workers' rights and women's equality while toiling in the mill and bringing up my dad.

My grandad, Wallace Acton, for fighting Rommel in the desert and not seeing his family for nearly six years. Then driving lorries and building reservoirs to give my mum a leg up in life. And the height genes too!

My grandma Norah for all the love, fun and big dinners and for being the best role model and friend a girl could ever have. I miss you every day.

My dad for his brains and all his words of wisdom and instilling me with self-belief, ambition and good manners.

My mum for my big healthy frame, joie de vivre and courage. She showed me how to be a party animal who lives every day to the full and takes no shit from anyone.

My brother Andrew. My friend, ally and inspiration. Thank you for encouraging me, by example, to grab life by the balls, to take risks and to enjoy all the adventures the world has to offer.

Cousin Linda Weekes for being like a sister, my partner in crime and such a laugh.

Binksy for always being there since I was three and still loving me warts and all. Baby we were Born To Run.

Dixon. (Still crazy after all these years). For a blast. And believing in me and encouraging my dreams while ultimately keeping me on the straight and narrow by showing me what can go wrong! I owe you.

Sheena for true friendship and all your emotional and practical support for me and now Paul, Sam and Joe too.

Radio Aire:
The boss Geoff Sargieson for giving me a break.
   Martin Kelner for egging me on ever since.

BT in Leeds:
Margaret Backhouse for pointing out that corporate bollocks wasn't for me.

The Yorkshire Post:
Howard for giving me a column.

BBC Radio Leeds:
Jeremy and Jan for sharing their show.

BT in London:
Gary and Joss for all your skill and hard work in the studios.

BBC in London:
Whistle Test's producer Trevor Dann for taking me under his wing and introducing me to the record industry and TV presenting. And presenter Ro Newton for getting us our gig on Radio 1.

Radio 1:
Head of Programmes Doreen Davies for signing us up there.
   Her successor Roger Lewis for believing in me.
   Stuart Grundy for letting me show what I could really do.

SIGNING OFF

Phil Ross my producer on The Evening show for teaching me the ropes of live radio.

Our Jane Buchanan for being such an asset, support, laugh and friend for life.

Peel and Walters (and his long suffering wife Helen) for taking Our Elizabeth into the family fold.

Bruno Brookes. What can I say Mate? What an absolute blast!

Johnnie Walker and Nicky Campbell for being enlightened men.

All 'The Girls' particularly Julie Ball, Cathy Mellor, Janice Wardrope, and producer Sue Foster (Our Brian).

BBC Radio 5:

Jane Birtu, John Yorke and Phil Critchlow for all the fun on The Vibe.

Frank Mansfield, Lynn McCadden, Gabi Fisher, Jane Shepherd and Ian Bent for your dedication and production values on The Crunch. And Adrian Goldberg for your journalistic excellence and continuing friendship and support to this day.

BBC Radio 5 Live:

Jenny Abramsky for taking me on and taking me with you as you climbed the management ladder.

Mark Whittaker, Adrian Chiles and Julian Worricker for being such generous co-hosts and friends.

Stephanie Harris and Beth Chesney for being brilliant producers and for being there for me ever since.

BBC Radio Northampton:

John Ryan for your vision in taking me on as a solo female on breakfast and being a mate ever since.

Joanne Griffiths for being a belting producer who didn't take any prisoners.

Nikki Holiday for being exactly the kind of boss the BBC needs.

David Clargo for knowing that if we work hard we need to play hard too. And for giving a girl the gig at...

BBC Radio Coventry and Warwickshire:
Andrew Bowman for your continuing inspiration and support. One to watch he is!

Fran Daly, Bob Brolly, Amrit Cheema, and Keith Wedgebury, for being good mates and true radio pros and 'getting it' when it comes to public service broadcasting.

BBC Radio 6 Music:
Antony Bellekom for recruiting me.

Jim Moir for letting him.

Leona McCambridge for being the best music radio producer I've ever had in the BBC.

James Stirling for being an ace boss.

Adam Hudson, my producer since those dark days of 2007, (that's long-term stuff in radio). For great teamwork and being so 'up for it'.

Huey Morgan, Tom Robinson, Guy Garvey, Bruce Dickinson, Brinsley from Aswad, Jarvis Cocker and Craig Charles to name just a few of the many guys who've made 6 Music a great station.

Not forgetting the girls – Cerys Matthews, Lauren Laverne, Mary Anne Hobbs and Nemone.

SIGNING OFF

BBC:

Sally Traffic for holding your own on Radio 2 and for being a party girl and pal.

Sally Williams at the BBC in Manchester. You're ace.

Tim Davie for being a modern man.

Director General George Entwistle for listening to me.

Director General Tony Hall for wanting the best for the BBC and for making this book possible.

MPs Tessa Munt and Nadine Dorries for fighting the fight for us girls.

My publishers:

Claire Brown and Steve Hanrahan who took me on when I cold-called in April, 2013.

And my editor and mentor, Chris Brereton, for your enthusiasm, encouragement, great company and all the laughs!

But most of all:

My Paul.

There's been scant reference to him throughout this book. But that's because it's been focused on my career. My public life. But the bedrock of all of that has been my friend of 34 years and my co-parent for 24 years.

Me and Paul met in 1980 when I returned to Leeds after a post-grad stint at Littlewoods in Liverpool. He was by then Our Andrew's best friend and so a toyboy to me by 15 months. I thought that, even though we loved each other's company, the same music and fiercely fought games of Scrabble, romance was wrong. But in the end we 'got it together' in 1986.

Paul is well-read, informed, curious, dry, calm, funny and witty. He's also honest, loyal, generous, supportive. And dead clever. And extremely wise. He always knew that I was a woman who wouldn't be caged. That if he tried to clip my wings I'd just fly before he could.

So although I've been a dedicated mother and homemaker, he's known that I could never be the little woman.

And so I've been given enough rope to go on nights out and holidays with my friends. But I've never hung myself. Because I know what's good for me.

We've never actually married. Mostly for practical reasons. Like neither of us could invite both our mums and dads. Both being from broken homes we couldn't see both parents together in the same room. But yet we have created a more stable, loving, and enduring home for our children than many couples who do 'tie the knot'.

And I know that whatever happens I can come home to a nice cup of tea, a welcoming and warm home, a comfy bed and an episode of University Challenge. Sorted.

Thank you Paul for all your love, support and mainly friend-ship and companionship for the last three decades.

And...

My boys
For all the fun. The joy. The pride.
You are wonderful young men who now tower over and protect your little 'Mamma' fiercely.

Thank you.

WISE WORDS, MATE...

Jack Kershaw:
'Education education education'.
'You can get whatever you want in life if you want it enough'.
'Money can't make you happy but it can
save you from being miserable'.
'Being well dressed is being suitably dressed'.
'Always judge a man by his shoes'.

Sheena Bullen:
'Never take your clothes off in front of someone you have to
sit in a meeting with'.
'Never put sex before friendship'.

Andy Bell of Erasure:
'You have to be psychologically damaged to want to be famous'.

Edmund Burke:
'The only thing necessary for the triumph of evil is for good men
to do nothing'.

Lord Reith:
'He who prides himself on giving what he thinks the public
wants is often creating a fictitious demand for low standards
which he will then satisfy'.

Our Andrew:
'If you let them treat you like shit they will'.

Unknown:
'It's not who you are. It's just what you do'.

THE BIRD and THE BEEB

LIZ KERSHAW

Trinity Mirror Media